T0235702

Posthuman Property and Law

This book analyses the phenomenon of digitally mediated property and considers how it problematises the boundary between human and nonhuman actors.

The book addresses the increasingly porous border between personhood and property in digitized settings and considers how the increased commodification of knowledge makes visible a rupture in the liberal concept of the property owning, free, person. Engaging with the latest work in posthumanist and new materialist theory, it shows how property as a concept, as well as a means for control, changes fundamentally under advanced capitalism. Such change is exemplified by the way in which data, as an object of commodification, is extracted from human activities yet is also directly used to affectively control – or nudge – humans. Taking up a range of human engagements with digital platforms and coded architectures, as well as the circulation of affects through practices of artificial intelligence that are employed to shape behaviour, the book argues that property now needs to be understood according to an ecology of human as well as nonhuman actors. The idea of posthuman property, then, offers both a means to critique property control through digital technologies, as well as to move beyond the notion of the self-owning, object-owning, human.

Engaging the most challenging contemporary technological developments, this book will appeal to researchers in the areas of Law and Technology, Legal Theory, Intellectual Property Law, Legal Philosophy, Sociology of Law, Sociology, and Media Studies.

Jannice Käll is Senior Lecturer at the Department of Sociology of Law at Lund University, Sweden.

Posthuman Property and Law

Commodification and Control through Information, Smart Spaces and Artificial Intelligence

Jannice Käll

Routledge
Taylor & Francis Group

LONDON AND NEW YORK

First published 2023
by Routledge
4 Park Square, Milton Park, Abingdon, Oxon OX14 4RN

and by Routledge
605 Third Avenue, New York, NY 10158

Routledge is an imprint of the Taylor & Francis Group, an informa business

© 2023 Jannice Käll

The right of Jannice Käll to be identified as author of this work has been asserted in accordance with sections 77 and 78 of the Copyright, Designs and Patents Act 1988.

All rights reserved. No part of this book may be reprinted or reproduced or utilised in any form or by any electronic, mechanical, or other means, now known or hereafter invented, including photocopying and recording, or in any information storage or retrieval system, without permission in writing from the publishers.

Trademark notice: Product or corporate names may be trademarks or registered trademarks, and are used only for identification and explanation without intent to infringe.

a GlassHouse boook

British Library Cataloguing-in-Publication Data
A catalogue record for this book is available from the British Library

Library of Congress Cataloging-in-Publication Data
A catalog record has been requested for this book

ISBN: 978-0-367-68795-3 (hbk)
ISBN: 978-0-367-68801-1 (pbk)
ISBN: 978-1-003-13909-6 (ebk)

DOI: 10.4324/9781003139096

Typeset in Bembo
by Taylor & Francis Books

Contents

Figure

Acknowledgements

This book is the result of many years of work where countless of inspiring and generous persons have helped me shape my thinking on legal philosophy, property, and digitalization. The work has furthermore been carried out in my transition from a PhD candidate in legal theory at the Departement of Law, Gothenburg University, towards a post doc and senior lecturer in the Department of Sociology of Law, at Lund university. I am therefore particularly grateful to these institutions, which has made it possible to challenge the boundaries of what legal research, and sociolegal research might imply. Ulf Petrusson, Eva-Maria Svensson, Håkan Gustafsson, Merima Bruncevic, Kristina Hultegård, David Jivegård, Sebastian Wejedal, Anna Wallerman Ghavanini, Erik Björling, Tormod Otter Johansen, Isabel Schoultz, Matthias Baier, Amin Parsa, and many more: you have all been vital during my work with this book.

My many friends in the critical legal theory setting have, furthermore, all been crucial both in terms of support and inspiration for seeking out the weirdest and most interesting sides of law and inviting me to innumerable special issues, workshops, and anthologies. Swastee Ranjan, Susanna Lindroos-Hovinheimo, Rob Herian, Danilo Mandovic, Fiona Macmillan, Daniela Gandorfer, Emily Jones, Matilda Arvidsson, Andrea Leiter, and many more: thank you!

Invaluable comments regarding to the initial thoughts in this manuscript have furthermore been provided by Maria Drakopoulou, Margaret Davies, Cecilia Åsberg, Kevät Nousiainen, Hanne Petersen, and of course, Andreas Philippopoulos-Mihalopoulos, whose thinking and existence this book very much depend upon.

Kristina, your always-open support hotline has been a lifeline in my writing (and in general) for many years now. No one knows friendship better than you and I am grateful to have the chance to learn from you daily.

My deepest thanks also to Jussi for motivating/forcing me to finish writing and have the book published, even in the middle of a global pandemic. It is a particular privilege have gotten to spend so much time together with someone who has such vast and deep knowledge about literally everything and in particular in relation to all things Deleuzian and digital. Thanks also for reading this manuscript not only once, but twice, on top of enduring my (long) monologues about how everything comes down to the question of property.

To Boel and Stellan, my most loyal companions in writing and in life: thanks for providing me with so much profound thoughts about all kinds of digital media, in a way that only persons who learned to navigate an iPhone before they could walk and talk, could do. I know we are all waiting for the moment when it will become cool to have a mother who is a researcher. Until then, thanks for your patience with yet another book.

Part One

Introduction

Chapter 1

Introduction to Posthuman Property

The digital economy is gaining new ground every day. We are faced with new practices, concepts and other materialities through the visible use of platforms such as Facebook and TikTok or the less visible logistic operations of Amazon, automated vehicles or smart cities. Then there are the even more hidden layers of digital economy such as the continuous need for natural resources including both rare minerals and labour. Previously, this development was described as a shift towards a knowledge economy or, in even more idealistic cases, it was called a knowledge *society*. Intellectual property and intellectual assets came to be understood to be the commodity forms under which value was to be created in this new form of capitalism.

The shift towards this new economy was early on met with critical interventions, particularly in relation to intellectual property rights. We can still briefly remember the resistance movements to the digital economy of the late 20th and early 21st century. These movements engaged both in calls for free software – including how code should be free from both patentability and copyright – and more explicit practices of piracy of cultural content as a way to demand cultural expressions should be free to access and distribute. In relation to the more traditional sciences, we also saw resistance to the patenting of the human body as well as, for example, of crops and seeds. As for the trademark construction, the measures against the global capitalist branding culture culminated in movements such as *Reclaim the Streets* and *ATTAC* and through pioneering insights like works such as *No Logo* by Naomi Klein (2002[1999]). To some extent, these critical interventions of the role played by intellectual property in advanced capitalism were also formulated as a critique of intellectual property rights in general (e.g. Kapczynski 2010; Wark 2019). However, the type of control that intellectual property opens up was still underestimated compared to the stage of the information capitalism we are witnessing today. This is evidenced in relation to research on the effects of smart technologies (Hildebrandt 2015), surveillance capitalism (Zuboff 2019), algorithmic governance (Pasquale 2020) and the general capitalist control of our digital communicative spheres (Cohen 2019). It is also evidenced in the struggle for the ecological resources needed for the digital economy to take

DOI: 10.4324/9781003139096-1

place (Cubitt 2016). While control of the body used to be about whether to allow patents for genes, we are now faced with biometric control systems that interlace our fingerprints, face prints and other bodily expressions with digital devices and their algorithms to interpret and produce increasingly digitized life-worlds.

From a consumer perspective, a good starting point to understand the digitally mediated economy is the old understanding in media studies revolving around the fact that if you are getting media for free, you are usually the one being sold. Consequently, if you get access to certain information goods for free, you are usually the one being sold (Wark 2019: 1). Hence, the access to our everyday social medias has come to be surrounded by the transfer of our personal data to platform and advertising companies. A similar understanding about the digital economy has recently been popularized, for example, in a documentary *The Great Hack* (2019) that covered the Cambridge Analytica scandal where personal data was transacted and used to affect the outcome of political elections. As Wark further puts it, it is important that we realize that the practices being deployed in current forms of information harvesting from consumers were also applied in the broadcasting era in which consumers' attention to media was what was being sold. The difference from previous forms of information harvesting and the new form of economy is that our attention is not only being held but recorded in a much more direct way. In this form of control, it is not just labour but our sociability that is being made into a commodity (2019: 1–2). Furthermore, as will be discussed throughout this book, this form of commodification extends to so much more than the control of information in social media. This particularly applies as the Internet of Things and smart cities are being rolled out (Wark 2019: 2; Sadowski 2020).

Meanwhile, the legal concepts pertaining to property are still focused on traditional ideas of what constitutes a commodity and the kind of control the right to such commodity implies. As a consequence, the critique of the commodity forms of advanced capitalism, rendering all these forms of control possible, remains scattered over different topics. The latest discussions focused on questions of control of personal data and privacy rarely touches on intellectual property rights, contractual regimes and technological designs that support the platforms that make data collection possible. Similarly, the discipline of intellectual property rights is entrenched in its conceptual definitions of what constitutes an object in each piece of legislation, even though economic disciplines have moved towards a portfolio that considers how to capture "intellectual assets" of different intellectual property rights and beyond (see e.g. Granstrand 1999; Granstrand 2000; Birch and Muniesa 2020; Adkins, Cooper and Konings, 2020). On top of this, the legal discipline still tends to treat property as a fixed object that can be transferred between contracting parties. This fixed understanding of the property object is contrary both to critical interventions in legal theory (Cooper 2007; Keenan 2015) and in theory in general showing that affective aspects of knowledge and information might be more to the core of what property control implies under this stage of capitalism (Massumi 2015). Examples of such affective form of control includes the ability to use data for analysing people's behaviours to nudge them into performing certain actions (including purchases, but also other social actions).

This book seeks to address this gap between how a shift in the commodity concept under digitalization and more recently, in relation to AI, has been suggested from several directions. In placing these insights in conversation with critical theory in general and posthumanist critical theory in particular a an alterantive view of understanding the commodty form under digitalization is captured and critiqued. The aim with this is to unfold an understanding of property that is more capable of grasping the range of commodification and control exercised via digitalization under advanced capitalism. As the book will show, such an understanding is necessary to capture what is at stake as it is by no means restricted to an increase in intellectual property rights anymore. In fact, as I will show, it is no longer even a question of property in any traditional sense. Paraphrasing Wark's famous quote: "what if we explored the line that this is not capitalism, but worse" (Wark 2019: 29), I will explore how we now may ask: what if it is not about property anymore, but something worse?

As mentioned, the theories that will be most profoundly made me follow such a line of thinking are those explored in the posthumanist theoretical tradition. For this reason, throughout this book I will investigate such forms that might not even be property anymore but *posthuman property*. In arriving at such a conceptualization, several posthumanist theoretical arguments will be made and redeveloped in relation to discourses and cases from the legal discipline, as well as many others in which the focus has been on the materiality of information. Before going deeper into that focus, some words should be said about what kind of posthumanist lines of thought will be pursued.

Posthumanism

During the past decade, posthuman/ist theory has become a hot topic in several fields of research. Spanning from philosophy to political theory, art, natural sciences as well as law, it certainly engages in one of its main promises to challenge disciplinary boundaries. Ferrando even goes as far as describing posthumanism as the philosophy of our time (2019: 1). However, as several writers have noted, the terminology used to describe posthumanism is still ambiguous (e.g. Wolfe 2010: xi, Braidotti 2013; Ferrando 2019: 1–59). Thus, *the posthuman* as a concept has become an umbrella term for posthumanism, transhumanism, new materialisms, new and old forms of antihumanism and object-orientated ontologies (Ferrando 2019: 1). In brief, what connects these different endeavours is a decentring of the dominating centrality of the human for society and theory. What joins this bundle of theories is, for example, the belief that binary boundary-making practices such as dividing matter into subjects and objects is too rudimentary. The materialist foundations that posthumanist theories rest upon furthermore address binary boundary making not only as a detached question of conceptual debate, but something that stems from the forms of power that structure life-worlds of humans and nonhumans alike (but in different ways). For this reason, a task for posthumanist theory is to make divisions between different materialities visible in order to challenge the regimes of power that produce them (Wolfe 2010: xiii; cf. Dolphijn and van der Tuin 2012). This creates a starting point for a theory that asks the question of how materialities come into being, how they are connected, and what they can do rather than, for example, starting from the perspective that everything human is under threat from the developments in the digitized world (such as robots, Artificial Intelligence etc., cf. Darling 2021).

To make posthumanist endeavours more concrete, Braidotti suggests that a posthuman condition can be outlined and approached as four plateaus. The first plateau that she suggests works with the assumption that Western culture thrives on the myth of the beginning of man and that in the beginning there was a He, a man, as the foundational image. Braidotti attributes this to the line of thinking from Protagoras that formulates man as the "measure of all things" and Leonardo da Vinci's Vitruvian man. As she puts it, what is common for this tradition is that it continuously produces a very specific (and narrow) understanding of what it means to be human. Braidotti further argues that these ideals belong to the specific construction of *humanism* as a doctrine that "combines the biological, discursive and moral expansion of human capabilities into an idea of teleologically ordained, rational progress" (2013: 13). This ideal of the human is furthermore modelled on antiquity and values stemming from the Italian Renaissance that function as a standard for both humans and human cultures (ibid.: 14–15). As she argues, discussions within humanism and the humanities have centred on the themes put forward by e.g. Descartes, Marx and Freud but not necessarily those put forward by Darwin. Braidotti therefore argues that, in the humanities, one is not even able to think both via, as well as beyond, the human at the same time. Instead, it is the humanist philosophy tradition that gains precedence (Braidotti 2019: 40–61) An often-referenced starting point for posthumanist theory is furthermore to be found in the philosophies of Nietzsche, Foucault, Deleuze and Guattari and their questioning of a particular figure of Man. An example of such a theory is the history of man pursued by Foucault in *The Order of Things: An Archaeology of Human Sciences* in which he points out that "man is an invention of recent date. And one perhaps nearing its end" (Foucault 2002[1966]: 422). These starting points implicate a critique of liberal social and political theories as well as theories of scientific knowledge as they both stem from the idea that the world is made up of individuals. In law, such ideologies are reflected in assumptions about individuals as pre-existing before the law, or the discovery of law as awaiting and inviting representation as, for example, Barad expresses it (Barad 2007: 46; Dolphijn and van der Tuin 2011: 302–393).

The second plateau of the posthuman condition is a form of inhuman humanism which points at how being post *human* may ring false to those who have never or barely been considered as fully human in the first place and, are still not considered to be. This plateau sheds light on the assumptions of the category of the human and how it excludes those who do not fulfil the philosophical prerequisites of being human. As Braidotti suggests, such creation of a nonhuman within the human includes how human subjectivity tends to be based on "the Cartesian subject of the cogito, the 'Kantian community of reasonable beings,' or in more sociological terms the subject as citizen, rights-holder, property-owner, and so on" (Braidotti 2013: 1). To move beyond this kind of excluding form of humanism, and move towards posthumanism, implies to take into particular account how those who were never fully counted as part of the human species to begin with, may be accounted for now. This in turn has consequences from a legal perspective, not the least in relation to human rights discourse (ibid.), and how it now is becoming integrated also in digital settings. The construction of the human as not as all-inclusive-as-perceived in liberal theory, echoed, for example, in the words of Wendy Brown when she reminds us that both persons and states today are construed on an idea of the firm as capital value maximizers (Brown 2015: 22). Another obvious example on the lack of substance in both the concept of the human and human rights is how nation-states and regions such as the EU increasingly tightens their borders to let humans die, even in regions that philosophically adhere to a humanist idea of the territories on which their societies are built (Esposito 2015: 33). For this reason, Braidotti argues that a more critical approach to the posthuman condition cannot be carried out with a humanist ideology (alone) as, in her words, it has become over-inflated and excludes too much (also cf. Braidotti 2013: 45). From the perspective of digitalization, we can witness these types of border controls via biometric passports that can be scanned by machines at the border of many airports, as well as the ongoing discussions about implementing specific COVID-19 vaccination passports for those who have had the privilege to receive vaccines. As of writing this in the end of September 2021, a situation has arised where the same types of vaccination have been recorded in different digital national systems, and used to hold free flow of persons stuck to both national or regional borders. The role of nationalism is not the least visible in the political game of accepting UK vaccine passports in the EU, a country that was part of the inner border, as late as when the pandemic started. There is furthermore no doubt that relations between humans, is less important than economic goals, as business venues have been opened, while borders remain closed via (arbitrary) rules on what digital copy is to be accepted as the outmost border of private persons' travels. As for example Bratton puts it: "Among the most decisive and disturbing realities of the pandemic was a big filtering whereby whole populations of people, otherwise mobile and intermingling, were *re-sorted back into their countries of passport,* often with only a few days' notice" (Bratton 2021: 15).

The third plateau also connects the theme of the posthuman to *advanced capitalism* that renders the posthuman subject as a being into a technologically mediated one (Braidotti 2013: 57). In the words of Braidotti: "[a]dvanced capitalism and its bio-genetic technologies engender a perverse form of the posthuman" (Braidotti 2013: 7). As practices of capitalism are vital starting points for this book, the concept of advanced capitalism and other forms of capitalism will be further explored in the next section. However, an important point to note already at this stage is how Braidotti via this plateau of the post-human as a concept directly references how capitalism is not only about extracting economic value from labour and the production of commodities, for example, but about the potential to govern life as part of advanced capitalism also extends to the control of, and increased exercise of power over, *death* (Braidotti 2013: 122, drawing on Mbembe 2003). As Braidotti further points out, in the post-Cold War era there has been both a dramatic increase in warfare and a transformation in how war is carried out. Thus, wars have now become intensified to a degree where they have reached a new level of administering the bodies and populations that may be destroyed (ibid.: 8–9, cf. Lindholm-Schultz 2002; Kaldor 2000). In relation to digitalization, this plateau is visible not the least in the killing of persons via drones and the technologies deployed to identify whether a person is a civilian or a military combatant (Gunneflo 2016).

As a fourth plateau of how to identify and move beyond the posthuman con-dition, Braidotti argues that we need to consider new ways to *visualize subjectivity*. To do this, she further suggests particular attention to a form of anti-humanism as a means to object to the unitary subject of humanism. In specific, she suggests that via an increased anti-humanist engagement the subject of humanism should be replaced by a "more complex and relational subject framed by embodiment, sexuality, affectivity, empathy and desire as core qualities" (Braidotti 2013: 26). Thus, in this vein, subjectivity is directed towards a less fixed idea of the human as being the unitary subject around which society is constructed towards under-standing how power that both human and nonhuman bodies exercise is the basis for how subjectivity emerges. Accounting for power differences related to the production of subjectivity is what has the capacity to bring something new also to technology studies where it is otherwise easy to fall back on the "all too human" fantasies about transcending the human capacities both in relation to the human body and mind (ibid.: 12) The post-anthropocentrism advocated in posthumanist theory also adds an intensity to *anti-humanism* since post-anthropocentrism engages further with science and technology studies, new media and digital culture, environmentalism and earth-sciences, biogenetics, neuroscience and robotics, evolutionary theory, critical legal theory, primatology, animal rights and science fiction in a manner which anti-humanism did not (Braidotti 2013: 58). Further-more, post-anthropocentrism distances itself from the human, as it aims to leave the idea of taking human *species* as the point of departure, for theory and world-making. This possible end of man is obviously a controversial topic that can be seen either as the end of the world or in a more affirmative light: as an end to a very particular world order and the worlds it has made (im)possible. Either way, both the posthumanist idea as well as factual developments of new materialities such as digital media, and the artifacts that embody them, are increasingly connected to human bodies. In this way, the human is already pushed towards a post-anthropocentric constellation where the body does not anymore end at the human skin (Haraway 1991: 178).

In particular, the last plateau also paves the way for a new form of ethics and political connection based on the posthuman condition where relationality between human and nonhuman bodies becomes central, as opposed to an ethics based on human superiority and inviolability. This potential for a different kind of ethics also lingers in the entire posthuman theoretical endeavour, not least in relation to the consideration of the possibility of actively constructing/affirming different new forms of posthuman *subjectivities*. Besides in the work of Braidotti, this is also a prominent feature in the posthumanist accounts developed by Barad, MacCormack and Wolfe (Barad 2007; Mac-Cormack 2012; Wolfe 2010: xii–xiv; Thiele 2014). A particular aspect of elaborating posthumanist ethics and subjectivity includes to pay increased consideration to nonhuman matter as being more fluid and livelier than in traditional humanist accounts. This implies that matter is considered to be independent within their own limits. In this way, all matter is considered to have self-organising and affective capacities (e.g. Braidotti 2013: 158). A common critique against perceiving of matter in this way is that accountability is removed from humans if all matter is understood to have (equal) agency (Ahmed 2008). While this critique is possibly well directed towards certain impulses of object-orientated thinking, the streams of feminist new materialisms and (critical) posthumanism have to large degree been developed by feminist theorists that are explicit about mapping out matter and materialization via the power regimes they seek to criticize. In brief, such posthumanist endeavours consequently imply a heightened awareness of how humans and other matter become entangled in the manner that they become able to act in certain ways against or in relation to each other. In doing so, attention is drawn, for example, to how advanced capitalism shapes matter as well as how capitalism intersects with other power regimes such as patriarchal, racist and speciest norms (Braidotti 2013: 159; Barad 2007, 224; Haraway 1991: 210).

The consequence for focusing on matter in a posthumanist setting here is furthermore that matter which has previously been thought of as being either digital *or* human can be studied in conjunction and with increased attention to what is afforded via their emerging relations towards each other. A classic example of bridging such a passive notion of matter comes from Butler's theory on how gender should be understood as being performed rather than enacted through nature (Butler 2011). Performativity as a concept is in posthumanist theory however further developed as a tool to show how materialities also perform themselves and affect the performativity of "social" aspects such as language (Barad 2007: 46). Matter here therefore becomes more than something passive, awaiting human inscription or representation, (Bennett 2010; Morton 2013). Simultaneously, narratives in innovation focused discourses highlights ways of increasingly perceiving information as being "alive." Today, this is quite visible in the hype of artificial intelligence in general and robotics in particular. These discourse are currently met as much with hope as with fear that robots will take over everything from our jobs to the world in general (see e.g. Pasquale 2020). To again quote Haraway, we factually however can conclude at least that "(p)re cybernetic machines were not self-moving, self-designing, autonomous." But already in late twentieth-century it had become clear how machines had made unclear the differences between "natural and artificial, mind and body, self-developing and externally designed, and many other distinctions that used to apply to organisms and machines." As Haraway famously concludes, one can even say that: "[o]ur machines are disturbingly lively, and we ourselves frighteningly inert" (1991: 152).

This book aligns to some extent with performative accounts of matter as I explore how digital materialities come about, how they become relational towards each other as well as different forms of humans, and how they affect (and are used to affect) who can act in which way. As such, the focus on materiality is an important starting point, since discourses of digitalization traditionally have been imbued with ideas of immateriality and disembodiment, which risk creating a form of forgetfulness of the continuity of power. As, for example, Nakamura and boyd highlighted early on – there is however a tendency and risk in disconnecting technology from "human" affects" (Nakamura 2002: 31; boyd 2012: 203–222). The idea of the internet as being disconnected from the human has also been advanced by Brians by pointing out that as cyberspace evolved, it was understood as "a place where the user would be free of the material limits of the body, while also exercising an enhanced control over his virtual environment" (Brians 2011: 121).

A perceived liveliness embedded in the performativity of the commodity is however not something new in a critique of the effects that capitalism produces (Marx 2013[1969]: 62–73). Just like previous forms of capitalism, commodities, whether they be robots or other machines, do not come to life by themselves. However, a difference between the commodity forms in a previous setting compared to the focus here is that their materialities equip them with traits which, in the Western understanding, has been (even more) exclusive to humans (and no obviously, not all humans). In posthumanist theory, this difference in what a materiality affords is important to both understanding which forms of power may unfold, as well as being a means of reimagining a world beyond commodity production. For example, when nature is understood as something not just there to be passively exploited by capital but something with its own life force, it becomes something to consider for human survival, but also in relation to other nonhuman kinds of species (Haraway 2016; Parikka 2015).

The account to be made here is however not of the vitalist kind suggested by, for example, Barad (2007) or Bennett (2010) but rather has the aim of showing the particular material aspects that digitalization affords for new forms of property control to emerge. As will be discussed next, this implies that the understanding of digital matter is analysed in particular with a focus on how advanced capitalism shapes the materiality of digital elements. This does not mean that such description should be understood as a final account for the performativity of digital matter. As will be discussed throughout, digital matter can be many things, and consequently also could be very different without the forms of control that will discussed as examples of proprietary control here.

Advanced Capitalism

This book works as both a description of, and critical intervention against, the currently emerging property form, which I refer to as *posthuman property*. As such, this intervention is pursued through posthumanist theory and follows the diagnostics of why, and how, we can argue that this form of property has emerged and continues to emerge. In this intervention, *advanced capitalism* functions as an essential concept to understand the unfolding of a posthuman condition. Furthermore, this concept of capitalism is used here to show that the form of capitalism we now find ourselves in, both connects to, as well as exceeds, previous forms of capitalism. Outlining such continuation, yet excess, of capitalism is vital for the purpose of the property theory that is being developed here, as it connects property to a historical setting while pointing at the particular transformations it is undergoing under this stage of capitalism. The privileging of advanced capitalism as opposed to other forms of descriptors of capitalism here is to great degree inspired by the biopolitical aspects and technological combinations under advanced capitalism as outlined by Braidotti. As Braidotti puts it, in her understanding: "[a]dvanced capitalism and its bio-genetic technologies engender a perverse form of the posthuman where Life itself – is the main capital" (2013: 7). This idea, which Braidotti develops from Cooper, furthermore suggests that the Earth as a whole is being capitalized through inter-connected operations (Cooper 2008: 3). Braidotti also suggests a connection between advanced capitalism and how personhood is being commodified under advanced capitalism in the manner that it produces differences in order to commodify them. These differences are thereafter packaged as "new, dynamic and negotiable identities" and as endless choices of consumer goods (ibid.: 58). As such, this is obviously a practice highly connected to the current forms of digitalization, in particular where influencers populate our social media communities and sell us both goods and the possibility to identify with, and become like, them. As an example of the extent of this type of commodification, one can highlight the fact that, both feminist critiques and more recently, the ideas and messages from the Black Lives Matter movement, have witnessed how their core political thoughts are being picked up by brands and influencers to sell goods based on "radical" identities.

The capitalization of the Earth, beyond the human body, as part of advanced capitalism, is furthermore also a prominent feature of how digitalization has come to be realized. Meanwhile the digital economy is often described as an immaterial one, whether we talk about the free flows of data or the knowledge needed to be created, it is pertinent to point also to the natural resources needed to run it. This includes everything from the materials that go into consumer devices to the logistics and infrastructures of media such as server halls consuming vast amounts of energy to be kept cool as well as the recently popularized understanding of the amount of energy that encrypted currencies such as Bitcoin requires. As will be discussed later, there is very little that is intangible about intangible goods. Possibly even more than continuous capture of information and knowledge, the current form of the digital economy requires exploitation of the Earth and those that extract for example rare minerals for our smart devices to work. As the development of data extraction for everything from behavioural advertising to machine learning shows, capitalism is certainly no longer (if it ever was) about capturing surplus from labour power and other natural resources to extract capital value. Instead, it is to be understood here as a complex order of control, wtih forms of exploitation and domination that works in alliance with other orders such as colonialist and patriarchal form of exploitation.

To consider how advanced capitalism works on multiple registers of control and exploitation is furthermore a vital starting point for developing a theory around its property form. It has, to this stage, been too common to stay within legal disciplinary boundaries such as the different intellectual property rights laws to describe the commodity form in the information economy. The biggest limitation with such perspective is just that it affirms an idea of how information or intangibles, or possibly the production of these, are the actual commodities that make advanced capitalism or digitalization thrive. To move beyond this perspective, a first step is to show that digitalization works on the capture of different materialities, where some, but certainly not all, are today understood as assets that can be captured via intellectual property rights.

Activating this theoretical idea of capitalism, is also important in the manner that it enables a view of advanced capitalism as something that engages in a multitude of discursive and material political techniques of population control, which transcend Foucault's idea of bio-political governance (Braidotti 2013: 61). More specifically, this implies to identify how a techno-scientific culture as a dominant culture is constructed at the intersection between biotechnology and information technology. This is notably visible, in the scientific field of *bioinformatics* and as noted by, for example, Vandana Shiva early on: the capitalist culture of biology and how it is closely linked to other post-colonial practices. These practices take form, for example, in the construction of what Shiva refers to as *monocultures of the mind*. Thus, in several instances, the practises of controlling biology through capitalism (foresting, seed control) are identified as a culture of reducing biological difference in order to achieve market benefits

(Shiva 1993). Haraway has developed a significant understanding with regards to such forms of advanced capitalism through the ideas of "Technoscience" and "Informatics of Domination" as well as arguing that a concept of advanced capitalism is not enough to capture the forms of power in play (Haraway 1991: 161–162). Following a posthumanist vein, both these concepts can be understood as valuable understandings of "biopower" that directly affect the intensities of posthuman bodies, at least to some degree, in advanced capitalism (Braidotti 2013: 58–59, 61).

The concept of biopower connects to Foucault's theories on governance in modern society. According to Foucault, governing as biopower may be understood as a plethora of techniques that regulate "Life" itself. The understanding that the West has moved towards a stage of power that can be described as biopower is outlined by Foucault as the idea that "deduction" is one of many other forms of power which also involves "working to incite, reinforce control, monitor, optimize, and organize the forces under it: a power bent on generating forces, making them grow, and ordering them, rather than one dedicated to impeding them; making them submit, or destroying them" (Foucault 1984: 259). Braidotti depicts a difference between Foucault's perception of biopower and her understanding of the posthuman predicament as the latter is interested in a greater variety of forces. Furthermore, as it is not merely the bodies subjected to power by humans such as "states" that are considered in posthumanist frameworks, a necessary implication is that biopower is considered not only as a governance logic of states within "socially" constructed boundaries, but that power always needs to be considered in its global dimension (and beyond) (Braidotti 2013: 63, 89). The difference between the forms of biopower outlined by Foucault and those that are interesting to the posthumanist theorists of today can also be exemplified in the manner that we have now moved away from the Foucauldian form of biopower towards "a society based on the governance of molecular *zoe* power" (ibid.: 97). Furthermore, she stresses that in the same way we have moved from disciplinary to control societies and from the political economy of the Panopticon to the informatics of domination (ibid.: 97).

This latter concept of *informatics of domination* developed by Haraway further suggests that the current form of capitalism radically changes how production and *reproduction* is carried out. Haraway proposes this understanding as implying a reworking of Marxist theory as she argues that the materialities of capitalist production lead to/continuously reproduce this new condition (Haraway 1991: 9). In particular, Haraway outlines a modular logic with regards to the commodification of information as part of the current form of capitalism (Haraway 1991: 161–162). As Wark suggests, this development can also be understood as leading towards the development of a vectorial class that controls the modulations that can be made through the control of vectors, rather than factories and natural resources (these too, of course) (Wark 2019). The informatics of domination as a form of control society exceeding both commodity production and state control of life was also famously predicted by Deleuze and Guattari in their later works (Deleuze 1992; Guattari

2008[1989]). As Deleuze writes, the societies of control are characteristic in the way that passwords as points of entry becomes key and entry into a space is either rejected or passed, never anything in between (Deleuze 1992). Furthermore, under advanced capitalism, as noted by Haraway, the logic is to arrange not only humans under this form of governance but anything that serves the mode of biocontrol (Haraway 1991: 161–162). A conceptual consequence of this understanding of control over bios is that the boundaries between humans and their others, which also inform much of Western law, become disrupted (cf. Esposito 2015). This makes for a complex form of becoming as, for example, Wolfe writes, where every week we are faced with new remarkable complexities of the life around us and "everything we have learned about how a wide range of nonhuman creatures are more complex, both biologically and phenomenologically, than we ever imagined" (2016). As later critical and posthumanist work has shown, this is also, and obviously, not only about a displacement of binaries, but highly material practices in which we have entered into the Anthropocene, Capitolocene and many other similar understandings of the irreversible damage that humans have caused both towards the possibilities of human life on Earth as well as to other forms of nature under capitalism (Braidotti 2013; Parikka 2015; Haraway 2016; Moore 2017).

The Relation between Advanced Capitalism and Other Descriptions of Capitalism

While advanced capitalism is the term I have opted to use here, there are several other recent theorizations of how to describe what characterizes the current stage of capital/capitalism based in the digitally mediated economy as compared to other forms of capitalism. Such examples include cognitive capitalism (Moulier-Boutang 2011), surveillance capitalism (Zuboff 2019), platform capitalism (Srnicek 2017) and, of course, digital capitalism (Sadowski 2020: 49). As briefly mentioned above, Wark furthermore suggests that the combination of power and capitalism that we witness today should possibly not even be called capital/ism anymore but something worse (2019). All these descriptions have their own merits and connections to advanced capitalism in the manner that has been outlined above. There are however also reasons from a posthumanist agenda to use the concept of advanced capitalism and its connection to ideas about capitalization of life itself, as well as orders of biopower such as the informatics of domination, to create a revised concept of property. Different ideas about capitalism in the digital economy are however also informative of how to situate as well as develop the concept of advanced capitalism further, why some vital aspects of these concepts also will be discussed briefly here.

To start with, cognitive capitalism, as coined by Yann Moulier-Boutang, is one of the oldest of the more recent ideas about the current capitalist stage we find ourselves in (2011). In summary, Moulier-Boutang outlines 15 markers specific to cognitive capitalism, including the growing role of the immaterial and services related to the production of immaterial, digitalized data such as input of information, processing and storage in digitized form in the production of knowledge and production itself, the depreciation of material labour as a strategic asset via the capture and transferability of know-how and technological progress and appropriation of knowledge as embedded in information and communication technology systems (ibid.: 50–51). As such he stresses both the networked and digitized aspects of the transformation towards a knowledge-based – or in his terms – cognitive economy. Like many others, he identifies a shift in the economy from industrial capitalism in which accumulation was mainly based on machinery and the organization of manual labour towards cognitive capitalism in which accumulation is based on knowledge and creative forms of immaterial investment (ibid.: 56–57). By cognitive capitalism he means: "a mode of accumulation in which the object consists mainly of knowledge, which becomes the basic source of value, as well as the principal location of the process of valorisation" (ibid.: 57). Whereas this account goes further than many others in connecting the capture of immaterial assets to also imply a production of bio-control, the theory is different from the post-humanist account in that it takes the cognitive as basis for what distinguishes the current form of capitalism from the previous one/s. This implies a risk in terms from a posthumanist perspective in the way that a focus on immaterial labour can get too caught in knowledge-based production and what is needed for this in a narrow sense such as innovation and creativity. This in turn reiterates rather than bridges the challenge of showing how the digital is created via layered extraction of many types of resources (cf. Parikka 2015; Crawford and Joler 2018).

Platform capitalism, on the other hand, focuses on an idealized logix of organization which companies take on as form under advanced capitalism, as opposed to capitalism built on the idea of the company or market as a means of organization. As Srnicek puts it in one of the latest contributions to this view: "[t]he platform has emerged as a new business model, capable of extracting and controlling immense amounts of data, and with this shift we have seen the rise of large monopolistic firms" (2017: 6). Srnicek furthermore affiliates this shift towards platform-based business models with the shift from tangible assets to a focus on data. As he puts it "platforms became an efficient way to monopolise, extract, analyse, and use the increasingly large amounts of data that were being recorded" (ibid.: 42–43). He also suggests that platforms at the most general level may be defined as digital infrastructures that enable two or more groups to interact. For this reason, they tend to position themselves as intermediaries bringing together different actors such as customers, service providers, advertisers, producers, suppliers and physical objects (ibid.: 43). Furthermore, what is significant with platforms is that they are both products and markets at the same time since platforms can be understood as being a basic infrastructure to mediate between different groups (ibid.: 44).

A prominent logic of platform capitalism is to make the platform grow through so-called network effects (ibid.). This implies that connectivity between different actors as well as different elements (including human users) is a key factor for expanding the platform. The rationale in general is that the more parts that a platform manages to connect to it, the more users and other actors will want to connect to it and expand it further (ibid.: 45–46). This may then be contrasted with both organizational logics for companies under industrial capitalism as well as their value propositions to customers. As for example Chesbrough points out, under industrial capitalist logics, the company is focused on offering a certain type of goods or service (Chesbrough 2011). Platform capitalism on the other hand connects to ideas in innovation theory of Open Innovation (Chesbrough 2003; Gianopoulou et al. 2010; Huizingh 2011), as well as intellectual capital management (Teece 2000) in the way that it aims to move away from innovation logics related to a specific type of goods or service and instead view the value proposition as consisting of more dynamic and knowledge-intense elements. To support such knowledge-based offerings it has become key to regard the company exactly as a platform combining different competencies rather than as the single organising unit that aims to perfect the production one type of goods or services. Consequently, one moves towards thinking of the company more as an intermediary in a network rather than as placed in a value chain in which each entity fulfils a role of producing or offering one specific thing. (Chesbrough 2003; Chesbrough 2011; Petrusson et al. 2010; Gianopoulou et al. 2010).

What distinguishes both the business models structured as platforms, as well as the capitalist logic assigned to their organizational structure, is that the logics of closure and boundaries of the firm as an organizational unit are replaced by a form of structured openness towards other actors. Possibly needless to state, this type of openness comes with the purpose not of a general perspective of growing benefits for all, but for expanding businesses, including (intellectual) assets. This logic will here be identified continuously as a recurrent theme in how advanced capitalism produces posthuman property. However, I also regard the platform logics as a form of organizational mode that supports rather than characterizes advanced capitalism. This implies, for example, that it is vital to connect how extraction of resources related to digitalization as being part of with are of platform-oriented business logics. However, the way that such extraction and commodification is made possible exceeds both the organization of such extraction via platforms, as well as the legal tools to capture assets as property for platforms. Furthermore, it should be noted that platforms as means to organize persons or resources do not need to be part of advanced capitalism at all; they can be used to produce non-capitalist research collaborations, counter-movements, etc. (Gawer 2009).

Surveillance capitalism is furthermore a concept that more recently has become popularized as a term to describe certain practices deployed by digital platforms. Zuboff describes this form of capitalism as a type of practice which unilaterally claims human experience as free raw material. Characteristic for surveillance capitalism is how data is captured as a form of "behavioural surplus." Hence, data is treated as something that organizations can harvest from the persons or things made into data points. This data is then fed into producing "prediction products" including machine learning, which become equipped with the capacity to anticipate what the user will do (based on data over previous behaviours from its own or similar users' behaviours). This assessment of behaviour creates what Zuboff calls "behavioural future markets," which is what companies trade upon (ibid.: 8). The effect is that "surveillance capitalists discovered that the most-predictive behavioral data come from intervening in the state of the play in order to nudge, coax, tune, and herd behavior toward profitable outcomes" (ibid.: 8). This implies a reorientation of capitalism where the goal with automated machine processes for example is no longer to automate information flows about humans but to automate the humans as such (ibid.: 8). Zuboff also significantly extends the media theoretical insight discussed above in relation to the fact that if a media is free, then oneself is the product being sold, by suggesting that "[w]e are the sources of surveillance capitalism's crucial surplus: the objects of a technologically advanced and increasingly inescapable raw-material-extraction operation" (ibid.: 10). In her diagnosis of surveillance capitalism, Zuboff furthermore cautions against conflating surveillance capitalism with the technologies it employs. Even if digital technologies enable surveillance capitalism to a degree that is unthinkable outside the current technological milieu, it is still the particular market logics of extraction of human social life that is at the core, rather than the technologies as such. This can be contrasted with the term "digital capitalism" as used by Sadowski for describing this stage as capitalism and its (more intrinsic) relationship with digital technologies. The reason he gives for using such terminology is that it is a broad enough term to incorporate other variations of how capitalism at this stage is being described while not being too narrow about specific functions of digital capitalism such as the platform capitalism by Srnicek or the surveillance capitalism by Zuboff (Sadowski 2020: 49–50). Similar to Zuboff, I however argue that this term is too narrow as the digital milieu does not just concern itself with the elements that are making it digital per se, but rather extends the previous logics of capitalism while accelerating via (some) new tools.

The capitalist logic described by Zuboff has merits to a posthumanist take on advanced capitalism since it focuses on extraction and affective control beyond the logic of labour via industrial production. This particularly connects to the idea of the informatics of domination suggested by Haraway, as described above. However, the limitations in Zuboff's analysis from a posthumanist perspective is that it focuses on both the "human" and the humanist layers of communication technologies. Even if such focus on the human and the extraction of data from human relations to some extent is also the focus of this book, advanced capitalism as a concept affords a wider focus on the multiple other layers of extraction involved in the emergence of posthuman property. Furthermore, posthumanist theory is to a larger degree also focused on the differences between humans in how they become captured by surveillance capitalism. As Braidotti puts it, we are all posthuman at this stage, but we don't become posthuman in the same way (Braidotti 2013).

In considering further the connection with other diagnostics of capitalism, Wark's thesis about the current situation as being no longer about "capital but something worse" is the closest kin theory to the posthumanist stream. In developing this diagnosis, Wark focuses on the Marxist tradition in outlining both a new form of producing and owning class. As briefly mentioned above, she argues that this development suggests the emergence of a new type of class relation subsisting in the class that owns the vectors along which information is gathered (2019: 2). This important insight into how capitalism today entails technological governance, or as I would call it – property control – can also be understood as a performance via a stack of layers. As explained by Bratton, such stacks can in relation to digitalization bet understood as taking place via the Earth Layer, Cloud Layer, City Layer, Address Layer, Interface Layer and User Layer (2015). As Wark describes it, one can imagine Amazon Echo as being the top layer in such stack in which the user's desire has to be parsed into a form that a machine can understand; that is the job of this interface layer (Wark 2019: 9). However, in Wark's understanding of vectorial power, there is also an added understanding about how layered media give rise to certain flows or intensities, which maps well onto the posthumanist interest in relational movement between matter as means of control or release, as will be discussed further below. As Wark explains, the vector is "the way and means by which a given pathogen travels from one population to another. Water is a vector for cholera, bodily fluids for HIV. By extension, a vector may be any means by which anything moves" (2004: note 315–316). As such, this understanding of capital consequently has informative value for a posthumanist take on advanced capitalism, in particular in relation to digitalization.

Posthumanist Knowledge and Kinnovative Thinking – Methodological Commitments

Posthumanist theory engages in several distinct methodological commitments which place it within the broader field of critical theory. One point of convergence between posthumanist theory and several other critical approaches is the questioning of the disjunction between epistemology and ontology. In posthumanist theory this is expressed as a particular commitment to *posthumanist ethics* as embedded in its research focus (e.g. Barad 2007: 86–87, Braidotti 2013: 190–197; Braidotti 2019: 153–173; Ferrando 2019: 128–132). In terms of research method, this implies that a normative orientation towards this particular ethics functions as a cornerstone in the selection of material in order to ground the concept of posthuman property. In doing so, a number of methodological commitments is emphasized to create what one could call a framework for *kinnovative thinking* (Haraway 2016: 209). These commitments are all utilized in order to move towards a different understanding of what property as a concept and as a bundle of control practices imply under the posthuman condition. In particular, I engage with the binaries of modern Western law and society that have been criticized in posthumanist thinking. This includes questioning the body/mind binary, the physical/immaterial binary, the human/nonhuman binary, as well as the individual/social binary and the role they play in legitimising property forms and property law.

The commitment to posthumanist methodologies may also be expressed as an affinity with *situatedness, cartography, radical disciplinarity* and *monism* (Philippopoulos-Mihalopoulos 2015: 28, 34–35, 59–65; Braidotti 2013: 56). A posthumanist epistemology of law is a situated epistemology (Haraway 1991: 59; Philippopoulos-Mihalopoulos 2015: 59). Haraway is particularly known for advocating such an epistemological perspective, which rejects both universalist ideas about objective knowledge as well as relativism. Just like objectivism, relativism is identified as a disembodied way of understanding how knowledge is produced and perceived (Haraway 1991: 191). Both relativism and objectivism are what she refers to as "god-tricks" (ibid.). In Haraway's words, in particular objectivism implies "a way of being nowhere while claiming to be everywhere equally" (ibid.). The alternative to both these perspectives in her view is "partial, locatable, critical knowledges sustaining the possibility of webs of connections of solidarity in politics as well as shared conversations in epistemology" (ibid.). Furthermore, situated knowledge requires that *the object of knowledge* is pictured as an actor or agent and "not a screen or a ground or a resource" (ibid.: 198) and "never finally as slave to the master that closes off the dialectic in his unique agency and authorship of 'objective' knowledge" (ibid.). However, this does not imply resorting to "realism." As she points out, the world can neither speak for itself nor disappear in favour of a master decoder. Thus, methodologically, one cannot proceed in a manner in which the codes of the world are treated as something waiting to be read by humans or as a form of raw material for humanization (ibid.: 192–193, 196–200).

Furthermore, situatedness in posthumanist theory is particularly aligned with feminist research in which the ontological stability of a specifically gendered reality and the relationship between space, place, bodies and the law have been explored (e.g. Valverde 2014 and for a review of these discussions in the Nordic legal discipline Käll 2021). Such projects have promoted an idea of ontological vulnerability which, in new materialism, can be described as a form of the *fragility of things.* As noted by Philippopoulos-Mihalopoulos, this movement towards considering entities, or bodies, as always fragile, entails the beginning of *the posthuman* in law (2014: 18). Also, epistemology in the posthumanist school is, as discussed, thought to unfold parallel to ontology (cf. ibid.: 10). Barad argues that one therefore cannot even speak of epistemology and ontology as separate, even in theory since "knowing is a material practice of engagement as part of the world in its differential becoming (2007: 43)". It therefore also implies that questions regarding ethics are always embedded in a posthumanist and situated epistemology (ibid.). Barad also refers to the posthumanist epistemology explicitly as an onto-epistemology (ibid.: 86–87).

The situated aspects of posthumanist epistemology unfolds here via an engagement with a number of formations related to the altered entanglement between mind and body, as well as to altered entanglements between persons and things. This in turn also entails questioning the divide between human/nonhuman and human/inhuman (Philippopoulos-Mihalopoulos 2016: 193–195). In practice, this means that this book aims to go beyond divisions of what constitutes the field of property law and other similar legal constructions in order to show how key conceptual divisions within property law are carried out between human (or rather, in tandem with a specific notion of "the human") and nonhuman bodies related to a specific idea of human subjectivity. The situating of law inside these phenomena is furthermore carried out in a posthumanist spirit in which certain encounters are of more interest than others, since they point to questions fruitfully embraced via posthumanist theory. One way of putting this is that the methodological aim in the election of cases and legal constructs is to create what can be broadly described as a posthumanist cartography (cf. Braidotti 2013: 164). Creating a cartography here paves the way for a re-evaluation of the boundaries of property under current forms of humanism described as *advanced capitalism* and *anthropocentrism*. Thus, the cases utilized here are informed by the interest in the specific dichotomies being challenged through advanced capitalism, with the focus on commodification of knowledge, as well as convergences between materialities such as digital and non-digital matter, and persons and things. The selection of examples – to some extent seemingly mundane and not at all embedded in the rigorous ideas about what constitutes an interesting legal case or example – also folds into a general ethical aim of disrupting what e.g. MacCormack has called "the Majoritarian language of law" (2012: 120). Such Majoritarian language of law tends to be, as will be discussed in chapter two, focused on the legal order in a narrow sense which involves legislations, court cases and similar.

The aim to enable a different understanding of law is also expressed here in the second methodological commitment to *radical interdisciplinarity*. Radical interdisciplinarity in a posthumanist sense involves engaging several fields of theory to create new knowledge in the interface between, for example, the humanities and science (Braidotti 2013: 169). As posthumanist theory is closely allied with critical theory, it is important to problematize the boundary-setting mechanisms of the legal discipline, which is continuously produced and reproduced in legal theory and practice. A traditional way of engaging in interdisciplinary research in law has been to advance so-called law and- perspectives such as law and literature, law and society, law and economy, law and gender, etc. This type of interdisciplinary work has been criticized, for example, by Davies as a way of assuming a separation (Davies 2008b: 281–282). To exemplify, when pursuing law and-perspectives in relation to social sciences, one risks continuing an idea that there is a separation between law as an entity and the external sphere (ibid.: 281). In continuing this division, including in critical legal research, one can notice that positivist assumptions of law remain (ibid.).

As Davies further suggests, the feminist legal research tradition has made important contributions towards situated approaches of law by asking questions of inclusion and exclusion such as "Who is represented in the law? Whose stories are told and heard? Who is in control?" (ibid.: 282) Also, other perspectives within socio-legal studies have a more fluid perception of law as something inseparable from the social landscape rather than something being superimposed upon it (ibid.). The engagement with technologically and market/trade-orientated legal fields has furthermore for long required a practical engagement with law (e.g. Wilhelmsson 1994; Wilhelmsson 2001; Glavå and Petrusson 2008). As we will see, this is also the conclusion from the development of control based on proprietary structures in the digitally mediated economy, as these forms appeared much earlier in business practices than in the legal field in a narrow sense. Also, even now when these questions are being raised in several fields of theory, we are unable to see a corresponding development of what is actually being enacted *as* law openly if only studying law in a narrow sense. In this way, the legal discipline of law may be blind to the developments in other fields in relation to *de facto* proprietary control. This runs the risk of sterilising legal discourse and underestimating the forms of control that legal concepts are supposed to, as a minimum, balance. Therefore, "the law" as generally outlined as property law is studied here through the identification of legal conceptual divides, but also the business discourse and practices, etc. that relate to the production of posthuman property. Thus, the aim is to highlight a diversity of practices that challenge the liberal legal concepts of subjectivity as expressed in property concepts in a digitally mediated society.

A third main theme in new materialist and posthumanist philosophy, is the focus on monism, which "pushes dualism to its extreme" (Dolphijn and van der Tuin 2011: 386). This methodological commitment involves a questioning of binary divides as a tool for pursuing research and ethics in a posthumanist manner. This approach to dualism has specific affiliations with the theories of Deleuze and Guattari, methodologically (for example, as ways of conducting philosophy), as well as ontologically (a materialist spirit). An often-quoted passage in which they describe their methodology they express this commitment as invoking one dualism only in order to challenge another and to employ a dualism of models only in order to arrive at a process that challenges all models (2013[1998]: 21). This implies a further commitment to making visible the *connections* between bodies that otherwise have been thought of as separate. Furthermore, the aim of challenging the very particular dualisms of modernity is to arrive at a philosophy of difference that paves the way for a "new" ontology beyond power regimes, such as anthropocentrism and capitalism, which may be directly connected to modernity (Dolphijn and van der Tuin 2011: 386; Braidotti 2013: 89).

This theoretical standpoint here unfolds through a methodology where I engage with different conceptual dichotomies related to the person–thing divide in legal theory in general and property law in particular. Besides the person–thing divide as such, the mind–body and human–digital divides will also be of particular concern. The specific aim with this methodological focus is to show how property law is not only a legal textual, or conceptual, apparatus but also something that is produced through digital technologies and advanced capitalism. Focusing on the enactment of law through digital matter is a highly beneficial focus with regards to technology-related law as the way in which law as a social construct has already been questioned in the digital sphere during the past two decades is already old news (e.g. Lessig 1999; Zittrain 2006; Hildebrandt 2015). Also, the questions of digital subjectivity as embedded in digital milieus were at an early stage researched within the fields of digital media studies and digital humanities (Nakamura 2002; boyd 2012) and, to some extent, law (Cohen 2012) but have gained increased intensity with the recent developments of smart objects, spaces, algorithmic government and, of course, artificial intelligence (AI).

Property

Property as a concept plays a key role in the Western liberalist conceptions of law. This has been expressed in a very illuminating way, not the least, by Bentham who proclaimed that: "[p]roperty and law are born together and must die together." In fact, he even goes as far as to state that: "Before the laws, there was no property: take away the laws, all property ceases" (Bentham 1846). In spite of statements like this, there is naturally not just one way of pinpointing what property actually *is* as a legal concept, not even in the Western liberal legal tradition. However, two particularly prominent ways of understanding what the property concept implies involve *either* considering property as something that grant control over things in absolute terms *or* to regard property as a "bundle of sticks/rights." The first understanding of property perceives property as the absolute domination over external things by the property owner. People other than the property owner are entirely excluded from controlling or using the asset which a property owner claims as property. In this form, the property right functions as an absolute control over both the property object as well as over others who could, for example, be interested in just a limited use of the asset in question. Property is understood here as a bubble of control that trumps other rights to a certain asset. This perspective is akin to what can be called a general understanding of property, particularly outside the (dominant) legal discipline (ibid.). (e.g. Rose 1990; Davies 2008a: 20).

The alternative idea, in which property is conceived of as a bundle of sticks, tends to be considered as a more nuanced way of explaining how property functions as a legal concept: as a combination of different rights and obligations between parties. Such understanding is also regarded as offering greater sensitivity to the particularities of property rights related to the qualities of the property object. This should then be viewed in light of how the first perception of property is represented as a full right to exclude others in relation to a specific object. The idea of a disaggregated concept of property has notably been pursued with reference to Hohfeld's idea of property as a bundle of rights, rather than one single right of control (1913; 1946). This understanding follows rationalizations of conflicting rights of different kinds that limit and consequently effectuate a form of property which is not superior towards all other interests. Interestingly, it can also connect to the differences in materialities between property objects that make property holding more or less effective, making, certain property objects more difficult to control. Such way of reasoning involves by statements that it is more difficult to steal a house than a small item (Davies 2008a: 20–21; Boyle 1996: 47–50; and Lessig 1999: 130–135). The bundle of rights perspective is more widely used in modern liberal jurisprudence as both a way of describing property in practice and, as mentioned, critiquing the dominion concept of property. Davies adds that the bundle of rights perception of property as a form of the denaturalization of what a property right entails may also offer a way of developing property into a more socially responsive concept (Davies 2008a: 21).

As Boyle further points out, a disaggregated understanding of property is also a cornerstone in the construction of intellectual property rights. This is easily recognizable in the way that intellectual property rights are conceptualized by the direct limitations enacted by each specific intellectual property rights act. Such limitations comprise, for example, the scope of an intellectual property right set out by the intellectual property law in question, as well as, for example, by how long a specific intellectual property right may be claimed in accordance with each individual law. Another example of a limitation of intellectual property rights includes how they are directly balanced towards social interests in recognising the creator's moral interests (in some, but not all IPRs), as well how to not suppress the innovation and diffusion of science via too far-reaching property rights (Boyle 1996: 47–50). Consequently, it is intuitive from the perspective of intellectual property rights acts to endorse an understanding of property as something that does not give the right to keep an intangible asset as a right over an object without any limitations. Therefore, the intellectual property right constructs are easy to recognize as a bundle of rights, rather than one well-defined right to exclude everyone from the use of a specific (property) object.

It is furthermore fairly common that the bundle of rights concepts, are understood as beneficial from more radical perspectives of property. As I will show in Chapter 4, this disaggregated understanding of property rights, can however also imply a risk under forms of intellectual asset-based capitalism, since the property objects as such are disaggregated in a more complex ways, and control is built around different types of legal design of combined property rights via e.g. contracts. This understanding of perceiving the bundle of rights-perspective of property as a tool for more commodification rather than the opposite, in turn resonates with a point by Davies on how a disaggregated concept of property rights might make the concept of property more flexible. And this in turn means that an increased number of things can become property (Davies 2008a: 21).

In relation to the topic of this book, the understanding that property rights are disaggregated can be understood as a starting point in considering how we can construct a concept of property for our posthuman age. This is particularly so since my own background both in Scandinavian intellectual property rights scholarship, as well as in the Scandinavian legal realist school in general (see e.g. Glavå and Petrusson 2002; Glavå and Petrusson 2008) is oriented towards outlining the actual power vested in legal concepts. This implies for example a scepticism towards the meaning of concepts such as property in general, with the purpose of showing which different types of rights that are used by which actors to establish control over things as well as societies. The Scandinavian legal realist understanding of property can in this way be summarized as a disavowal of using legal concepts such as property rights to explain which interests are *actually* playing out between parties in a transaction. However, what is more important for the purposes in this book is that property but manifests itself in a differentiated manner where a number of rights and interests create weaker or stronger property rights for the property holder and *how* property per se is being transformed in relation to the developments of advanced capitalism in a digitally mediated society. To investigate the transformation of property under this form of capitalism, which orders of dominance it is embedded in, and how it is being deployed to build control, is crucial for an analysis into whether we can even call the emerging forms of property anymore or if it is something else, and worse. In relation to such transformation of the property concept under advanced capitalism, it should also be noted already here that Davies also suggests that property in the digital economy could potentially no longer be understood as property in the modern sense, but is possibly more a feudalist type of "property". The reason for this is that she finds that property control now, just as in the feudal society can be understood to collapse concepts of ownership and sovereignty and in doing so property controls both a thing as well as who has political standing in society (Davies 2008a: 81–82). This idea of property as something akin to feudal power is also something I will return to in Chapter 4.

Another important starting point for reconsidering property in the posthumanist vein is the minor tradition of property in which alternative themes in how property is theoretically and practically enacted have been explored (Davies 2008a: 10). What connects these themes is that they criticize the liberalist political project in which property is key to the constitution of citizens as political actors. Under this liberalist project, the private sphere is seen as a separate zone from the public sphere. The private sphere here functions as a form of zoning to protect individuals from intrusion by the state (ibid.). Consequently, in such liberal thought, property combined with other rights granted to the individual is generally understood to be inviolable, as it functions as a protection for the individual against the nation state. A theme in this type of theory is hence to show how the concept and practice of property works as a means of strengthening liberal individualism and privatising the power that is embedded in it. This theme is particularly focused on how to criticize the understanding that persons are equal and free to accumulate and defend their property rights as a form of private right, whereas the political or public sphere is simultaneously understood as something that all citizens have an equal right and access to. Consequently, this theme aims to show how political indifferences produced by property rights connected to very particular property-owning individuals, against the rest of humankind, are being erased (ibid.: 10–11).

A second theme of an alternative property theory theme outlined by Davies concerns the connection between property and class status. Davies calls this theme "propriety and the proper" and builds on the role that property has played in stabilising the political order, at least from feudal times when political status and authority had to do with "family heritage, position in a hierarchy of landholdings, and inalienable connection to a (generally) male-controlled estate" (ibid.: 12). This idea of property goes well beyond the idea of property as something that is pinned down by law as a form of human ownership over a thing. Instead, it focuses on how ownership is embedded and performed also via other orders of domination and control, even if we would have to stretch to say that the feudal system as such still prevails today. This is also a key point in the theory of posthuman property developed here, even though the focus is on posthumanist analyses of power rather than the direct ties to old and new feudalist forms of power. As Davies puts it:

> property as propriety enters further into the construction of social identity than simply being about what we own: regardless of whether we are owners, the notion of property, with its boundaries and exclusion zones, helps to define "me" and "you" within the liberal cultural context.
>
> (ibid.: 13)

This axploration of how property control functions as hierchacical domination certain persons over others is also associated with the third theme of property outlined by Davies (Davies 2008a: 13–14). This theme, which recently has been popularized by Esposito relates to the construction of subjects and objects via property (ibid. and Esposito 2015). The distinction between persons and things, which also feeds into property theory, rests, for example, on a Kantian philosophical idea of which bodies can be considered ends in themselves versus those bodies that are only a means to an end. In law, this implies that persons are those who are considered to be legal subjects as they are moral ends who can own property and consequently are not property themselves (besides *persona ficta*/juristic persons constructions which are placed on some kind of middle ground) (Davies 2008a: 13; Davies and Naffine 2001: 127). A way of expressing this is that property is based on the person–thing divide. This line between the human subject and all other matter (Hayles 1999: 2; Braidotti 2013: 2) is further utilized as a divide to rationalize control by those considered persons over everything that can be considered property.

These types of processes unfold through practices of dematerialization, in making something into property (from otherwise being considered as part of something else, that was not property). Such dematerialization is also characteristic for cybernetics in general (Hayles 1999), as well as property control of information in particular. Furthermore, the processes of dematerialization come to shield anything else that goes on in relation to property besides the commodification it very clearly makes possible (whether or not through a bindle of rights). This leads to what we can call a third position, besides property as domination and property as a bundle of sticks, in considering what property as a concept is about (and consequently what it is not about), namely, that it is about a human (person) owning something (a thing). In turn, this assumption implies that property is understood to be a mere tool for owning a commodity. If the commodity turns out to have a life of its own, this does not hinder property as a concept as such. As Keenan argues, such neutralising notions of the commodity, and ownership, implies a lack of sensitivity in property theory for how property functions as a means of control in much more dynamic ways (Keenan 2015: 6–7 and passim). The affective or otherwise lively aspects of property is instead generally classified under market law or, to some extent, contract law in which the message of how a property is sold and which emotional registers it should be attuned to, are regulated and to some extent, limited. Or in terms of animals or the environment, it is other laws that regulate the safety and health of such (joint or private) commodities. The passivation of a commodity on a person–thing scale however fits badly with considering information as a commodity, in general. The reason for this is that information has the capacity to slice through this idea when a commodity is both communication, knowledge, labour and affective production circulating between both human and nonhuman bodies.

With all these three dominant aspects of property ruptured, we therefore need to follow and recreate a stream of property theory that gives us the capacity to capture and critically engage with our posthuman condition.

Posthuman Property as a Concept

A key theme of the legal concept of property is that it builds upon and enforces a distinction between persons and things, or owners and property objects. Persons as concepts in the legal discipline are furthermore fundamentally entangled with an idea of the human as described above (even if legal personhood today has developed into something very far from human personhood in the everyday understanding of the term) (Radin 1993; Radin 1996; Davies and Naffine 2001). This means that property as a theoretical concept in Western forms of law is conceptually bundled with the exact ideas about both humans and nonhumans that the posthumanist theoretical discipline in general is trying to get rid of, or at least: decentre. From a posthumanist perspective, a property theory that, as a fundamental principle, divides persons from things is less capable of understanding the forces that property engages with. Furthermore, a standardized divide between either a human, property-owning, subject or a passive nonhuman object, is not sensitive enough in articulating differences within the groups of humans and nonhumans. To return to the thoughts on the posthuman advocated by Braidotti, it is vital to visualize how the becoming human, and subsequently posthuman, does not occur in an equal way for all humans. The idea that humans are on the one side of the property concept, as owners, whereas only nonhumans are on the other side, consequently iterates an idea of sameness that obfuscates the extreme inequalities of property control today. Following posthumanist theory, a starting point for articulating a concept for property involves to start from the position that who is a property subject versus who is a property object does not automatically arise based on who "has" a human body. As such, this assumption may sit uneasy with the legal discipline, including critical legal theory, since much work has been put into defining the human, and human rights, as means to provide a framework for how humans are not to be traded as commodities. However, assuming that humans are not possible to commodify runs contrary to the less clear boundaries of what constitutes the human, or even the human body, as will be discussed throughout. In particular, this perspective makes less sense in contexts where it is not "natural persons," "data," nor "personas," but rather entanglements between humans and digital bodies that are at stake, as will be discussed throughout.

Posthuman property as a concept therefore seeks to visualize how property control in a digitally mediated society works on levels beyond our traditional understandings of property. In doing so, a vital starting point is that the commodity form as such is neither given nor eternal, and that this is mirrored today in the way that commodification, as suggested by Wark, now means

> not the appearance of a world of things but the appearance of a world of *information about things*, including information about every possible future state of those things that can be extrapolated from a quantitative modelling of information extracted from the flux if the state of things, more or less in real time.
>
> (Wark 2019: 15)

The concept of posthuman property constructed here is particularly affiliated with different critical positions within property theory. It also builds its posthumanist position in affiliation with theories that underlie posthumanist thinking such as feminist theory. The feminist property tradition has significantly highlighted how personhood and community is assumed or excluded from property. In particular, the concept of posthuman property draws inspiration from accounts on how property can be understood as an affective force to sustain certain forms of belonging. As proposed by Keenan, an alternative notion of property can be developed around the understanding that property sustains and produces power in a way which "holds up bodies as space" (2015: 71–72 and passim). This conceptualization of property has the purchase of enabling a posthumanist reconsideration of what property implies in the sense that it disrupts the focus of general property theory's alignment with subject–object distinctions. Another way to express this focus is to frame property as performative in the sense that it creates part–whole connections (Cooper 2007; Keenan 2015: 6–7). As Keenan shows, this reshuffling of property theory makes property "less about the subject and more about the space in and through which the subject is constituted" (2015: 74). By considering property as something that holds up bodies, it also becomes possible to consider a wider array of control practices as being *internal* to property.

This positions property as having a performative, affective, relational as well as nonhuman function as it does not start from either a humanist divide between persons or things, or as a fixed idea of property power as something coming from above. This in turn affords a framework for visualising the continuous reshaping of the commodity form that digital materialities afford. Furthermore, it enables, in particular, a focus on the affective dimensions that property both produces and unsettles via the commodification of information/information about everything and everyone. This focus is furthermore deeply needed when investigating the potential for both law and property in the latest stages of digitalization, as they involve the use of information about things to effectuate certain forms of politics as well as more soft nudging of behaviours based on information. As such, the commodity form and the property control form become significantly entangled with both *the production of* bodies besides holding them up as space. This focus disrupts the linear or fixed temporality embedded in all of the assumptions of conventional property theory as described above, in which property is taken as given to, and is enacted via, human subjects, reaching through both time and space (Keenan 2015: 66). Such understanding of property here therefore also functions as a form of spatio-temporal re-ordering of relations between both humans and nonhumans, via the forces related to advanced capitalism. In order to develop the concept of posthuman property in this direction, I further utilize three posthumanist tools: body, entanglement and ethics. The purpose with these tools is to illustrate both how bodies are being produced, held up and relate to each other as posthuman property.

Body

The centrality of the body as a concept for posthumanist theory was identified early on, for example, in the essay collection *Posthuman Bodies* from 1995 edited by Halberstam and Livingston (Halberstam and Livingston 1995: 1). The theoretical ground upon which this concept rests furthermore implies that "a body can be anything: it can be an animal, a body of sounds, *a mind or idea:* it can be a linguistic corpus, a social body, a collectivity" (Philippopoulos-Mihalopoulos 2015: 193). For the sake of property theory, the conceptualization of what a body is and which bodies are disposable has consistently played a role in rationalising proprietary control. Haraway exemplifies a similar line of thought by arguing that from the 18th to the mid-20th centuries "the great historical constructions of gender, race, and class were embedded in the organically marked bodies of woman, the colonized or enslaved, and the worker" (Haraway 1991: 210). In turn, the bodies marked with such forms of power have traditionally been seen as more part of, or subject to, nature and therefore as a resource in general (Haraway 1991: 210).

The first move to visualize posthuman property is therefore to theorize property as the production and reproduction of bodies. This starting point is particularly useful as a critical intervention in property, as this concept invites an exploration of the boundaries of matter. At the same time, the monistic rendering of the body concept in its posthumanist theorization avoids reinstituting divides between binaries of matter such as body/mind and persons/things.

Such idea of body is furthermore interesting from a processual idea of property as the body here is understood as having fluctuating boundaries based on how it connects and moves in relation to other bodies. A famous statement which captures this capacity of bodies to transform themselves and their relations to other matter can be found in Deleuze's widely cited statement that "[w]e do not know what a body can do" (Deleuze 1988 [1970]: 17–18). This understanding of the body, holds within it both that the material conditions of bodies can variate as well as that there is always a level of uncertainty or excess, in the knowledge about how such variations may come about. The ethical implication of this, is as will be discussed further below, that the indeterminacy of bodies, disengages the god-view kind of observing and governing, which runs through both legal theory and more recent AI narratives alike.

To study how matter expressed as bodies come to fluctuate in this way is furthermore possible only via an investigation of the desires that bodies produce (individually and in connection to each other). Desires, stemming from bodies, and keeping them together in turn, can become so persistent that they are to be understood as regimes of power, or *atmosphere* (Philippopoulos-Mihalopoulos 2015: 107–173). Such regimes of power or atmosphere, can furthermore have such substantial effects on bodies, that they seem entirely natural, while strictly determining what a body can be at a certain time. This implies that meanwhile the body as a concept is used in posthumanist theory to shed increased light on materiality, it also bundled up with an understanding that matter is shaped also via more incorporeal aspects such as collectivized desires as power, or distributed excess between bodies (cf. Grosz 2017: 5–6).

The body concept as a means to articulate posthuman property therefore enables a critical engagement with the body that offers something more than a conceptual but constantly overridden idea that the human body functions as boundary for commodification (cf. Cooper 2007). Another implication of focusing on matter in the vein of articulating posthuman property as a concept is to interrogate the concepts taken for granted in intellectual property theory such as the division between body and mind. To question the divide between matters of the mind, versus matters of the body is particularly vital when faced with digitalization and the data-driven economy. The reason for this is that much research has made clear that such economy is only possible by the exploitation of (other) material resources. Furthermore, the affective aspects of digitalization, effectuates changes also in what is possible to think, or access as knowledge (see e.g. Parikka 2015; Pasquinelli 2018; Noble 2018). Consequently, a concept of intellectual property needs to be grounded in a theoretical understanding that it is not only a tool for the commodification of knowledge, but for example of culture, science, love and life itself. As will be discussed, neither intellectual property, nor intellectual property theory was obviously never really blind about these aspects. However, as will be made clear, the assumptions about intellectual property as a property of limited expressions of knowledge, detached from context and use, needs to be broken down even further now. The reason for this is that the proprietary control embedded in AI technologies such as algorithmic governance, machine learning, blockchain etc., have a capacity to reprogram the world in the image of capitalism in a way that is simply not possible to capture as merely a control over knowledge, or an expression of knowledge. As several authors show, the differences in what data that an algorithm is trained on, creates a continuation of the material condition in which said data was collected. This means that if datasets are compiled in a society where racism and sexism exist, our machinic intelligences risk perpetuating this (cf. Noble 2018; Benjamin 2019).

By developing posthumanist understandings of the body as part of the concept of property, it becomes possible to both see the appropriation and uses for information as workings on matter themselves, but also to analyse how this activates very specific affective regimes or forms of power that hold up bodies as space. To engage such concept of materiality as a basis for a property theory is furthermore pertinent in facing critical algorithm studies as regards to for example questions of racialization and gendering in the datasets being used for automation. Here, such continuation of power via desires and affects of bodies is intimately treated as a concept of property via the formation of bodies.

Building on the body concept in this theoretical vein also enfolds the other two concepts put in motion here: entanglement and ethics, which function as an important means of disrupting the dominating development of posthuman property.

Entanglement

In posthumanist theory, the concept of the body has the function of both foregrounding materiality as such, as well as to revitalise it with questions of its relational placement towards other bodies. This is useful in producing a critique of both in Western law in general and property theory in particular, where the smallest unit often is understood to be the individual, independent, property-owning, human. The body concept breaks with this idea in the manner that the body is conceived of as being shaped by, and shape, other bodies (human and nonhuman) via desires, place-taking on behalf of other bodies, etc. By giving primacy to how relations are formed according to the terms for the bodies engaged in these relations, posthumanism foregrounds the connective potential between bodies that are otherwise treated as different and therefore non-connectable (Braidotti 2013: 159). This relational onto-epistemology folded into posthuman property and the body concept is here expressed as *entanglement*. Barad expresses this theoretical standpoint as that

> [t]he very nature of materiality is an entanglement. Matter itself is always already open to, or rather, *entangled with*, the "Other". Not only subjects but also objects are permeated through and through with their entangled kin; the other is not just in one's skin, but in one's bones, in one's belly, in one's heart, in one's nucleus, in one's past and future.
>
> (2007: 392–393)

In this way, *relationality* is something bodies cannot escape. As Philippopoulos-Mihalopoulos puts it "there can no longer be a pre-given boundary between a body and its environment" (Philippopoulos-Mihalopoulos 2015: 199). Such understanding also reflects the conception of assemblage or *agancement* in the theories by Deleuze and Guattari. A body is consequently always "an assemblage of various conditions and materialities" (2013[1998]: 296–304).

In discourses related to the digitalized society, the concept of how materialities are connected to each other often takes the form of the fantasies of networks or our later digital "communities." The idea of thinking about the internet as a form of network is, as Jonathan Zittrain shows, already from its start in 1969, embedded in an idea of functioning as a means of "subsuming heterogeneous networks while allowing those networks to function independently" (2006: 1975). Zittrain further argues that this implies that from the beginning the internet was both a set of building blocks as well as a "glue" holding the blocks together (ibid.). As he also points out, this structured openness of the materialities that become entangled as networks were also constructed in a way that: "any sort of device: any computer or other information processor could be part of the new network so long as it was properly interfaced, an exercise requiring minimal technical effort" (ibid.: 1976).

As will be particularly discussed in Chapters 5 and 6, this view of digitalized society as built on networks has paved the way for reconstructing how property control is exercised as a form of architectural control of networks. With more theoretical water under the bridge compared to the early 2000s, we can now see an increased number of legal theorists that considers digital networks not only to be about internet or other more visible forms of networks, but also its connection to natural resources, human data etc. (see e.g., Cohen 2012; Cohen 2019; Vatanparast 2020). Such developments towards expanding the entanglement of matter beyond a narrower idea of what constitutes the digital is vital for articulating what is at stake in terms of property control. Consequently, the tool of entanglement in posthuman property seeks to highlight how proprietary control is both about control over segments of the internet via e.g. intellectual property, as well as about targeting users for their data and extracting natural resources. In this way, posthuman property can be explored as a concept with both architectural expressions as well as with ecological and even geological properties (cf. Parikka 2015). This relational understanding of property is furthermore complemented with a normative register via the posthumanist focus on ethics.

Ethics

The third tool for theorising posthuman property that I will utilize here is the specific form of ethics developed in posthumanist theory. This idea of ethics can be explained in relation to the previous concept of entanglement in the manner that connectivity does not have a positive for the connected bodies (Deleuze and Guattari 2013: 5–11). It is particularly important to stress this here because convergences between human and digital matter tends to be conceived of as *intrinsically* good for society, which is not the least evidenced in the current boom towards AI. Ethics here is therefore engaged to evaluate at which costs (and for whom) that certain bodies, and their relations, come into being while other entanglements of bodies may be destroyed. This type of ethics is generally perceived of as an *immanent* rather than a *transcendent* form of ethics, morals, and values (Spindler 2013: 43–45) via its connections to Deleuze's writings on Spinoza (Deleuze 1988; Deleuze 1992; Braidotti 2013: 55–57; MacCormack 2012: 1–2). This implies that there is no external and definite framework against which for example a certain law is measured against. To specify further here what such ethics might imply, we can contrast it with the most common takes in intellectual property theory, as well as in the legal discipline in general, where law and economics inspired ideas of distribution, efficiency of markets and similar, are used as external norms which the value of IPR laws are measured against. Traditionally, also religious views of what constitutes justice, has functioned, and still functions today as means to establish a transcendent idea of what is good in/for a society.

Other common ways of expressing normative aims with law is via procedural perspectives of justice, human rights, gender equality etc. Here however, the starting question is that we need a better understanding of how property works under the posthuman condition and the forms of power that is involved in expressing it. The normative guiding point for the ethics that is applied here is consequently to highlight processes of materializations that disrupts the general understanding of property, and what this leads to. Starting from posthuman theory, this is not a pure immanent ethics in the sense that it comes without values or interests. The problem formulation of the posthuman condition, as described above, rests upon ideas of how to account for the ways that advanced capitalism affect bodies. The ethical dimension is about both developing theory around how such powers are connected with how we become human, inhuman and posthuman, as well as finding affirmative openings within such becomings. This affirmative side of ethics is described in posthumanist theory as an aim to contribute to create more radically sustainable ways of living than what is currently afforded (Barad 2007: 391–396; Braidotti 2013: 172–194). This can for example imply to question the liberalist/humanist individualist idea of property rights currently (at least theoretically) is encapsulating.

Another way that such ethics of affirmative kind unfolds is via the way that technology is approached altogether as having potential to contribute to a different kind of social order. In the words of Braidotti, such a view of ethics is particularly fruitful as a means of countering techno-optimism and the fear of technology (2013: 190–197). This consequently involves employing an ethical stance that is both critical as well as affirmative at the same time. As such, this type of ethics is also actively engaged with reshaping desires to move bodies in other directions than those that are currently keeping them in place via (from a posthumanist perspective) destructive power regimes. As a part of producing an alternative understanding of the world, Braidotti argues that it is important not to give into entirely negative accounts of informatics of domination as a form of bio-power or so-called "necropolitics." As she further points out, biopower and necro-politics can be thought of as two sides of the same coin. Thus, the interest in the politics of life itself also affects the geo-political dimension of death and killing as mentioned above (2013: 122 ff.). Braidotti proposes an example of a posthuman idea of ethics in her notion of *zoe ethics* or *radical relationality* (2013: 35, also see Philippopoulos-Mihalopoulos 2015). As Braidotti also notes, posthumanist ethics, in following a more experimental path, needs to be "enacted collectively, so as to produce effective cartographies of how much bodies can take" (2013: 191). For this reason, she also refers to the exploration of bodies in connection with ethics as "thresholds of sustainability." The aim of experimenting with such concepts is to "create collective bonds, a new affective community or polity" (ibid.).

It should be noted already at this stage that discourses on AI have interestingly also recently come to dwell on questions regarding ethics. However, what sets a posthumanist idea of ethics slightly apart from other types of ethics is that posthumanist is connected to a critical tradition in the manner described above. This implies not the least that it is less about making machines as ethical as humans, and more about changing society in a manner so that it moves away from the destructive forces that anthropocentrism and advanced capitalism give rise to and sustains. Consequently, while acknowledging questions of how to make, for example, big platform companies attend to ethical practices in relation to data collection or to secure a human-in-the-loop, as is the case in current forms of ethics (cf. Amoore 2020), posthumanist ethics attends to the wider entanglements enabling which resource extraction, and property control, is made possible and desirable. What is needed here is therefore a fuller programme for what is at stake in terms of the commodification and control of property, which relationships it allows and which relationships are hindered.

Chapter Outline

The book is divided into an opening introduction section that includes Chapter 1 and Chapter 2. In these chapters, posthumanist theory and posthumanist jurisprudence are introduced as a means of engaging with questions of property in digitally mediated societies. Whereas Chapter 1 sets out these premises in general, Chapter 2 focuses on questions of why it is important to understand the impact of advanced capitalism and digitalization on law itself, and how we can think of law in new ways via posthumanist theory. As stated in the introduction, a changed focus on the role of jurisprudence is as vital to understanding property in a new light, as it is to visualising the reshaped role of property theory. The reason for this is that Western law and property is so intimately connected that the dislocation of one, demands the dislocation of the other. As described in Chapter 2, law as such, has been understood to shift material form under digitalization. These narratives are here introduced via concepts such as "code is law," "blockchain as law" and algorithmic governance. With the backdrop of such developments, it has lately been advanced in legal theory that we might be witnessing the end of law as the Western legal order (have mostly come to) know it: as a text-driven, court-centred reality. Such insights in legal research regarding the transformation of, and possible end of, law is in this chapter read and developed further via posthumanist theory and posthumanist legal theory. The aim of this exercise is to suggest not only a reshaped vision of law's materialities but also an invigorated form of jurisprudence which manages to engage the ethical dimensions of posthumanist theory. In short, the chapter suggests that it is not the shifting materialities of law that are the problem, *per se*, but the loss of certain ethical diagnostics and motives. In relation to this loss, posthumanist jurisprudence is suggested as a means of reactivating law with normativity based on the ethics suggested here. In doing this, it becomes possible to reactivate law in more ways than before for the purpose of resisting both advanced capitalism and other power regimes.

Following the two introductory chapters, the structure of this book runs along the theoretical thread of the three tools, or themes, identified in posthumanist theory, which are presented as intermezzos between *body, entanglement* and *ethics*. These tools further unfold as means to challenge several dichotomies related to the dominant ideas of property that in practice are being displaced by digital technologies. The aim of doing this is to reshape the understanding of property in order to equip it with critical insights from posthumanist theory, and affiliated theories that foreground similar critiques. The dichotomies, in turn, are explored in relation to several cartographies as discussed in the methodological commitments earlier in Chapter 1. In terms of the structure of this part, the book is divided into two mirroring chapters per tool. These two mirroring chapters comprise a first chapter that engages with phenomena and practices – identified in both society and other disciplines than law – and a second chapter directed towards property theory and assumptions that can be questioned in relation to these. Both chapters are also embedded in the specific tool and placed in conversation with posthumanist theory and critical theories that are affiliated with posthumanist endeavours.

Chapter 3, which is the first to engage with the body tool, focuses on discourses and practices related to innovation theory and practices in which information has been pictured and produced as a resource. The aim of this chapter is to focus on discourses concerning the materiality of information, and the digital in general, to show how the disconnection of information from other resources (including human bodies) functions as a prerequisite for commodification and the shape that proprietary control can take. This type of de- and rematerialization of information (obviously) does not take place in one unified way, as this chapter aims to show. Several different narratives and business practices shape the turning of information into a resource that can be captured. This involves for example both narratives that dematerialise knowledge from the human mind as well as rematerialize them as individual elements to be controlled under contract or intellectual property rights.

As recent scholarship has shown, to produce a critique against information-based commodities, we further need to pinpoint both the asset logics that drives high-tech capitalism (Adkins, Cooper and Konings 2020) as well as the market/business models in which they are embedded (Srnicek 2017). This chapter seeks to do this, both with a focus on how digitalization becomes materialized as commodities in this vein as well as drawing from other examples in for example the biotech industry. Examples of such discourses engaged with in this chapter include theories regarding assetization via business management theories and practices such as intellectual capital management and open innovation. These two streams of business management theory for knowledge-intense companies both convey ideas of how to manage high-tech innovation in general. Such themes are today deployed in multiple ways related to for example the control of data and platform capitalism, as this chapter also shows.

Chapter 4 responds to the aspects discussed in Chapter 3 by outlining a number of conceptual challenges that property rights encounter in relation to treating information as an asset in general and how digital materialities trouble this further. The challenges are identified both in relation to the discourses outlined in the previous chapter as well as via following a theoretical orientation of progressive work on property. This involves identifying a number of conceptual divides that have been conceived of as boundaries against commodification, including the conceptual divides between intellectual vs. physical property and property vs. personhood. As shown in the previous chapter, control over knowledge or information builds upon, and establishes a disembodied idea of information, from both its context and from the bodies from which such control is developed. The disembodied, yet human-derived, character of intellectual resources have also previously caused conceptual problems in liberalist property theory. The reason for this is that liberal ideas of property entails that each person has ownership of their (human) body. When information is collected as data or when information is derived more explicitly from human body material, one can therefore argue that such conceptual boundary is being displaced to the benefit of a more general enclosure of information. An example which is also discussed in the chapter is the ironic twist of recent data protection legislation which conveys how personal data is made into a business asset on the basis that is not personal (enough). Examples such as these are here put forward to suggest that posthuman property emerges just when the ambiguities of information as an asset is to be captured as a commodity.

Chapter 5 is the first chapter on the theme of entanglement. This chapter outlines a number of practices and discourses in which digital materialities can be conceived of as entangled both to each other and humans. Recent developments of such logics of entanglement, which are addressed here, includes the smartification of both objects and spaces. Examples of this development are now visible in many parts of our daily lives in which smart objects, such as smart phones, have come to be accompanied by domestic robots, and in which entire cities are planned to become smart. As the chapter outlines, this is also where the platform-based business model as such reaches new intensities, as market actors connect new digital materialities to their networks. Besides connectivity, between phenomena, this chapter also stresses how such development is intrinsically connected with a business logic that seeks to produce so-called network effects.

Reading this development of entanglement through posthumanist theory consequently aims to stress that what is at stake in terms of enmeshment between matter, is the subordination of matter to a larger platform logic. Here, such logics is identified and unfolded via discourses on how platform control in general is strengthened by a number of emerging digital phenomena and practices. This includes a focus on encryption technologies that function both as a means of governance, as discussed in Chapter 2, and as tools for facilitating an interconnection between automated objects and spaces. Furthermore, phenomena such as smart cities and smart logistics are identified as further extensions of platform-based business logics, driven by connection and control over interfaces between digital and not-yet-digital matter. This chapter therefore argues that in order to understand the logics of advanced capitalism, one needs to understand how it pursues a number of practices in order to entangle different matter to each other and then control and expand such entanglements.

Chapter 6 explores the idea of entanglement via property theory by questioning concepts of spatial boundaries as a boundary for property. As the chapter exemplifies, property in digitized settings is generally coded via a platform-logics that disrupts Western liberal assumptions of spaces while drawing other bodies together. In performing such a role of drawing bodies together, property can also be considered as actively creating entanglements, or belongings, rather than just defining narrow rights of ownership control of different elements (whether formalized or not, as discussed in Chapter 4). This understanding of property now moves from the person–thing divide towards a control of both locating parts in networks, as well as how they can be conceived of as whole assemblages of bodies. As discussed here, posthuman property when appearing in this shape is both a spatial form of property that produces architectural control points for bodies to access and disconnect, as well as changing spaces of community and privacy. Furthermore, the chapter paves the way for further elaboration of the affective aspects of such governance of the interface between bodies, to be further explored in the final theme of ethics.

Chapter 7 opens the final section covering the theme of *ethics*. The focus here is on the discourses on ethics currently emerging in artificial intelligence in the wider sense of the term. As such research has shown, there is a need to assess the normative functions that automation plays. The posthumanist idea of ethics is utilized to suggest a reorientation from the humanist values re-emerging in ethics discourse in relation to AI. This implies a shift in focus from the general discipline on AI ethics towards addressing relations at the human-nonhuman continuum as they are enabled via automation. This need is here also connected back to the discourses in Chapter 2, regarding the shifting focus and role of jurisprudence under digitalization. Consequently, this chapter returns more deeply to questions of normativity, by moving through and beyond discourses of AI ethics that are currently unfolding. The notion and use of affect (human, nonhuman and other variations) and affective governance is here furthermore identified as a particular theme for advocating AI ethics in a more posthumanist way.

Chapter 8 connects the chapters by adding a layer of affective control as a particular register by which also posthuman property is enacted. This chapter again engages property theory and its conceptual boundaries towards other legal constructions such as advertising laws and freedom of speech, to show how the common view of property fails to recognize property's affective characteristics. Such lack of recognition to how property produces affects that reaches beyond more than just ownership over a thing, is a flaw if one is to analyse how property control is produced in the digitally mediated economy. This is particularly so in relation to the vast amount of AI related technologies such as behavioural advertising, but also in relation to the general optimization based on sensors that automation requires. This chapter consequently advances the ethical role of posthumanism to be able to visualize how property de facto, at all times, could be considered to take place as a tool for distribution of posthuman bodies. An affirmative consequence of such ethics is furthermore that it opens up for a possibility to consider the redistribution of property under automation in a wider sense. This could be compared to other alternatives of redistribution such as suggestions for the sustainable use of the resources needed for the production of devices, or for fairness and anti-discrimination on social media and other platforms.

To summarise, all these chapters suggest a way of understanding the different forms of property power that advanced capitalism exercises in a digitally mediated society. It does so by highlighting how a much more complex form of property control has emerged compared to what the standard perception of property and control under industrial capitalism would capture. However, this turn of capitalism and property, which produces a form of posthuman condition, together with other orders of power and domination, also opens up for a new ethics to emerge: an ethics of full redistribution along posthumanist ethical lines. Such redistribution then includes the re/production of a world beyond the human as we know it. Property here is fully considered as taking the shape of being something worse than it has generally been perceived: as ownership of things or knowledge. However, it also suggests that by understanding property in this way, it can also more clearly give way for something better, from a posthumanist perspective. This is the emergence of property as a forceful tool to redistribute bodies through affect and against forms of control that may otherwise render them entirely expendable. In other words, this is the emergence of posthuman property.

Chapter 2

Code is Law and Posthumanist Jurisprudence

A key starting point in Western modernist forms of jurisprudence is that law is a discipline that concerns the identification, interpretation and application of laws in accordance with a pre-set system of rules. This idea of law involves many assumptions about how law comes into being, how it is expressed, how it ends, and naturally who oversees it all. It is uncontroversial to say that the law's identity and the identity of practising lawyers rest upon an idea of law as a privileged system of rules that those of us trained in such systems are best equipped to handle. Ultimately, this system is described in the form that law is something that happens in courts, in which lawyers settle conflicts in accordance with the rules. In doing so they activate the rules they are trained to handle by appealing to arguments in predefined legal sources. All these legal norms are considered to be possible to express in texts, whether they are laws, previous court cases (precedents) or preparatory works used in the development of a legal act. It is the lawyer's role to know which norm to invoke, and the judge's role to assess the validity of the arguments presented (including the strength of evidence supporting the legal claims). In accordance with this dominant understanding of law. he legal sources to be used depends on the legal system in question, and the legal discipline in particular,

This perception of law has come to be criticized widely during at least the past 100 years, in influential schools of legal realism and critical legal studies. Douzinas and Gearey, has expressed this as an obsession of generations of jurisprudence writers as defining what law is. Furthermore, as they point out, this has resulted in theories and histories if law where the meaning(s) of the word "law," the "concept" of law, the "idea" of law, and "law's empire" make up some of the field's most influential textbooks. Furthermore, it is clear that this focus on law's proper place indicates an insecurity, or at least a kind of anxiety amongst legal scholars working hard to establish an essence of law, assuming that law even have such essence (Douzinas and Gearey 2005: 4). In this chapter, such insights of both how law is presented as having an essence, as well as further theorization (and possibly further anxieties) about how to think about law from a posthumanist perspective will be developed. This perspective will be developed from the standpoint that the (still) hegemonic view of law and jurisprudence is

DOI: 10.4324/9781003139096-2

problematic from the context of digitalization as well as in relation to posthumanist theory. In short and as will be further explored this depends on the fact that digitalization and the actors in charge of these processes involve a number of other materialities in the construction of what *de facto* works as law. This is expressed in many discourses around digitalization and law as "code is law" (Lessig 1999), "blockchain as law" (De Filippi and Wright 2019) and similar as will be discussed further here. Posthumanist theory, in turn, engages in a view of both matter and normativity that does not put textual expressions *ex ante* in front of others, in assessing how matter comes into being. Consequently, there is a correlation in these differing fields of research in relation to reconsidering the performative capacities of matter that has a technological or otherwise less linguistic basis.

Another assumption involved in our dominant idea of law involves the view that nation states are sovereign to legislate within the boundaries of their jurisdictions, which follows the borders of the nation state. This implies that states have the right to exclusively decide who is a legitimate legal subject and on what grounds (both conceptually and physically) within their borders. In this view, law is intrinsically connected to the state apparatus and its multiple carriers and expressions. Needless to say, there is nothing uncontroversial about the idea of the nation state nor the idea of sovereignty as explored in much legal theory and recently in relation to law/governance and digitalization (see e.g. Bratton 2015: 19–31; Cohen 2019: e.g. 108–137). This will be explored here through an understanding of the shift of power towards particular market actors under advanced capitalism. However, what is also interesting in relation to a posthumanist perspective is how the control of space is embedded in new types of materialities and an array of actors backed by the state. In most cases such state-backed power in digital settings occur via codes for capital (c.f. Pistor 2020) such as property rights and contract law. However, as is being increasingly discussed, there is also a variation of governance between different societal context such as in the case of China, where the state is understood to have a more direct influence of governing digitalization.

To reach towards the idea of law in a posthumanist vein, we start from the insight that both of the above-mentioned dominant perceptions of law and jurisprudence can be considered to be forms of "restricted jurisprudence," as coined by Douzinas and Gearey (2005). By this they mean that law under these assumptions is constrained by a view of law and legal thinking that is limited in both scope and time in relation to a more general form of jurisprudence. As they show, general jurisprudence can be understood as a form of law which is more concerned with questions of justice in a wider sense, including other materialities than those often described as "law in books" or legislation. This involves, for example, an increased interest in several fields such as literature, cultural theory and psychology as being vital to formulating an understanding of law and law's rule in a wider sense than rule-of-law perspectives offer (ibid.). In digital settings, the restricted pre-conception of law has been decentred for at least three decades as digitized matter has been found to have a capacity to function as laws in its own right. This decentring has not gone unnoticed in terms of critiques from legal scholars. More recent interventions have included the belief that we will see the end of law when machines automatically take on roles over which law and lawyers have had exclusive control. This chapter however outlines a different perspective of law related to digitalization in the manner that it asks the question of the effects of the normative orders emerging, rather than whether a human should be in charge of it (in order for it to be law). The aim here is consequently to open up for an understanding of how these views of law can enable an affirmative point of departure for posthumanist jurisprudence. In brief, posthumanist theory is elaborated here as a response to the understanding of digital technologies as law by infusing law with a perspective of posthumanist materiality and normativity.

Code is Law

It has now been more than two decades since Lessig coined the famous insight and phrase that code is law (Lessig 1999). His analysis shows how digital spaces differ from physical spaces as code replaces, or forms the function of, law. A well-known example that Lessig gives in relation to the difference between physical and digital spaces is the one in which he discusses how the cultivation of flowers has different properties depending on whether they are grown in a digital or physical garden. The case with which he illustrates this relates to a person, Martha Jones, and a dispute between her neighbours in a cyberspace setting. The conflict between Martha and her neighbours circulates around Martha's practice of growing extraordinarily beautiful flowers with the added feature that they are poisonous to the extent that they could even be lethal to anyone who touched them. In the story, this leads to the death of a virtual dog whereby its owner urges Martha to just change the design of the flowers so they will not risk killing other beings (ibid.: 9–10). What is at stake here is the way that the materiality of the flowers has normative effects in a way that sets the rules for how persons in the game can act. No legislative act states that one has to make one's flowers poisonous or not, but as an extension of each actor's property right, the players coded in different properties into their objects. By (simplified) comparison, in a physical setting we usually have laws that govern what is allowed, including in terms of which plants can be legally kept in one's garden. This example therefore points to a central idea of digital governance: that the entanglement between objects and the norms that govern them are conflated when the norms of governance are literally encoded into its objects. This insight was further theorized in connection with Lessig by Zittrain in relation to how locks and openings are created in relation to the internet, through digital design (2006) as will be further discussed in Chapter 6.

Building on subsequent technological developments, Mireille Hildebrandt pinpoints the migration of coded logics of law to enmeshed digital and physical worlds via smart technologies. Hildebrandt does this by first setting out different scenarios of how living in a smart world in which parenting, work and other pleasures could take place when cared for by a digital assistant. The assistant consequently functions as the mediating element in the enhanced environment in which the code is seamlessly embedded into everyday life, yet governs or possibly arranges human lives by human will (Hildebrandt 2015: 1–7). She continues this understanding by showing that norms become encoded into smart objects to an extent where they also enact these norms in the next layer and in non-digital worlds (ibid.: 41–61). In this way, smart objects become extensions of the code-is-law perspective into previously non-digital life-worlds.

Another characteristic of this type of governance which was identified early on is that there is a form of plasticity (Bhandar and Goldberg-Hiller 2015) in the matter of code, which modern modes of governance, such as legislations, do not afford. Looking strictly at matter, this implies that digitized spaces are easier to alter and that the governance connected to them tends to fail since they can always be reshaped into another technological form. This is mirrored, for example, in both the way that Lessig perceives of code as something that can be altered to change cyberspace. It is also noticeable in how Zittrain perceives the internet as being constructed by building blocks that can be combined in ways to produce more or less generative effects (2006). As a next phase in the process of digitising society, this logic of governance has also come to encompass what Hildebrandt, in borrowing a term from Adam Greenfield, describes as a move towards code as law as "everywere" (Hildebrandt 2020: 7). These subsequent discussions about how digitalization can replace or at least distort the capacity of law as the sole order with the capacity of regulation society. Besides the fact that digitalization makes more spaces readable and codable, other materialities beside code are also involved in the move towards making objects and environments smart. This involves both technologies in the wider sense, such as old and new forms of biopower, as will be discussed further, but also other technologies to make the digital happen.

The enmeshment between objects, spaces and regulation happens via digitalization because objects and the spaces have both become embedded in digital technologies. This embeddedness in digital layers via smartification of society shifts the performativuty both with objects and spaces in the way that they need to be designed towards interoperability in order to function. For example, for autonomous vehicles to become integrated into the spatial register, their capacity to read physical space requires a change in the material layer of both the vehicle and the space surrounding them. A car needs to be able to understand what is happening around it if a human does not perform that interpretation for it. Naturally, even if a human is operating the car, they are embedded in a machinic constellation that enables the car to respond in certain ways to certain situations, for example, by braking when the car needs to stop. As Bratton also remarks "the integrated design of driverless cars includes navigation interfaces, computationally intensive and environmentally aware rolling hardware, and street systems that can stage the network effects of hundreds of thousands speeding robots at once" (Bratton 2015: 12). In autonomous vehicles, the interpretation of space is supposed to be conducted by the vehicle. In order for this to happen, cars need to have some way of sensing the city, and cities, in turn, via some technologies, have to be perforated by an extensive range of wireless signalling capacities (Parikka 2020). As Parikka puts it, a camera eye is stuck to an autonomous car, making it see in ways that are not "just seeing but modelling, mapping, measuring, predicting, and a range of other cultural techniques that pave the way for a wider set of infrastructural implications" (ibid.: 187). This type of seeing and interpretation via WiFi signals, radar or camera can all be understood as a form of operational imaging that does not focus on seeing in a traditional sense but "in the connected networks where multiple feeds are a part of the dynamic formation of an image in real time" (ibid.: 188). As a consequence, the current layering of digital technologies stretches into physical spaces in ways that are both invisible and more multiplied than can be imagined when considering the term "code" in code as law. Here, it is not only the code but also the sensors, signals and everything else that make objects and spaces smart and hence reshape the materialities by which law currently emerges.

Of course, the intensity with which automation takes place also leads to the possibility of automating law in the narrower sense. In a similar manner, Deakin and Markou point out how machine learning is currently being implemented to replicate certain aspects of what in the dominant understanding of law is perceived as being legal decision making, including adjudication (Markou and Deakin 2020). Numerous new projects on AI and law also show how different types of technologies in the wider spectra of artificial intelligences are now being tested to produce automated decisions for the otherwise non-digitized world. An example of this is the automation of asylum decisions, which is now being trialled by the Swedish migration authority (Arvidsson 2021). The spatial metaphor as well as governance via digital technologies is even more prevalent at the time of writing this book because states have adopted inherently national regimes for governance as well as for tracking the COVID-19 pandemic. The movement of bodies between spaces and the digital layers in which they are mandated to be embedded conveys a plethora of ways that code is becoming law, and very strict law at that. In the early stages of the pandemic, social media was full of videos of drones circulating Chinese cities urging people to return home and isolate. This was later followed by smartphone applications for tracking infections and sending alerts to those who may have been exposed to risk. The connection to states and their remaining capacities to mandate certain forms of codes as law has also become blatantly clear as suggestions are being made to create "vaccination passports" to be embedded in one's smartphone as an added requirement to the already doubtful technology of passports as a requirement for movement across the borders of nation states (cf. Keshavarz 2019).

The development of the digital layering of an increasingly large number of objects and applications, however, is only the first way in which we are now seeing an intensification of what digitalization means to a shift in law and jurisprudence. A more recent transformation is the effects on digital governance via the role played by data collection and refining. Hildebrandt also reminds us that "cyberspace as such refers to cyber (steering) and connects with cybernetics (remote control of one's environment by means of feedback loops)" (2020: 6). As she points out, this implies more than just a shift in materiality from speech, writing, printing and mass media since it is both hyperconnective as discussed in this section, but also works via producing computational pre-emption loops (Hildebrandt 2020: 6–7). The latter type of how digital materialities produces law in new ways via a logic of prediction and pre-emption has also recently been explored under the topic of algorithmic governance.

Algorithmic Governance

Algorithmic governance as a concept has emerged more recently as a means to describe how algorithms order the contexts in which they are embedded. From a legal theoretical perspective, the emergence of algorithmic governance both as a concept and practice can be understood as a development of the code-is-law perspective. Just like such perspectives, algorithmic governance is based on understanding that computational regimes have the capacity to act on expected behaviours and govern them in relation to certain desires (cf. Hildebrandt 2020: 7). As Kalopkas puts it, algorithmic governance "is characterised by its tackling of problems through 'their effects rather than their causation'" (2019: 2). In order to do this, this kind of governance is also slightly different from the general code-is-law stream since it needs data to establish robust correlations by "decoding underlying essences by way of establishing connections, patterns and predictions" (ibid.: 2). All these correlations can then be utilized to algorithmically organize decisions and courses of action, whether it involves changing the digital architecture for governance, as described in the previous section, or via nudging strategies. There are, in turn, many layers of technologies related to digitalization that enable algorithmic governance, some of which engage the increased availability of sensorial nodes that can collect data, the increased availability of storage in "the cloud," as well as improvements in hardware and, of course, algorithms (ibid.: 2).

From a legal perspective, an important starting point is that algorithmic governance appears to be more similar to what is often seen as sociology of law. This is because, as described in the introduction, law is perceived as a text-based and (to lawyers) visible system of rules. The actual functions of laws tend to be studied as sociology of law. Here, such "actual" functionality (or lack of functionality) is replaced by direct pattern recognition via sensors that can optimize this pattern according to the instructions of the algorithm (Hydén 2020). When governing by algorithm, one identifies and uses the patterns of behaviour as direct input for how to govern towards a certain goal. Even if this kind of idea of law as a tool to engineer society is not new (e.g. Svensson 1997; Glavå and Petrusson 2002; Glavå and Petrusson 2008), the efficiency with which this can be done is new in the sense that it builds on larger information input or data sets. This is because algorithmic governance works best when there is data from which it can optimize towards certain effects. A way to pursue such data collection is to equip products, spaces and our bodies (Internet of Things, smart cities and smart homes, internet of bodies) with sensors that make this possible. Even simple smart machines such as vacuum cleaners are fitted with these types of sensors (e.g. Kalopkas 2019: 3).

In this way, algorithmic governance is also connected to the need for good data sets (Kitchin 2014). This implies that collecting large amounts of data in itself is necessary in order to produce "better" forms of algorithmic governance, or rather to make possible the algorithmic governance desired by those who pursue it. In brief, this implies using large amounts of data and optimising the results for the algorithmic outputs that one wants, and then going back and forth in a way that also optimizes the algorithmic accuracy. The data-driven ordering that passes through algorithms both implicates and further allows for training of the system or object in case. This training is furthermore the basis for automation, via for example machine-learning, which consequently renders systems and smart objects independent or semi-independent. From a legal theoretical perspective, in turn, this means that we move towards what could be described as an (at least increased) automation of norm creation, which paves the way for something that is both through and beyond the "code-is-law" narrative as governance happens through a large number of materialities, as well as objects and spaces, which we could tentatively call *lex ex machina*, a law executed by machines (cf. Markou and Deakin 2020). As we will see next, this automated law is also increasingly bundled with questions of secrecy as a form of control and, more specifically, cryptographic techniques to keep automated objects or objects interfacing each other locked into certain behavioural patterns.

Lex Cryptographica

Besides the question of the automation of goods, work, spaces and everything else that occupies modern capitalist human lives, recent years have also seen a surge in digital currencies, such as bitcoin. It is also through bitcoin that most people gain a remote (if any) understanding of the encryption technologies that make decentralized currencies possible. *Blockchain* is an example of such a decentralized encryption structure. What is interesting for our purposes here is that the vision for blockchain as a technology by no means is limited to digital currencies but has also been regarded as an evolution of the code-is-law perspective towards a code as *lex cryptographica* (De Filippi and Wright 2019). In this understanding, cryptographic technologies such as blockchain not only connect and encrypt information transactions between devices to authenticate monetary exchange, they also restrict certain smart objects to what they can do, who can intervene in their operations and so on. Even though it is notoriously obscure what blockchain exactly is, and even more so what it means in terms of regulation (Herian 2018), a general understanding is that it enables a more rigid structure of encrypting the information transactions between different digitized devices since the authorization process demands it. In brief, it could also be said that the rationale behind encryption technologies is to enact openings and closures between different elements through passwords. Successful decryption subsequently opens access between each side of the encryption chain. A basic form of encryption technology is the regular lock, which produces a barrier between what is inside (e.g. a locker containing papers and books) and what is outside (e.g. a human). For the human to access the elements inside the locker, a key is needed to unlock it. In comparison with a regular lock solution, blockchain could be understood as being a significantly more advanced lock (see e.g. Herian 2018). As it is a digital lock, it can also be added to everything that can be combined with a digital layer.

By adding more advanced encryption technologies such as blockchain to digital layers, one can argue that encryption technology itself may function as a mode of (very efficient) law that makes possible or prevents certain enactments. de Filippi and Hassan have already pre-empted and developed this analogy by stating that what blockchain signifies is a movement in which *law itself* becomes code rather than vice versa They base this understanding on the perception that "law" may be coded into products, for example, through smart contracts (2016, see also Swan 2015). In turn, this implies that control is designed into, and enforced via, objects or even entire environments. The integration of the means of encryption into property objects and how this renders them tamper-proof and placed into a pre-determined decision pattern may also be read in light of the now well-advanced discussions regarding Digital Rights Management (DRM). DRM is famously known as the technology popularized in the 2000s to control the digitalization of content such as music, films and video games (e.g. Schollin 2008). As de Filippi and Hassan write, in this way, DRM came to replace textual/positive law as the means of controlling the distribution of content (de Filippi and Hassan 2016). Just like algorithmic governance, blockchain and other advanced encryption technologies can be understood as a new turn in code-as-law perspectives. It is also important to understand the link between these two latter perspectives in the way that they both afford a form of concealed automated governance. However, as will be explored, the level on which these forms of governance are concealed works on more layers than what is restricted to these technologies. From a legal theoretical perspective in general, this involves an important point since the less opaque a technology and the way it orders is, the less possible it is to regulate it via the standard understanding of law.

Instead, what the possible emergence of lex cryptographica further highlights in relation also to algorithmic governance is that we are about to face a much more complex ecology of code as law than previously. This implies furthermore, as will be discussed next, that we are entering a form of governance that can only be readable and made sense of by machines, whether or not we can decrypt and understand its data inputs on a general level. I have decided to refer to this perspective as *Governance via Operational Images*, based on recent work in media studies (Dvorak and Parikka 2021).

Governing via Operational Images

An intuitive understanding of data as well as code is that it consists of words. These words are then put into a computational machine which, in turn, is based on texts (code) and hardware. This is also visible in the forms in which law supposedly becomes increasingly automated via algorithms and encryption technologies, as described above. Even if code notoriously difficult to pinpoint as objects, for example, in intellectual property law, it is both understood as being a form of literary work, rather than anything else, in copyright law. Another object type known to copyright lawyers is the *image*. Images can be both photographic and more traditional, such as painted, drawn or something else; they all represent different types of images that are protected under modern copyright statutes. Just like literary works, these types of works are endowed with an understanding that they have the capacity to generate both values and affects to a larger degree than what is literally represented by a flat image (cf. Bruncevic 2017). However, what is interesting in terms of the development of code-as-law perspectives here is that images as objects also have the capacity to double up *as* law in new ways of realising automated governance.

As hinted at above, automated objects need to make sense of their surroundings – and this unfolds via many different media. A significant way that machine learning is made possible is by training machines, including algorithms, on image data sets. As described by Crawford and Paglen (2019), machine-learning systems intended to recognize objects, including faces, are trained on data sets comprising multiple images. As they put it, in order to build computer vision that can differentiate between different fruits such as apples and oranges, a developer needs to collect, label and train a network by feeding it with thousands of images of apples and oranges. These images are then used to make an algorithm conduct a "statistical survey" of the images whereupon they develop a model to recognize the different classes of images: apples or oranges. If the training works, the model will be able to recognize and differentiate between images of apples and oranges even in cases in which such images did not belong to the predefined image data set.

Data sets can also comprise, for example, several images that are classified according to certain linguistic categories such as the famous dataset, ImageNet. ImageNet can be described as a catalogue comprising a huge number of images, mapped onto WordNet, a catalogue of nouns (ibid.). As even the most traditional lawyer would know, nouns can contain a multiplicity of meanings, all of which are highly context dependent. Legal training as a text-orientated profession teaches us to react to words such as "goods," "consumer" and similar as they trigger an array of legal understandings via arguments in cases, laws and other "legal sources" as to how to interpret such otherwise seemingly innocent nouns. In image data sets, nouns are mapped onto images without any such legal definition as a foundation, but rather by using micro work systems where labour is performed by huge numbers of people to map out a meaning for each image. This process of mapping nouns onto images is by no means uncomplicated. The reason for this is both the normativity in mapping, as well as the output of the exercise in terms of its normative effects that such data set systems may produce. The complexity in how to interpret something, and evaluate it, as well as which normative effects an evaluation has, is not the least easily recognizable for a person trained in how to interpret legal language. This does not as such mean that the normative dimension of description may cause much worry in the case of oranges and apples. However, as discussed by Noble, the same classificatory process is more controversial for example where images of black people were classified as pictures of monkeys or animals, including a case in which Michelle Obama's face had been replaced by the face of an actual ape (2018: 6).

This aspect is also explored, for example, in relation to image data sets by Crawford and Paglen on how the mapping and categorization of images has often been deeply problematiç in the manner that it presents a form of objectivity, which is not objective at all. As they write:

> You open up a database of pictures used to train artificial intelligence systems. At first, things seem straightforward. You're met with thousands of images: apples and oranges, birds, dogs, horses, mountains, clouds, houses, and street signs. But as you probe further into the dataset, people begin to appear: cheerleaders, scuba divers, welders, Boy Scouts, fire walkers, and flower girls. Things get strange: A photograph of a woman smiling in a bikini is labelled a "slattern, slut, slovenly woman, trollop." A young man drinking beer is categorized as an "alcoholic, alky, dipsomaniac, boozer, lush, soaker, souse." A child wearing sunglasses is classified as a "failure, loser, non-starter, unsuccessful person." You're looking at the "person" category in a dataset called ImageNet, one of the most widely used training sets for machine learning.
>
> (Crawford and Paglen 2020)

The fact that governance through images is part of the increasingly digitally mediated society is evident from the expansion of facial recognition. A case recently in media concerned the way that a chain of food retail stores in the UK, Southern Co-op, had introduced facial recognition in its stores to identify and alert its employees about such persons entering the store who had previously been banned from the store or engaged in suspicious activities on the premises. In the case of Southern Co-op, it was using technology from a London-based start-up called Facewatch. The service is set out to function in the manner that every time someone enters one of the shops in which the technology has been deployed, the tech cameras scan their faces. These scanned images are then converted into numerical data that is compared to a watchlist of "suspects" for the detection of matches. If a match is made, employees in the store receive a notification on their smartphones (Burgess 2020; Privacy International 2020). As what seems like a legal defence, with direct or indirect support by the EU General Data Protection Regulation 2018/1725, GDPR, Facewatch also defends the legality of its business as it doesn't add everyone's faces to a central database but create watchlists of "subjects of interest" based on the companies with which it works and only stores data of subjects of interest for two years; that it carries out legitimate business by minimising the impact of crime and improving the safety of staff; and that data is only held and shared proportionally with other retailers, not the police, for example (ibid.). Of course, facial recognition also plays a role in border control between nation states, in which passports contain photos of persons passing a border, as well as increasingly being captured and read in automated passport control systems (cf. Keshavarz 2019). Another example is how artificial facial recognition and face reproduction have been turned into achieving an ironic twist in the image generator: "This person does not exist," based on data sets of images of existing persons and generating an image of a fake person/portrait every time someone clicks on the site (https://thispersondoesnotexist.com).

As hinted at above, governance by images also operates in many ways that are less recognizable by humans. For example, Parikka shows that there is a growing literature that understands how WiFi works to map, visualize and model space, humans, animals and any other object that reflect signals back from WiFi traffic and antennae (2021). Sensing here becomes a form of technological modelling and "(t)he image, then, is a sampling of a spatio-temporal situation: a constantly produced entity that cuts across the dynamics of a city as part of an operational processing of what is being seen, at what time, in which relations, and to what ends" (ibid.: 186). This technical modelling, which naturally also has normative consequences, is carried out via, for example, laser mapping, which, by nature, is invisible to the human eye. This can be illustrated by the way that autonomous vehicles operate on roads, as discussed, by sensing and making sense of the environment via either laser scanning technologies such as LiDAR or machine-learning based on image data sets (Käll 2020; Parikka 2021). Also, the way in which machines render images understandable is not always linked to such clear ways of image recognition as via the image data sets described above (via categorization of two images based on a noun). Steyerl even goes as far as claiming that

Not seeing anything is the new normal. Information is passed on as a set of signals that cannot be picked up by human senses. Contemporary perception is machinic to a large degree. The spectrum of human vision only covers a tiny part of it. Electric charges, radio waves, light pulses encoded by machines for machines are zipping by at slightly subliminal speed. Seeing is superseded by calculating probabilities. Vision loses importance and is replaced by filtering, decrypting and pattern recognition.

(Steyerl 2021: 139)

Machine vision therefore also involves interpreting and creating new images that only machines can understand. Examples of such different images created by machines to read their environment can be found in works by artist Trevor Paglen. The potential to map spaces in a different way via laser technologies has also been widely explored in both art and research by the research group, Forensic Architecture. The latter's works also show how alternative normative understandings can be produced by providing new models than those previously produced as evidence in several criminal cases (Weizman 2019). Thus, the role that images will play in relation to how law plays out in the digitized society cannot be underestimated.

The End of which Law?

Just like advanced capitalism and digitalization are understood to create the end of man as well as mankind and the beginning of the posthuman condition, so have digital technologies functioning as law been understood to activate the end of law as we know it (Hildebrandt 2015). This can be contrasted with the understanding that Chun puts forward in relation to code-is-law narratives. As she argues, the rendering of code into law should not be understood as being particularly profound as the move to materialize code was made possible through narratives that embed computers in "logic" and reduce all machinic actions to the commands that supposedly drive them (Chun 2011: 27). To this she adds that code should not be understood as law but rather "every lawyer's dream of what law should be: automatically enabling and disabling certain actions, functioning at the level of everyday practice" (ibid.). This bleak view of law and lawyers is certainly sustained in most of the current love for and paranoia about technologies related to artificial intelligence as law. For example, Hildebrandt voices the fear of losing written law as in the manner that an onlife world which is based on data driven agency that taps into a digital unconscious which we cannot access, may easily turn written law into a paper dragon (2015: 226).

With the clear evidence that digital technologies are governing our everyday lives, there seems to be a lingering fear that we are losing law and consequently also justice (or at least ethics) (see e.g. Hildebrandt 2020: 283–315). This potential loss of law as the means of creating justice and other kinds of seemingly universal goals, such as legal certainty and purposiveness, is heavily dependent on a liberalist view of law, which is also recognized by Hildebrandt (2015: 226; 2020: 17–37). It can however be noted that Hildebrandt explicitly argues that "regulating, influencing or even enforcing behaviours has little to do with legal normativity" (ibid.: 226). She goes as far as to state that if one cannot disobey law it is not law but discipline. While Lessig compares the code that makes up "cyberspace" with codes that make up societies in general and argues that they are just different forms of regulations, his general understanding of law also remains trapped within a similar understanding as Hildebrandt (1999: 28). For example, he discusses that online gambling could be adapted to different regulations imposed by different states (both nation states and US states) merely through the inclusion of specific certification technologies. He refers to this rupturing of the larger digital space "zoning." Also, as early as 1999, he argued that such practices would become increasingly relevant as more commercial interests entered the internet and states became dependent on each other for imposing regulations on companies to comply with specific laws in their different territories. This view of law is manifested not least in a belief that law has a democratic element which is fundamentally different than if the market could govern digital spaces by code (ibid.: 222–230).

Cohen, in turn, criticizes "cyberlaw scholars" for paying too much attention to technologies as a form of governance in digitized settings. As she puts it, they forget how many layers of law were involved in the construction of the internet and its constituent protocols and processes (Cohen 2019: 210). This nuancing in which law is a regulatory force involves showing how law is embedded in a number of standardization systems and similar (ibid.: 210–237). The realization that law also functions via standard-setting processes is naturally an important one, particularly in technology market settings in which much normative work is carried out in deciding which technological standards should prevail for new systems such as 3–5G standards for telecommunications. The way in which standards are important norm constructions in law and technology has also been widely discussed in the field of law and economics (e.g. Treacy and Lawrence 2008). Consequently, law in the form of regulations matter to what technologies can do.

However, changes in the terms of digitalization overriding our common understanding of law go much deeper than that, as has been discussed throughout this chapter. Something that could create more worry, and which is also what legal scholars tend to emphasise by insisting on "law," is the way in which these norms are actually developing to the detriment of social justice. However, if anything, law in the modern sense has been rightfully identified as delineating itself from justice, as a form of restricted jurisprudence hinted at in the introduction to this chapter. As Douzinas and Gearey state: "In the positivist world-view, law is the answer to the irreconcilability of values, the most perfect embodiment of human reason. Its operation should not be contaminated by extrinsic, non-legal considerations, lest it loses it legitimatory ability (2005: 7)." As they further show, a distinction between "pure law" and contexts, politics, economics and similar is continuously being produced, which is also what we see in much research law and digitalization. Law in the positivist way of thinking becomes limited to what they call "state law," only. This then, limits the potential for jurisprudence to engage with questions concerning "the legal institution with its practices and procedures, its rules norms and rights, in what can be called a legal interzone" (ibid.: 12). From a sociology of law perspective, on the other hand, (but on the same side of distinguishing between law and other norms), concerns have been raised about whether the possibilities to even study norms outside of legislations risk being lost, when algorithms are kept secret (as they generally are) (Hydén 2020).

The problem with restricted jurisprudence is not only its limitations regarding the different materialities that can be considered as law, but consequently also, and more importantly, the normative consequences that such a restricted/liberalist conception of law/rule of law may have. Even if perspectives of justice are generally not lost on anyone writing critical accounts of law in digitized settings, the remedies suggested for injustices often remain with a limited number of alternatives based on the law that is being critiqued. This can be contrasted with, the general thesis put forward by Cohen is that those who are in power over digitalization and digitized life-worlds also act on what becomes knowledge and truth in the digitally mediated society (Cohen 2019). Consequently, it is not only a question of power in the sense of having control over a particular setting, but that truth as such may be distorted via the practices that are allowed to produce knowledge in digital settings. Here we can again recount the normativity identified in the power to design algorithms, encryption, and images for machines to interpret, as having fundamental power to change what can even be known for those in power. To this, it should be noted that also Lessig highlights the risks of leaving power over code to market actors (Lessig 1999: 188–209) and Hildebrandt draws particular attention to the risks of perpetuating discrimination in machine-learning systems when law is not in control (Hildebrandt 2015: 191–199). Thus, they are all hinting at what could be a more acute question from a posthumanist perspective in the form of what we are witnessing is maybe not so much the end of law, but for whom law is ending, and for whom it might never have even started (cf. Braidotti 2013: 1).

In relation to this, it also becomes obvious to connect to recent research in critical media studies and digital humanities on how, for example, search engines reinforce racism through the algorithms they use (Noble 2018). As an example, Noble outlines what first started her working on the subject: her googling the basic term *black girls*. Back in 2010, this meant that she was met with both racist and sexist results (of a pornographic nature). Now Google has altered the algorithms that made such search results prioritized in its search feed. However, as Noble shows, racialization through algorithms and platforms goes much deeper than a mere Google search. Another example she highlights is the potential discrimination against black businesses by the Yelp platform, which appears to place businesses that pay or get many recommendations in terms of quantity higher than the qualified recommendations that a black community can give, e.g. a black hairdresser (ibid.: 171–179). Similar points are also made by Benjamin in relation to the how race and racism are not only an output of technologies such as algorithmic governance and surveillance, but a technology itself that leads to the digital inventions being produced (Benjamin 2019: 44).

As Amaro also puts it what we might call or might consider "algorithmic bias" is based on the fundamental principle of mathematics which is already predicated on the education of chance and contingency: namely, to regress, to clean, to normalize the unexpected, and therefore normalize and exclude the opportunities that live outside of the lines of political engagement" (Amaro 2021: 155). Consequently, the assumptions of what is normal in a society or at the market at large can continuously be iterated via the way they are mediated here, no matter whether they are harmful to some humans or nonhumans.

These recent revelations all show how technologies are creating highly normative worlds without the presence of law in the narrow sense. What needs to be remembered now more than ever is however that law has never served the purpose of creating justice for everyone. A legal positivist solution to current developments could be to call for new legislation or erect boundaries in relation to such developments. However, such a demand would, at least to some degree, ignore the fact that law has been dissolved into a more fluid regime of control, as anticipated by both Deleuze and Haraway around 25 years ago (Haraway 1991: 161–162; Deleuze 1992). When Hildebrandt warns that a law that cannot be disobeyed is not a law but a discipline (as discussed above), this also needs to be seen in light of the pressure by which the societies of control and the informatics of domination have unfolded. This implies that it is capitalist logics and other orders of domination, rather than non-hierarchical modes of governance that are the mode of ruling. Furthermore, as also depicted by Deleuze in relation to how control now operates (Deleuze 1992), the development of, for example, blockchain technologies, as a kind of technology that decentres law or "trust" in its previous sense, also entails the thorough production of passwords as a requirement for access between everyone and everything that is digitally "enhanced" (cf. Käll 2018). Also, in a platform economy, such control is vested in those who control the closure and openness of the data, images and codes in the respective platform (Srnicek 2017). For this reason, a more posthumanist response would be to take into account the connection between different regimes of governance, which effectuate the current situation evolving in relation to digitalization.

Moving Towards a Posthumanist Jurisprudence

The end of law discourses, whether they show how code becomes law or goes further to show how algorithms have the capacity to be discriminatory, highlights the loss of a certain legal technique as well as the loss of a perspective of justice embedded in law. As such, this loss builds on a positivist understanding of both what law is and has the capacity to become. The answer to getting out of this mess is generally either to argue for programmers and companies to be forced to comply with the legal norms that belonged to a previous form of capitalist society, or to argue that there is a need for a new kind ethics, as discussed above. The latter response: a call for a new kind digital ethics, is particularly popular with non-legal disciplines but is also becoming more prevalent in law (e.g. European Commission 2019; Bietti 2020; Hildebrandt 2020). This mourning and call for "old" ways of conducting law and the other perspective of calling for a seemingly apolitical type of ethics for the digitized society are both understood here as being problematic in their own right. This is because both law and ethics obviously are more political than they may seem, and cannot be enacted from a new universalist framework that disregards how many of the challenges we are facing are caused by advanced capitalism. The forms of ethics or laws suggested to govern AI technologies also tends to build upon an idea of the human as law-maker for his own needs. This includes for example the recent European suggestion of always having a human in the loop to control AI (EU 2021/0106 (COD)). As Bratton points out, critiques specifically directed towards algorithmic governance also replicate the presumptive of logics that is individuals as human subjects that are the only model and object of governance (Bratton 2019: 59). As such this can also be understood as a way of governing that reinstitutes anthropocentrism in AI starting from a point where "AI is intelligent to the extent that it is human-like." As Bratton further elaborates this idea about AI goes back

> at least to the Turing test, in which a speculative AI was asked to "pass" as a human, and to pretend to think *how humans think that humans think* in order to qualify as intelligent. What Turing meant as a sufficient condition of intelligence has become instead, especially in popular culture, a necessary condition: a threshold, an ideal, a norm against which AI is measured.
>
> (2021a: 94)

As he further puts it, this implies that the potential in such governance in terms of "artificial planetarity" or large-scale environmental planning, is therefore lost (Bratton 2019: 59). He further argues that what is needed is not the abolishment of algorithmic governance as such but a remobilization away from the individual's desires and micromanaging human culture, to instead move to dealing with bigger questions such as how to reshape the Earth into a habitable place (ibid.: 60 and passim).

However, moving towards post-anthopocentric goals like this, as well as facing the different forms of power taking place via the current micromanagement of human culture, also demands a radically different understanding of law and the law's role, which I refer to here as *posthumanist jurisprudence*. The aim of framing a perspective of posthumanist jurisprudence is to develop a theory that corresponds to the posthumanist impulse to consider the posthuman condition in both critical and affirmative ways. This approach is well suited to the attempt of posthumanist theory to place ethics and the identification of the affirmative potential of the topic being criticized in alliance with critique. Another way to express this is to use Goodrich, that the aim of critique is to pursue a true *love* of law (Goodrich 1999). As such, this perspective is furthermore affiliated with a number of theoretical developments along these lines such as Philippopoulos-Mihalopoulos' theory on spatial justice (2014), Bruncevic's Deleuzian/rhizomatic understanding of law (2014; 2017), Davies' quest for an unlimited concept of law along the lines of new materialist theory (2016), as well as many other critical perspectives of law (e.g. Gustafsson 1998; Gustafson 2011; Douzinas and Gearey 2005; Svensson 2013).

The implication of a posthumanist perspective of law is first, that law needs to be imagined in a manner that also breaks with the liberal humanist and also anthropocentric ideas that are currently in place. This implies, for example, that law is understood as manifesting in many ways other than "legal" texts. As Philippopoulos-Mihalopoulos puts it:

> the law is not just the text, the decision, even the courtroom. Law is the pavement, the traffic light, the hoodie in the shopping mall, the veil in the school, the cell in Guantanamo, the seating arrangement at a meeting, the risotto at the restaurant.
>
> (2015: 129)

In a similar way we can contend that law in the digital sense is not only in the code that makes up digital platforms but also, to paraphrase Wark, in the mineral sandwich in your pocket, your mobile phone, that generates information about all its (and your) movements (Wark 2019: 4). This entanglement of matter and norms make for a dissolving of law's inside and outside, which corresponds to the practices of digital technologies and law pinpointed above. However, here it also becomes possible to think further, that this is not a new event, caused by for example code, but that law has always had other materialities than those claimed as law.

Nor can law be understood anymore as the system we were once taught it was, which a human universal observer may interpret from an objective viewpoint. Instead, it is more like *lawscapes* sustained by an atmosphere produced by human and nonhuman bodies (Philippopoulos-Mihalopoulos 2015). Rather than being about what is or what is not law, legal or illegal, the lawscape functions as a continuum in which "the multiplicity of lawscapes are folded into the continuum of the lawscape." Each lawscape, in turn, can be understood as an expression where the manifold emerges via the in/visibilization of law and space "like a sound equaliser screen whose values go up and down depending on the song without, however, a main button to control what gets in/visibilised" (ibid.: 192). Bodies in turn "carry law and space, indeed generate law and space, through their moving on the lawscape" (ibid.). As discussed, this creates a rupture on the inside and outside of law, so often encountered in legal theory and legal practice. Law, just like code, can also become everywhere and it does so by a materialist turn, as integrated in all matter. In a similar manner, Davies has argued for the need of thinking of law as a flat ontology as she argues that by perceiving law as flat, one paves the way for other norms as having potentially equal or even more value for practices in specific contexts (2008: 284–284). From the perspective of posthumanist theory, an important note is that this perception of law into space and (other) bodies should not be seized as an opportunity to a move towards an even more universal perception of law (as a god's view). The lawscape, just like the legal researcher's position, is conditioned by how it is held together, and which folds and affects one manages to recreate (cf. Philippopoulos-Mihalopoulos 2015: 4). Building on such understanding, posthumanist jurisprudence moves away from criticising legal concepts from, for example, their lack of "coherence" with an emerging technology, or other societal practices. The question here becomes more: which lawscape is being produced here, by whom and which combination of bodies and affects affords change?

This form of jurisprudence is also constructed upon the affirmative endeavour of posthumanist theory in which it has consistently been argued that we need new ways to both criticise and think more affirmatively about the ongoing processes of world-making. The aim of discussing law in this way is therefore not to leave law's conceptual or linguistic domain altogether. For example, as I will show throughout, the idea advocated here is to break down the conceptual divides between subjects and objects by showing that this rupture has already been produced through digitalization and advanced capitalism. Show-casing such cracks in the concepts from a posthumanist theoretical position takes us somewhere else. (cf. Haraway 2016: 30). Consequently, the aim of posthumanist theory as used and developed here is not to erect a new form of human to answer for the negative effects caused by advanced capitalism. Rather, it aims to show that this change has already occurred and that the way out of the troubles caused by the breakdown of these divides is available precisely *via* such processes.

In this way, what is produced is a deeply relational ethics in the posthumanist vein, in spite of, but also deeply *through*, the developments in advanced capitalism. Thus, posthumanist jurisprudence is developed here to challenge specific conceptualizations of matter, as well as in relation to which role law plays in these constructions as it does not consider law's objects in traditional ways of understanding matter as being something fixed, and does not consider law to be vested in textual/nation-state founded ideas of law only. Through this understanding of law, posthumanist jurisprudence is better equipped to visualize and reshape lawscapes held together but also falling apart by advanced capitalism and other atmospheric elements of the Anthropocene.

Part Two

Body

Matter and materialisation are concepts that are key to posthumanist theory in highlighting how power determines which relations can take place. In alliance with such a starting point, the body concept is used here to highlight how matter fluctuates and is being captured as assets. As introduced in Chapter 1, the body is understood here in a non-anthropocentric way, implying that both information and media transmitting information can be understood as bodies. As described by Haraway, the materiality of the digitally mediated society is continuous, as communication via information technologies is not only about linguistics in the narrow sense but depends on electronics (1991: 165). To this we can now add several other bodies such as algorithms, data, minerals, gig workers and of course, platforms.

The following two chapters engage with some of these materialisation processes, configurations and transformations of matter, or bodies, in order to show what counts as a human and nonhuman body, as well as what they can do, are in flux when information is understood as a commodity. The way that bodies come into being and come together along posthuman lines depends on continuous flows and pauses of such flows. The forces that create and prevent bodies from materialising are equally many. Here, the forces released under advanced capitalism to treat information as a commodity in digitised settings are of particular interest, as a means of pinpointing certain characteristics of posthuman property.

Processes of materialisation are vital in how to shift imaginations and desires regarding what can be claimed as property – whether or not these processes are visible to others than those making property claims. An irony in advanced capitalism is that the embodiment of property does not stand in opposition to disembodying its property objects or, to put it in simpler terms: to think of it as something intangible does not prevent it from being captured, embodied, as property. This is repeated again and again in narratives about the liquidity of code, data, digital spaces and similar, as we will see throughout. Thus, the focus on the production of matter as independent serves as a point of departure to further show how the emergence of digital technologies, such as software,

DOI: 10.4324/9781003139096-1b

through processes of commodification is strictly connected to the ideas of making code a form of law or even *logos*, as described by Chun. As she puts it:

> Software emerged as a thing – as an iterable textual program – through a process of commercialization and commodification that has made code *logos*: code as source, code as true representation of action, indeed, code as conflated with, and substituting for, action.
>
> (2011: 19)

This emergence of the digital as an object is a vital process for understanding the posthuman logics that are at play here.

Chapter 3

The Dematerialization of Information

In the beginning, there was body and mind, or so the Cartesian story is told (e.g. Hayles 1999: 4–5). The division of Mind versus matter has indeed become such a successful ontology that it is difficult to see anything else than a divide between thinking human subjects and the rest of life and the physical world (e.g. Davies 2017: 8). The Cartesian split, makes for a pervasive philosophical basis for dividing the human mind from the body to prove that existence and superiority is simply based on the capacity of the human mind. The division between mind and body can be understood to fill many functions in the idea production of what it means to be human or nonhuman. However, to summarise the division one can say that it consists of a two-fold boundary. First, it implies a separation between mind and body, within the boundary of "the human". Thus, a human being is divided into consisting of part body, part mind. Second, this delineation functions to advance an idea that the mind is in superior control of the body. In this idea fodder that we could generally assign to Western values, the *possibility* to think also grants humans a form of thinking substance (*res cogitans*) that renders them with superior capabilities to other nonhuman bodies (Esposito 2015: 109).

The body can also be considered as being what the subject recognizes inside itself yet as something different for itself. A subject consequently separates itself from the body and keeps it at a distance (ibid.). In this way, the human/body distinction may also be considered in a unified manner in which the capacity of having a mind was what separated humans from the rest of the world. This connected effect of perceiving the body and mind as distinct leads to what Braidotti describes as: "The Cartesian subject of the cogito, the Kantian 'community of reasonable beings' as intrinsically connected" (2013: 1). The posthuman condition discussed in Chapter 1, puts both these assumptions into question since knowledge, information and now data as objects, are all objects of the mind but have to be separated from human bodies to be considered as such under advanced capitalism.

These kinds of more recent ways of arguing for knowledge to be disconnected, or dematerialized for increased economic production, can be understood as a prolongation of modern cultural narratives in which the mind is considered to be separate from the body. In more recent discourse, the mind takes on an even more

DOI: 10.4324/9781003139096-3

expansive independent existence through sci-fi story-telling in which the mind is transformed into a substrate that can circulate freely on its own, as Hayles (1999) argues. Haraway also links the fact that the world can now be perceived of in this way to a theory of language and control in which the key questions revolve around how to determine "the rates, directions, and probabilities of a flow of a quantity called information" (Haraway 1991: 164). This understanding is also mirrored in economics theory in which the aim of the economics of knowledge has been identified to analyse and discuss the institutions, technologies and social regulations that can be utilized to facilitate the efficient production and use of knowledge (Foray 2006: 18). Today, the processes in disconnecting information and "the mind" have reached a new level of intensity via the "extraction" of data from bodies to produce automated machine intelligences (e.g. Crawford and Jolan 2018; Sadowski 2020). To talk with Wark, one can certainly conclude that

> [i]nformation is a rather strange thing. Contrary to the popular under-standing, there's nothing ideal or immaterial about it. Information only exists where there's a material substrate of matter and energy to store, transmit, and process it. Information is part of a material world.
>
> (Wark 2019: 5)

The obliteration of human and other bodies involved in the commodification of knowledge therefore also links into the processes in which both old and new forms of capitalism conceal multiple histories and geographies necessary to produce a commodity for consumers. As Marx identified, the commodity in its finished form as a product hides all the material aspects, including labour, involved in its production (2013[1969] 2013: 62–81). Today, this means, for example, treating knowledge as a separable product from the materialities needed to produce it. For this reason, advanced capitalism is involved in creating an idea of knowledge, information, data, etc. as being separate from its sites of production, transformation and distribution (e.g. Graham and Haarstad 2011: 1; Crawford and Joler 2018). Whether viewed as a pattern to flow freely across time and space, as extracted memories from human brains possible to download on computer disks, or as this chapter will show, as a knowledge-based commodity, "the great promise of information is that it can be free from the material constraints that govern the mortal world" (Hayles 1999: 13). In any case, this "freeing" of information may be understood as a disconnection of the mind from the human body. This disconnection of the mind, or rather "products of the mind" is traced here as being a first step needed to render human bodies and minds expendable and information as (re)materialized posthuman property.

Thus, this chapter engages with a trajectory of how knowledge is being framed as disembodied, starting out in cybernetics discourse, exploited in innovation management theory, and becomes intensified in artificial intelligence discourses. More specifically, the chapter is focused on considering what, and how, information as a "product" of the mind has been transformed into a commodity through continuous and multiples processes in which knowledge has been dematerialized from human and other bodies. The body as a conceptual tool is used here to shed light on how such processes of dematerialization can be understood in a way that does not prioritize the human mind or human body, yet remains critical to the very particular processes of (de)materialization that advanced capitalism engages in. This chapter consequently also argues that even if we may now speak of a disembodiment of the mind from humans, an *embodiment* of mind as *products* also occurs. In Chapter 4, this kind of embodiment is suggested to produce new bodies in the form of *non-human objects* of matter previously considered human. It consequently highlights how dematerialization of aspects considered internal to humans are increasingly captured, and embodied, as commodities. It is also suggested that these commodities still can be considered as part of human bodies, in the sense that they become extended through posthuman embodiment. A posthuman concept of the body is therefore also activated here in relation to showing how what is at stake here is not only a process of increased commodification, but an intensification of biopolitics in which very particular human, nonhuman, and posthuman bodies are controlled as well as sacrificed.

The Making Immaterial of Knowledge

The digitally mediated society, and property in intangible elements, are both dependent on the production of information as something that can be treated as a materiality separate from other materialities. On a daily basis we witness vast dematerialization processes on a large scale and in new ways. What previously was just a face, a finger, a photo in an album or the wall or a letter, today forms both content as well as interfaces to machines. In order to perform as such, these different materialities need to be captured and analysed as resources for both market actors and governments, as information. The possibility of pursuing this kind of capture rests heavily on the advancement of technologies that make it possible, as well as the desires to do so amongst both ourselves, as well the ones pursuing the capture. However, it also relies on the possibility of thinking that this separation is both possible and feasible. This means that something needs to be perceived of as an object, or as an object in new ways, to materialize into something new. A starting point to consider such a rationalization of all kinds of matter into information, data or intellectual assets, is that those in charge of such processes find a way to express a need and method for pursuing such a capture. As Hayles points out: "a defining characteristic of the present cultural moment is the belief that information can circulate unchanged among different material substrates" (Hayles 1999: 1). In theories about innovation and intellectual capital management, we already have a long history of such rationalizations for why and how information can be captured, as will be discussed. As one can expect, not all these forms of rationalization come via linear narratives.

One vital form of dematerialization can be detected in the coding discourse that perceives of knowledge or information as a liquid asset that is partially extremely hard to capture and partially flows, almost as if it was a force of nature. Ironically, the description of information as liquid also comes from "critical" perspectives on cyberspace such as: information wants to be free! The expression is almost impossible to assign to one single source, as it is widely used online and functions more as a meme or general critique of intellectual property than anything else. However, the expression has been credited to Stewart Brand for using it at a conference for hackers in 1984 and subsequently as a means of advocating joint coding by sharing computer code rather than competing with each other (Levy 2014) Yet, what is also constantly reiterated in these narratives is that even information has the capacity to be free. A later move in such a dematerialization of knowledge and information is allegedly when data is considered as something disconnected from material substances. It is a resource that can be "extracted," (Srnicek 2017: 40) or it is an object that can belong to a data subject (while, of course, being balanced against the "free flow of personal data"), as in recent data protection regulations such as the GDPR (no ()). In a similar manner, the dominant narratives of data, including those considering data as a raw material, tend to disconnect data from other types of physical matter – such as geological matter (Parikka 2015: 1–28). In this way, objects of knowledge are dematerialized from both the human mind, as well as other processes required for its production.

The disconnection of mind from body in relation to knowledge-based business can be understood to also be entangled with a narrative that argues that knowledge is a difficult resource to commodify compared to physical resources. Foray, for example, argues that due to the specific materiality of knowledge, knowledge needs to be understood as a *fragmented* resource, both with regards to its functions and with regards to geographical reasons. In accordance with such reasoning, knowledge is also to be understood as difficult to capture, as some of its *parts* should be understood as "tacit" and difficult to codify (Foray 2006: 14–19). Within the framework of understanding knowledge as a resource that is difficult to commodify, business theories have been developed to suggest how knowledge can be *captured* and *packaged* in order to reach a degree of firmness that is similar to physical goods (e.g. Petrusson 2004: 187). Narratives like this (related to dematerialization and the subsequent objectification of knowledge as a business asset separate from the physical) are also reflected in the way that businesses are being *organized* and more specifically, how one speaks about the value of business, not as a form of the production of products but rather as offering services, values and increasing business through innovation (see e.g. Petrusson 2004: passim; Chesbrough 2011; Srnicek 2017).

A common reasoning in economic theory revolves around the difficulties of turning knowlege into an economic resource. Such arguments are, interestingly, similar to how "information wants to be free" expressions allude to the difficulties of information, as matter, locked up. In a similar manner, critical intellectual property scholars tend to argue against the ownership of knowledge since it is seen as a particular type of resource. However, as Granstrand lucidly put it:

> [o]ne may argue that information cannot be owned. Neither can humans be owned. However, ownership per se is not the primary issue. Rather it is how private agents (companies, individuals) can control (manage) the rent streams derivable from immaterial resources and turn these streams into intellectual capital.
>
> (Granstrand 1999: 123)

The dematerialization of knowledge resources into tradeable assets consequently occurs in many different ways in which immaterial resources may be captured as (intellectual) capital, which will be discussed in more detail below. This understanding furthermore aligns with recent insights that it is assetization that is characteristic for technoscientific capitalism, rather than commodification (Birch and Muniesa 2020: 1–2). However, as we will see here, assetization also aligns with concepts for commodification such as property, as well as a general tendency to dematerialize information from humans/human bodies.

Turning Intangibles into Objects of Trade: Intellectual Capital Management

The theme of perceiving both knowledge and information as an inherently liquid and very particular resource in comparison to physical objects is reflected in numerous other discussions related to knowledge management and innovation theory, for example, in the emergence of specific scientific disciplines discussing how to best manage knowledge in order to capitalize on it. One example of such theoretical developments is the so-called intellectual capital management stream, which bridges business, technology and legal research. The implications of the findings made in this field are vital to understanding how information goods are captured as objects of their own, as this logic permeates both business models recently popularized as platforms, as well as through the more recent forms of data mining, using data sets to shape new technologies and so on. The fields provide both tools and rationales for utilising such tools to create what mostly means capital value, but is also translated into other values such as transitioning societies to new means of production to benefit society at large (e.g. Glavå and Petrusson 2008).

Thus, the overarching aim of intellectual capital management business-orientated research is precisely to "explore" how one may treat knowledge as a business, or at least, a societal, asset. Examples of how to conduct such packaging of knowledge into intellectual assets include, logically, increased attention to intellectual property rights (IPR) and the strategies behind deciding what (and what not) to protect as IPR, but also other more refined understandings of how knowledge may be controlled as an asset. Particularly noteworthy is that intellectual capital management includes not only the general (lawyer-orientated) understanding of control of knowledge through IPRs but also through human resource management/strategies/documents, shareholders agreements, licensing agreements (which may go further than the mere out licensing of IPRs), branding strategies, technology development strategies, etc, (Petrusson 2004: 187; Bruncevic and Käll 2016).

A simple way of illustrating, or rather mapping, how dematerialization of knowledge occurs via management of innovation practice and discourse, is through the intellectual asset mapping tool. This tool is meant to help visualize the intellectual assets that one could claim through intellectual property rights but also through contracts or other means such as capturing something by its physical nature, establishing standards, policies, etc. In doing this, one can make an assessment of either the intellectual assets (IA) one already control, or need to acquire in order to make a certain venture possible. One version of an intellectual asset mapping tool could look like this:

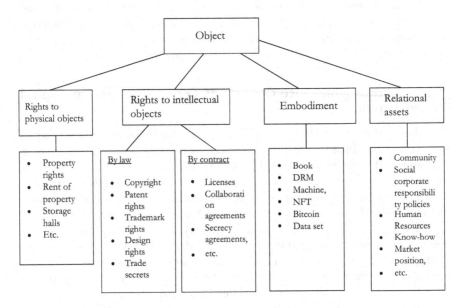

Figure 3.1 Intellectual asset mapping
The entire table is a translation of an earlier version published by myself and Merima Bruncevic in the Swedish textbook, *Moden immaterialrätt*, Liber: Stockholm, 2016, p. 242 with some added examples relevant to digital settings.

The aim of tools such as intellectual asset mapping is arguably not demater-ialization as such but that they should function as a map for everything that can be considered to be elements of a bigger value proposition, or more narrowly: an innovation. Such disaggregation, in turn, makes it possible to consider how information can be controlled in other ways than intellectual property rights and as a consequence facilitate a dematerialization process beyond intellectual property rights. If we consider how data functions as an asset today, it becomes less surprising that companies can state things like: "At large companies, sometimes we launch products not for the revenue, but for the data. We actually do that quite often … and we monetise the data through a different product," as expressed by Andrew Ng, who has held top positions at several of the most famous information capitalist companies in the world, such as Google, Baidu and Coursera (as cited in Sadowski 2020: 30). In fact, this way of collecting information from what seems to be outside of the "main" business model in order to move into a more intellectually capital intense form of business had already been hailed as a success story when, for example, Millennium Pharmaceuticals was showcased in a Harvard Business School case some 15 years ago.

As the case is elaborated by Thomke, Millennium Pharmaceuticals was established as a company just at the transition from chemically-orientated drug development to biotechnologies in the pharmaceutical industry. In the early days of this transition, companies with a biotechnological profile were very happy at the prospect of developing technologies that could be of interest to the giant pharmaceutical companies and consequently bought out of the risks in terms of the investment that this type of drug development entail. Millennium Pharmaceuticals, on the other hand, has been hailed as a success story since it managed to *not* get caught in this product-focused way of developing biotechnology for the pharma industry. The common "error" attributed to other biotech companies at the time is that they did not have enough resources to market drug compounds or did not have a technology platform vast enough to not become "research boutiques," (2001). As Thomke further describes:

> The initial vision of Millennium was to marry molecular biology with automation and informatics. This would allow for discovering and processing huge amounts of information about genes, making thousands of new targets possible. A dramatic increase would also require quicker screening technologies in order to test many more compounds.
>
> (ibid.: 5)

The way to reach that place of merging molecular biology with automation and informatics was first to ensure that lab technologies, including software for analysing gene functions and machines that decode DNA sequences, were held as proprietary (Thomke 2001).

This move, in turn, can be described as a move towards a dematerialized, process-orientated understanding of what it takes to be a biotech company in the pharmaceutical industry. This production process could be translated into a technology itself in which each link in the chain leading to the capture of a compound could be made increasingly efficient. When identifying these technologies, they can all be further enhanced and linked together, as what was already then referred to as "technology platforms," which enabled drug searchers to speed the process of identifying a gene and render it into a product in the form of a treatment. Consequently, the products and businesses emerging from such logics are no longer limited to the object being traded. Instead, the focus is on how to capture parts of the process as assets, in which other actors could also be invited and grow the entire business model, and the assets that could be captured (Thomke 2001: 5).

As Thomke further describes, by creating a technology platform instead of just a service or a product, Millennium Pharmaceuticals generated enough revenue to keep its business (as a platform) ahead of the competition. This idea of knowledge in general, as well as intellectual assets as an opening for endless growth, beyond physical property, resonates with the rationale behind the push towards a "knowledge economy" from industrialized societies when the competition over production became globalized and factory workers "too expensive" to sustain within the scope of the nation state in this global race to the bottom. The platform-based business model, as will be further discussed later, is just one example of this kind of business logics in an "intellectual value chain" or "intellectual value network" (e.g. Petrusson 2004: 241–246). Also, what needs to be remembered when the materialization of new phenomena appears in this stage of capitalism is that it is never about finding that one new asset that is like oil (*The Economist* 2017) but that both regular capitalism and advanced capitalism in particular are constantly seeking avenues for further capture and exploitation. In other words, an asset economy (Adkins, Cooper, and Konings 2020).

This can also be exemplified by how the Google search business model became a business model on the prediction of behaviours or, as Zuboff calls it: surveillance capitalism (2019). In discussing how surveillance capitalism entered the scene via Google, she describes a story where Google at one point cracked that they could create a business model not only around being a dominant search engine, but also by the extra information it could collect about how and when searches were being made, in relation to events external to the particular individual conducting the search (Zuboff 2019). To speak in terms of intellectual management theory, this is not only a question of moving towards behavioural or surveillance-orientated business models and markets, but also a question of realising intellectual assets that seemed to be outside of the "product" generally was considered to be the main business. From a traditional intellectual property perspective, one can also see that it is not only the technology that comprises the Google search that can be covered via patents or copyrights but also the data derived from users' searches, which (as we know by now) in themselves did not even have a clear property status. However, in using them and analysing them, Google could create new value propositions, such as advertisement sales. Furthermore, Google is, of course, an interesting example from the perspective of intellectual capital management in the way that there are many layers of the Google venture that reach beyond the product of the search, such as the brand, the side products (Google books, for example).

To summarise these examples, both highlight the fact that in a form of capitalism in which assets of "the mind" are in focus, this follows a logic of claiming a range of assets that can all be leveraged in a way that disconnects such assets from the generally disavowed product logics, or material value chain logics. As such, this logic is more than just a form of platform capitalism, as the disaggregation and rematerialization of assets start with what in management discourse is called the *value proposition*, or *intellectual value proposition*. Starting from what is a "unique proposition," one can then map the assets and desired assets and construct the legal strategies for controlling the proposition (Petrusson 2004: 144–194). Consequently, one does not start from, for example, the innovation which one has developed in-house in order to map it onto intellectual property constructs, but from how one can maximize value and, based on this, then map the strategy and appropriate forms of control in order to receive venture capital funding. This is not to say that legal property constructs do not matter or that traditional innovations such as technologies that can be patented matter, since they indeed do. It is just that they are not the end –, or even the starting game. They are instead conceived of as pieces or elements that can be disaggregated and re-assembled on their own. However, as the intellectual asset mapping tool pictured above shows, this construction of "intellectual" objects is deeply connected to other matters of relations, storage and carriers, workers, etc., all of which are vital to dematerialising and realising these objects from individual minds, to commodities (Granstrand 1999; 2000).

It cannot be stressed enough how important it is to start from a perspective that understands these aspects of advanced capitalism if one wants to critique its property form. This is because different kinds of legislative measures to prohibit, for example, the extraction of personal data, or patenting of computer programmes, will always stop short of controlling the techniques under which the market operates. There are always other ways of controlling the business models and famous examples that, to some extent, escape the property form: trade secrets or contracts are only some of those ways. Just like the platform disaggregates the firm or the market (Srnicek 2017: 43–48), so does intellectual management disaggregate the commodity, in order to repackage it as a more refined and liquid value proposition, controlled in more elaborate ways than via simple ownership.

Knowledge as Material: A Co-Created Resource

The general understanding of the need to move towards a knowledge economy as well as leftist critiques of the same have both been occupied by the idea that knowledge is always a co-creative effort. As Terranova puts it in relation to the identification of network cultures, there is a persistent idea that we need to be online in order to form part of the hive mind of the immaterial of networked, intelligent subjects (Terranova 2011). As she points out, this need for online connectivity in order to grow knowledge early on included multimedia artists, writers, journalists, software programmers, graphic designers and activists together, as well as small and large companies (ibid.). In a similar to vein to the posthumanist theories utilized here, Hardt and Negri have described this shift as a stage in which ideas, images, knowledge, code, languages and even affects can now be privatized and controlled as property (2000: 40). Hardt, however, also points to the specific capacity of knowledge as a commodity, which has been continuously raised by critical theorists, i.e. that knowledge is more difficult to control, lock in, compared to physical property. As Hardt states:

> There is a constant pressure for such goods to escape the boundaries of property and become common. If you have an idea, sharing it with me does not reduce its utility to you, but usually increases it. In fact, in order to realize their maximum productivity, ideas, images, and affects must be common and shared.
>
> (Hardt 2010: 346–356)

Other researchers, writing from different fields of theory, have also produced many similar takes on what makes knowledge a particular type of resource, which makes it difficult to convert into a commodity (e.g. Foray 2006). Early on, there was also widespread celebration of how digital media, by replacing more expensive and burdensome carriers of content, made knowledge sharing available to a wider audience than before (Kapczynski 2010).

This defence of knowledge as a non-typical resource is interesting from a posthumanist perspective in the sense that it calls for exploring what can be considered as non-commodifiable based on the materiality of knowledge as such. A common example of such a defence is how knowledge is different in its materiality than other resources and can be understood as a resource that grows from sharing and not by enclosure. For this reason, one could argue that holding knowledge, as a commodity, risks creating lock-in, rather than openness or common ownership. This, in turn, is perceived as harmful in relation to trying to extract value from knowledge as a commodity (see e.g. Heller 1998). This is because this identified complexity is not necessarily identified in the fact that these goods are pictured as disembodied. Rather, they are understood as posing problems in relation to their materiality in the manner that they may not as easily be controlled as other "resources." Thus, it is seen as a problem or a hope, that *knowledge* cannot as easily be captured and traded with (Hardt 2010; Foray 2006: 14–19; Heller 1998; Heller and Eisenberg 1998). Key to these kinds of ideas and practices is that knowledge is something that grows from sharing.

In a similar theme, Foray also argues that knowledge is not subject to the same "tragedy of the commons" logic that may be attributed to physical goods if too many actors (over) utilize a physical resource (2006: 14–19). In brief, the tragedy of the commons is generally told as a story about why property is needed since common resources would otherwise be overexploited. For example, those who believe in these ideas have argued that if several herds all have access to a specific grazing area, they would all attempt to reap the most benefits from it. This would also lead to a situation in which the resource is destroyed due to overuse and no one would be better off in the long term as no one would be able to use the resource. The tragedy of the commons therefore implies that resources cannot be held in common as this produces overuse of such resources, since everyone with surplus would be prone to maximising their own use of such a resource. This idea builds upon several assumptions but probably most prominently that the people that jointly resides on a surface consists of a group of humans that are all so-called *homo oeconomicus*, or individual well-fare maximizers. Also, the idea that a "tragedy of the commons" emerges if property ownership is not designated to a joint resource as it otherwise would be subject to over exploitation, builds upon the idea that all resources are limited in use.

However, in innovation management, the communality of knowledge creation is (unsurprisingly) not mirrored in an idea to leave knowledge be as a too complicated resource to produce and capitalize. This is clear from the intellectual capital management discipline as described above, but also in the way that the commons were very easily co-opted by companies to both appropriate open-source software and build business mindsets such as Open Innovation/Open Service Innovation, as famously advocated by Chesbrough (Chesbrough 2003; 2011) In these discourses, the focus is how companies can grow their general productivity through business models orientated towards capturing knowledge in a more refined way based on understanding how some assets can be kept closed while others are shared. Open Innovation (OI) discourses emphasize the potential of treating knowledge as something that grows from unlocking certain parts of the business model that had previously been kept as assets within the boundary of firms or other organizations such as a university (Chesbrough 2003). The strategic aim of OI for companies is consequently not to grow knowledge in general, but exactly how to transform their previous product-heavy, or in-house-orientated value chain production logic, towards a more dynamic way of capitalising on their assets. As many early on set out to explain, this does not imply a move towards an openness in knowledge production such as waiving one's intellectual property rights, but rather to strategically analyse where in the business model certain intellectual assets can be expanded via an opening up towards other actors. Such actors could furthermore vary in kind and include for example (previous) competitors and consumers (Chesbrough 2003; Petrusson, Rosén and Thornblad 2010; Chesbrough 2011). Open Innovation as a form of technology management practice also aligns to a large extent with platform-based business models. However, what separates OI from more fully-fledged modern ICT platforms is the way in which OI is advocated by Chesbrough, in that he focuses to a larger degree on companies with more traditional products and ways of managing their business, such as automotive companies. Consequently, we find a more prominent understanding here that both physical and intellectual elements are part of a company's value proposition and can also, then, be subject to different levels of openness and closure to create new forms of control and the conversion of assets into capital. Thus, in making this argument, we find rationalizations for why companies and organizations need to think differently about the control of knowledge assets than they thought in relation to physical assets in the industrial setting.

The Open Innovation perspective, then, in turn, is ironically a way of controlling knowledge in new ways by deciding which parts of a business model would best benefit from being placed under which level of openness order, and how. Once again, we already find these practices in earlier forms of intellectual property management in which portfolio thinking and diversified licensing strategies existed long before they became part of these wider OI/sharing perspectives. For example, the licensing out of trademarks or bundled franchise concepts all run on the idea that a core asset is controlled by a company, while other parts of the production and product development process is developed by other actors.

The idea of knowledge being a collaborative effort that cannot be captured is in this way, quickly became a to go-perspective as more fluid forms of management styles, closely following the general idea of intellectual capital management discourse in which assets need to be objectified to as large a degree as possible so that they can be controlled. An example of a tool, besides the intellectual asset management tool pictured above, are those tools used to visualize the intellectual assets that actors bring in and out of a project, commonly called *Background and Foreground IP* (Granstrand and Holgersson 2014). Besides defining which assets are being covered in an agreement, the parties also state who should control what, how results are being shared and so on. When negotiated, such assets can later be defined in collaboration agreements, both between parties and in separate contracts in relation to other parties. Consequently, the level of control and openness can be defined in relation to a specific asset or several (Petrusson 2004: 178–182; Granstrand and Holgersson 2014; Bruncevic and Käll 2016: 255–279). In relation to digitalization, furthermore, the idea of the joint development of code, as well as the subsequent treating of code as a language not to be patented, also reflects such ideas about joint knowledge creation as being more or less a necessity. As expressed by Don and Alex Tapscott, for example, this came with a sentiment in which many people had high hopes of a change in the terms of control of *information*. The idea was potentially, as they point out: naïve, but still it was believed that "[l]ow cost and massive peer-to-peer communication would help to undermine traditional hierarchies and help with the inclusion of developing world citizens in the global economy" (Tapscott and Tapscott 2016: 12). The subsequent battles over which platform was "better" between iPhone iOS and Google Android, based on whether they were built on open-source software, furthermore reflects both an idealistic idea of open-source software as being more ethical, as well as the fact that none of these models were ever about being entirely open or closed, but about a layered understanding of where to place openness and where to place closure in co-creation.

To summarise both these standpoints, there is a persistent idea that knowledge is a non-rivalrous asset. This understanding is intuitive when we consider the cultural aspects that intellectual property rights cover, such as music, film and other art content. Of course, this also rings true in general if we consider the potential to grow knowledge, amongst both humans and certain other animal individuals, through education or other practices for teaching and learning. What characterizes this understanding of knowledge is that it does not depreciate the more people hold it but could instead grow more if more individuals hold similar types of knowledge and recreate it in new or mutual ways that benefit them. As Foray argues, knowledge in itself should be understood as always existing as a partly non-exclusive resource, which is independent from competition due to the fact that several actors may occupy knowledge at the same time without diminishing the value of said knowledge. As he puts it "[k] nowledge can theoretically be used by a million people at no additional cost because its use by an additional agent does not imply the production of an additional copy of that knowledge" (Foray 2006: 15–16). The refined understanding of knowledge as a resource in business management, however, forces us to realize that we cannot trust the materiality of knowledge to save us from the perils of the forms of advanced capitalism within which we live. Instead, a more fruitful avenue from a posthumanist perspective in further understanding which materialities are at stake when knowledge is dematerialized from the human body, as well as a collective of human bodies, is to also recollect its materialities in other forms that are generally disregarded in the knowledge economy and the narrower knowledge management discourses.

The Material in the Immaterial

As has been stressed throughout, the materialization of knowledge into an individual class of assets is the product of several narratives and discourses related to both critical theory and innovation management. A particularly vital intervention in these narratives is to stress the way that knowledge, by being an always embodied and human resource, always paves the way for something communal, or commons, to emerge (e.g. Hardt and Negri 2019; Negri 2019; Fuchs 2019). A challenge with this view from a posthumanist perspective is however that the continuous division between physical and intellectual assets rides on a humanist wave of also distinguishing between nature and humans. It is also problematic in the way that the overemphasis on the differences between intellectual and physical assets obliterates the hybridization which digital media makes possible. This, in turn hinders, an insight into how property as a concept is not so much about whether something is intangible or physical but how control is constructed whether the conceptual divides in property allow it or not, as will also be discussed further. One can at this stage say that work has gone into rationalising the differences between intellectual assets and physical assets there is a tendency to dismiss how there is nothing intellectual without the bodies that carry them, whether these bodies are human or not. To speak with Negri:

> [f]ixed capital appears now within bodies, imprinted into them and at the same time subordinated to them – this is even more the case when we consider activities such as research and software development, in which work is not crystalised in a physical product that is separate from the worker, but remains incorporated in the brain and inseparable from the person.
>
> (2019: 211)

Within several of the perspectives related to how knowledge could be treated as an economic good, or as a commodity, there is, interestingly, also a wide understanding of the material conditions that render knowledge less intangible than the more capitalist understandings convey. For example, the reasoning put forward by Foray that knowledge is "partially localized and weakly persistent" including that "new knowledge is most often not of general value for the economy because it has been produced in a local context for particular purposes" (Foray 2006: 17). Knowledge is also weakly persistent in the manner that people forget and knowledge can also depreciate through deterioration and obsolescence when communities break/are broken up (ibid.). Also, in models such as the intellectual asset management tool visualized above, it is clear that it is not only information or knowledge that are understood as being necessary to materialising intellectual assets. The innovation and entrepreneurship discipline also stresses the importance of human resources and combined knowledge creation as a means of creating new knowledge and the open innovation discourse is only one example of this (Chesbrough 2003; 2011). Such points of the materialization of knowledge are vital to moving towards a concept of posthuman property and to capturing more than just a critique of the commodification of knowledge. However, staying with these perspectives would also risk pursuing a continued disconnection from the media that transforms knowledge into a resource in digital societies. This may be particularly dangerous if disembodied ideas of knowledge feeds into discourses regarding artificial intelligence in which human intelligence is no longer viewed as embodied in humans, whether individual or collective (e.g. Dyer-Witheford, Mikkola Kjosen and Steinhoff 2019).

Instead, it is suggested here that it is via more clearly following the line of thinking which considers how an assemblage of different bodies makes up knowledge production that we can also find a further rematerialization against such commodification processes. To move towards this perception of how intangibles can be reconsidered, two fruitful avenues to further explore are the ecological as well as labour-orientated perspectives of the production of digital commodities. As a representative of the first, the ecological perspective critiquing the dematerialization of digital media affords many vital avenues that also link into the posthumanist critique of the Anthropocene – and its critical variations (Braidotti 2013: 5–6 and passim; Parikka 2015; Haraway 2016; Moore 2017; Yusoff 2019; Braidotti 2019: 156–158). Amoore, amongst others, have further suggested how the cloud in cloud computing, can be considered along its physical representations. As she puts it, when cloud computing is understood as an architecture where data and algorithms meet, "the cloud is actualized in data centers, located on places within economies of land, tax rates, energy, water for cooling, and proximity to the main trunks of the network" (Amoore 2020: 35). Along similar lines also Parikka points out that a geology of data also needs to start from the fact that cloud computing has very little to do with any metaphor of the cloud itself and has everything to do with keeping servers cool (Parikka 2015: 24). The choice of where to place data centres in cool areas such as Stockholm in Sweden, consequently points at the importance of geography in data storage. (e.g. Amoore 2020: 35–36).

In this way, abstract metaphors of the seemingly immaterial kind – the data is in the cloud – can be reconnected to the way that data and the digital economy are thoroughly dependent on so-called natural resources, just like any other commodity. When data is pictured as a resource that can be extracted in itself, such infrastructures necessary for its objectification are made invisible. In pointing at how digital technologies are environmentally embedded and have ecological effects, we also rematerialize these seemingly abstract products. Recently Moll's art project on The Hidden Life of an Amazon User traces the steps of a simple online transaction where an experiment where the book *The Life, Lessons & Rules for Success of Jeff Bezos* was purchased at Amazon on June 17, 2019. As she shows, in order to purchase this work, the consumer had to go through 12 different interfaces, built up of large amounts of different types of code. Moll was also able to track 1307 different requests of scripts amounting to the equivalent of 8724 pages of printed code and 87.33Mb of data. This also had the consequence that: "all the energy needed to load all this data was effectively unloaded upon the customer, who ultimately assumed not just part of the economic costs of Amazon's monetization processes, but also a portion of its environmental footprint" (Moll 2019). Her piece therefore conveys how a customer enters a "labyrinth of interfaces and code that allowed them to buy Jeff Bezos's book, while also revealing the rising energy costs that were unwittingly paid for by the Amazon customer" (Moll 2019).

A second classical way to rematerialize the commodity, which is also being pursued in relation to digitalization, is through an understanding of labour. As discussed in the introductory chapter, such a perspective has been advanced by Wark in her suggestions that what defines the current stage of "not-capitalism-anymore-but-something-worse" is the emergence of the vectorial class (2019: 45). This vectorial class, in turn, exploits a number of new forms of representatives of the working class, spread globally as well as engaged in a number of layers that are controlled by vectors, such as those enrolled in platform capitalism (ibid.; Srnicek 2017) Following the lead of Haraway, we can also identify how the informatics of domination runs on convergences between technology, labour and capital that all become unified under informatics-driven capitalism (Haraway 1991: 161–162. As furthermore argued by Terranova, the expansion of the internet gave increased support and material infrastructure to an increased flexibility of the workforce (Terranova 2011: 74–75). In recent years, critical interventions have made it increasingly possible to see how "the digital" is produced not only as code by hip engineers in valleys made of silicon (whether they are located in California or Stockholm) but on the streets in which gig workers deliver food and parcels, in mines in which blood minerals are being excavated, or in massive task forces ready to categorize images to be utilized for machine learning.

An example of the latter is the mapping of the images onto the previously mentioned ImageNet, as was carried out by Amazon Turk or MTurk. Amazon Turk (alluding to the original Mechanical Turk) is a well-known crowdsourcing platform on which people can post tasks and have them carried out by a number of workers, at a low cost. As described by the creator of ImageNet, what would have taken them 19 years to do was carried out through MTurk in significantly less time by simply paying 40 cents for every 300 images to a worker who "chose" to take on such work. Naturally, Amazon Turk, in turn, is a form of innovation management invention, which sustains both the knowledge communicated above in relation to how to disaggregate an object into many smaller pieces (tasks), as well as to not do everything in-house if there are more cost-efficient ways of doing it.

Another layer in how labour plays a continuous role in the digital economy is naturally also the work (or whatever one wants to call it) performed by users of digital platforms. In recent research, Qiu goes as far as describing the labour in the manufacturing of digital devices as a form of iSlavery. While the terminology of slavery as a form of labour in digital production has received critique (e.g. Goodwin 2019: 165–167), Qiu argues that one can still draw links to how the goal of slavery is to exploit the body or body parts of the enslaved under an abnormal labour-capital relationship. However, he also reserves the concept of iSlavery as being more of a *de facto* type of slavery (2019: 153–154). This terminology can also be compared to how Couldry and Mejias make reference to how data collection and processing also could be considered forms of *de facto* slavery (Couldry and Mejias 2019 e.g. xvi–xviii and passim) As for iSlavery, Qiu identifies two forms of slavery: the manufacturing or production-mode iSlave on the one hand and a manufactured iSlave/consumption-mode slavery on the other (ibid.; 156).

He further illustrates the different layers of such slavery in the manner that a connection can be made between the manufacturing domain and the "bowels of the earth" in a place like the Democratic Republic of Congo. Here, "blood minerals" such as coltan, essential to our electronic devices, are mined by workers, including children, under the control of warlords and even at gunpoint (Qiu 2019: 156). iSlavery is according to Qiu also embodied for example by the 1.4 million Chinese workers at the world's largest electronic manufacturer, Foxconn. As discussed by Qiu, Foxconn came under media scrutiny when reporters managed to get a view of Foxconn's "Peace" dormitory in Shenzen in the South of China, where they saw "300 workers sleeping in three-level bunk beds in one huge room without air conditioning" (ibid.: 156). Qiu also states that there is a practice at Foxconn in which "student interns" are sent by vocational schools in the Chinese hinterlands to the factory. These student interns, usually in their late teens, come to Foxconn for three months to work on assembly lines, including making iPhone back cases, otherwise they are not allowed to graduate. This in spite of the fact that they could be majoring in such diverse fields as accounting, English or pharmaceutics (ibid.). Tiziana Terranova paints a similar picture of work in the digital media industry outside of China. "Netslaves" of the "dot-com" boom also witnessed 24/7 sweatshops with 90-hour working weeks (Terranova 2011: 73). Another form of iSlavery outlined by Qiu that could also shed light on the material aspects of the production of information goods is what he calls the *manufactured or consumption-mode iSlavery*. In his terms, these are the consumers who are so possessed by the idea of owning and consuming the communication technologies being produced, as well as handing over their time to digital platforms, that they could sell a kidney and/or 653 billion hours of attention during one year (2014) (ibid.: 158–159). This type of work is also discussed by Terranova as a form of free labour in which "the activity of building web sites, modifying software packages, reading and participating in mailing lists and building virtual spaces" are all carried out for free (2011: 74).

A twist to these types of exhaustive and often "free" forms of labour can now be witnessed via the move towards the extreme abstraction promised by AI discourses. As discussed, AI runs on the idea that intelligence can be objectified to an even larger extent than before, to perform tasks previously carried out by humans. As critical theorists have pointed at, in this way, AI can be understood as an automation of labour, to the benefit of capitalists (for an overview of these discussions, see Dyer-Witheford, Kjosen and Steinhoff 2019: 1–29). This kind of abstraction of human knowledge into something that can be fully absorbed and executed by machines also ironically shows that what is at stake here is not only knowledge but the advancement of new embodiments of knowledge. The human-centred fantasies of AI reach their peak in the idea of robots, which will not only be able to be as smart, or smarter, than humans, but also have bodies of their own, move around, and naturally, perform work that renders an increasingly large number of workers expendable (ibid.: 5–6, c.f. Bratton 2021: 1). When moving towards increasingly embodied and artificial intelligences, it is more important than ever to not get caught in simplistic divides about knowledge as something abstract in capitalism, but something that can be objectified and claimed in many new ways.

From a posthumanist perspective, a task along these lines involve to become more engaged with all types of resources that make the endless commodification of knowledge possible, as well as the actual finitude of these resources – in both their capture and their mediation. Critical media studies such as the ones mentioned here in general facilitate seeing this finitude by centring on how knowledge and information never flow freely but always depend on various matter of mediation (Cubitt 2016; Terranova 2011). Furthermore, the material aspects for the production of the digital economy are deeply entangled with questions of racism, sexism and all its combinations with capitalism, producing boundaries for which bodies can become automated and how. As is well-known by now, gig workers are often under enormous pressure to deliver quickly and very few gig workers other than those who have no alternative, remain in this work for long. Workers performing crowdsourcing tasks are those who can do so for extremely low salaries, which naturally places such work in countries that are already exploited by global capitalism (e.g. Moore 2019). The sexism and racism further coded into our machine learning systems are expressions of the workers who have coded and trained the systems or designed the algorithms as discussed in the previous chapter (and see e.g. boyd 2012; Noble 2018; Benjamin 2019).

In this way, our intangible world carries both bodies from previous forms of capitalism as well as other systems of oppression further and produces a post-human condition which by no means transcends the body into a transhumanist vision in which the mind is abstracted from the body and reinserted as a form of increased knowledge for all humans (Bostrom 2011). Instead, we are reminded of the multiple layers in which posthuman bodies are in flux under the desires produced via advanced capitalism, and relate to each other, even when seemingly disconnected. As the following chapter will show, this dis-aggregated way of understanding matter, while still grounded in an increasing number of materialities, is also the opening for posthuman property.

Chapter 4

Coding Posthuman Property through Intellectual Property Law and Beyond

What is property and where does property start and end? This question seems both trivial and impossible depending on the position from where one is looking. In spite of the fact that, early on, cyberspace was claimed as a zone without the legal concept of property by the savvy folks who inhabited it. As Barlow put it in the 1996 Declaration of Independence of Cyberspace: "Your legal concepts of property, expression, identity, movement, and context do not apply to us. They are all based on matter, and there is no matter here. Our identities have no bodies" (Barlow 1996). In introductory legal textbooks today, property law is however (still) all about defining different objects that can be claimed by humans, not least in the form of companies, and what happens if several actors make conflicting claims over them. In this way, property is about fixating an object in order to make it controllable or, as Davies puts it, "*[i]ntrinsic* to the existence of private property is the power to control the object, whatever it is, and the power to exclude others from its use and enjoyment" (Davies 2008: 52). As such, many of the processes that make something into property are so taken for granted that it is not until law students encounter legal theory courses that they are able to start acknowledging the many layers of philosophy and power needed to back up concepts of property. So, where does one then start to consider property even further in accordance with the posthuman agenda, without getting lost in all the philosophies of property? A good starting point is to put it in what strikes me as a very new materialist kind of definition presented by Wark, in which she states that:

> To make something property is to separate it from a continuum, to mark it or bound it, to represent it as something finite. At the same time, making something as property connects it, via a representation of it as a separate and finite object, to the subject who owns it. What is the cut from one process joins another who owns it. What is cut from one process joins another process, what was nature becomes second nature.
>
> (Wark 2014: note 176)

DOI: 10.4324/9781003139096-4

This definition of property aligns with a posthuman perspective in particular because it sheds light on the processual or continuous flow that needs to be cut for something to be rendered property. Starting with such understanding implies to consider how enclosure of objects functions as a means for those in control seek new enclosures for property (Boyle 2003), similar to the cases of assetization and dematerialization described in the previous chapter. Speaking with new materialist theory, the process of cutting a continuum (Barad 2007: 42) naturally also applies to producing any kind of legal concept, including law itself. As Douzinas and Gearey remind us, law is etymologically connected to the Greek word *krinein* which "means also to cut; critique is a diacritical or cutting force, a critical separation and demarcation. It aims to distinguish between the just manifestations" (2005: 38). In spite of this general awareness of law's necessary processual orientation, the way property is enacted via the person–thing divide in Roman law is almost taken as given in the ordering of, and by humans. For example, Esposito shows the historical roots of this divide as:

> [w]hen the Roman jurist Gaius, in his *Institutes*, identified persons and things as the two categories that along with actions constitute the subject matter of law, he did nothing more than give legal value to a criterion that was already accepted.
>
> (2015: 2)

Esposito further argues that because of this, the distinctions between persons and things have, since Roman times, "been reproduced in all modern codifications, becoming the presupposition that serves the implicit ground for all other types of thought – for legal but also for philosophical, economic, political, and ethical reasoning" (ibid.: 2). This has the effect of creating a "watershed" that divides the world of life, "cutting it in two areas" defined by their mutual opposition (ibid.: 2). However, both the digital economy and advanced capitalism create a cut in this divide, and create new bodies, beyond the divide between persons and things (ibid.: 136)

The legal forms of intellectual property rights to all kinds of novel information both respond to and further enable the changes in the forces of production running on this divide (e.g. Wark 2019: 15–16). Cohen echoes this insight by showing how all forms of intellectual property rights have come to grow more similar to each other during informational capitalism. As she describes it, this can be understood as a form of dematerialization sped up via a portfolio thinking related to claiming more and more parts as intellectual assets rather than specific intellectual property rights (Cohen 2019: 23). As discussed in the previous chapter, this is by now an old insight for those who have worked in the field of making such dematerialization and subsequent commodification of information happen.

In relation to platform capitalism, it has also been highlighted that we might be approaching a more feudal type of economy, in which power over assets is held by a few landlords and most people only rent their share of the lands, whether they are digital, physical or converged (such as AirBnB, Foodora and Uber) (Sadowski 2020: 61–66). Because of these developments it is increasingly possible to say that the concept of property is no longer about owning a certain thing, but rather building a form of power in which the one in control sets the rules for access. As already described by Drahos and Braithwaite in 2002, we can ask whether what we witness in terms of control of the knowledge economy is a form of information feudalism since "(t)he redistribution of property rights in the case of information feudalism involves a transfer of knowledge assets from the intellectual commons into private hands" (2002: 2–3) and

> (t)he effect of this is to raise levels of private monopolistic power to dangerous global heights, at a time when states which have been weakened by the forces of globalization, have less capacity to protect their citizens from the consequences of the exercise of this power.
>
> (ibid.: 3)

The conflation between property and cultural power via feudal ties, comes into particular force when it comes to property in knowledge, as Drahos and Braithwaite discuss, in the sense that copyright has played a role in dictating what can be spread as truth (ibid.: 2–3). This is in spite of the fact that property and contract rights, even if it is difficult to remember now, were initially construed in order to limit monarchical authority (Cohen 2020: 270). To this it can also be added, as remarked by Davies, that feudalism never really disappeared entirely, which is reflected in certain forms of property such as in heritage law, which protects both the financial and the cultural values of the elites (Davies 2008: 13) and today, also via the physical property markets in many countries, as they increasingly demand the intergenerational transfer of wealth, if one wants to enter it (Adkins, Cooper and Koning 2019: 26–28).

As Cohen argues, what is needed to further such understanding of property power as being more than a right of a person over a thing involves to reconsider "the logics of dematerialization, datafication and platformization" in order to disrupt such logics (2019: 270–271). For this reason, theories advancing the similarities between feudal times and advanced capitalist forms of control align with a posthuman theory of property in the manner that they highlight the fact that property is no longer only about a subject owning an object, but a more fundamental change in control of both numerous assets and life-worlds, including truth. However, a transgression also occurs by affirming liberal theories and meanings of property by pushing them to their extremes, while keeping them in place. To reach further into an understanding of how this transgression towards posthuman property (or indeed something worse) is being coded, this chapter focuses on how legal conceptual divides between intellectual versus physical property, as well as the divide between personhood and property, can be further understood as processes for dematerialization, datafication and platformization against unfolding forms of capitalism.

Intellectual versus Physical Property: Knowledge as Property

A fundamental starting point here is that intellectual property rights play a key role in the information economy and advanced capitalism alike (e.g. Lessig 1999; Boyle 2003; Wark 2019: 42–43; Cohen 2019: 11). An important divide for the information economy, as discussed in the previous chapter, is to capture knowledge into separate objects for commodification by claiming their difference in relation to physical objects. More specifically, this divide manifests itself in the manner that it is continuously iterated that intellectual property rights consider the protection of intellectual efforts, or even, *ideas* and not *physical* objects/things. Whereas different descriptions of the emergence of copyright exists (e.g. Madero 2010: 1–4), modern copyright is conceptually constructed upon philosophical fundamentals vested in Enlightenment values in which the importance of providing protection to intellectual efforts (of varying extent) to support the cultural and scientific progress of society is often emphasized (Chon 1993). Thus, the general conceptual binary between material and immaterial matter in property theory extends back to the more general idea in society in which ideas are perceived as being part of the activity of the mind and are thus disembodied, or intangible. In this way, intellectual property rights are also intrinsically connected to the perception of the human as a rational being "of the mind," which is so vividly criticized in posthumanist theory (e.g. Braidotti 2013)

The reification of such values is visible even when considering the terminology used to describe intellectual property rights as *intellectual* or, in German based languages: *immaterial* (rights). In the Nordic countries, this difference is also echoed in many examples of legal conceptualizations regarding law related to trade in which the sale of goods is understood as being the typical category of trade. This leads into an actual state of law in which intellectual property rights depend on the division between tangible and intangible things (Pottage and Sherman 2013: 11). As Boyle also puts it:

> [o]wnership of an individual physical thing is not enough, whether that thing is a lump of tissue, a faded photo of a compromising position, a confidential prospectus for a takeover, or a book like the one you hold in your hand. Each presents us with an attempt to control information, to restrict access, to delimit control.
>
> (Boyle 1996: 17)

In this way, all intellectual property laws build upon the premise that knowledge can be separated from the human mind and controlled (while limited in time, space and other embodiments). In the intellectual property law sense, a new knowledge object is understood as an object that can be patented, copyrighted, trademarked or design protected. The categories in intellectual property laws directs exactly what kind of knowledge each law may objectify and treat as an object subject to intellectual property rights protection, and how. In modern times, these differences between the different intellectual property laws and their objects have functioned as fairly strict disciplinary lines between lawyers and legal theoretical work alike. Hence, just because one is an intellectual property law scholar or practitioner, does not mean that one knows as much about patents as one does in relation to copyrights. Furthermore, the legal fields of patents and copyrights are extremely rich in their own right as they cover vast numbers of different knowledge objects. It is fair to say that in the discourses of intellectual property rights in other disciplines, these differences have, to some extent, been glossed over (e.g. Wark 2019: 42–43). However, as many have noted, there can be a point to understanding intellectual property rights as a system (Drahos and Braithwaite 2002; Boyle 1996; Cohen 2019: 18–23) today, as this is how market actors treat them, which is also obvious from the previous chapter. Furthermore, the system of intellectual property rights in the digitalized world also includes the use of contracts to a degree where one can say that intellectual property rights and contracts have systematically collapsed into each other (Radin 2003; cf. Elkin-Koren 2005; Radin 2013). This implies that the objectification processes taking place in the production of knowledge as a property object, while having some kind of legal origin in intellectual property taxonomies originating in a previous form of capitalist production, have now come to be both blurred and extended through other legal tools such as contracts (Cohen 2019: 23). However, what unifies the dominant underlying thoughts about intellectual property rights discourse, whether combined with contracts or not, is the idea that what is being controlled is a limited form of a knowledge object. This equips intellectual property law with a view of it as being disconnected to material circumstances, in spite of the fact that the laws are legitimized via support for very specific material conditions (innovation, the dissemination of arts, literature, etc.).

In recent times, the extraction of information from matters previously considered as belonging to individual bodies has shed light on the materiality of intellectual property. For example, an early debate was about the dematerialization of human bodies into genetic information, leading to a discussion about the connection between access to knowledge and access to medicine (e.g. Kapczynski 2010). An often-discussed case in which the materiality of patents over human bodies is made visible is the so-called "hairy leukaemia case." This case started in 1976 when a called patient John Moore initiated treatment for the disease, hairy cell leukemia, at the University of California. After his doctors became aware that some of his blood cells and components might have commercial value, they performed tests of all types of bodily fluids, without informing Moore. In the end, they also removed Moore's spleen, for medical reasons, but also in order to reassure themselves about how to keep a spleen for research purposes. In 1981, a patent was filed based on the information derived from Moore's T-lymphocytes by the University of California, with his doctors listed as inventors (Boyle 1996: 22) Afterwards, the doctor who performed the surgery claimed this material as property to be used as research material (without the patient's explicit consent) since it contained information about the rare cancer for which the patient had been treated. With reference to his lack of consent, the patient further claimed that the material should be seen as a part of his body. In the ensuing court-case however, the court ruled in favour of the doctor and consequently the material was seen as information and not as a part of the human body (Boyle 1996; 22–24; Bhandar 2012: 112–116; Davies and Naffine 2001: 11–12).

What happened in this case exemplifies exactly the way in which a dematerialization of the human body, or at least the concept of the human body and its boundaries, is activated in creating an object for intellectual property. In this case the object to be dematerialized was genetic sequences. When these could be considered as "derived," and detached from the physical body, they could also more easily become reduced to codes or information. At that point, it is no longer the human body that is at stake but "rather the control of information derived from the body" (Davies and Naffine 2001: 123). As Boyle shows, this understanding is also made possible by the court in the specific case in which body parts are partly understood as something that one cannot own after they have been separated from the body and partly by perceiving information in the human body as something that is not unique to one individual in particular and therefore cannot be owned by Moore (Boyle 1996: 23). For this reason, Davies and Naffine contend that the trick performed by intellectual property is to state it is not the human body that is at stake, since intellectual property concerns abstract objects and not physical things. The object of IPR inside a person is not about the body but "rather abstractions of the self which are intrinsically repeatable" (Davies and Naffine 2001: 125). In the case of John Moore's cell-line, as well as in many other cases in relation to biotechnology, this distinction has generally developed towards a view in which what *could* be considered as (parts of) human bodies, are instead treated as "information."

Similar dematerialization processes have recently come to actualize the point at which data becomes a separable object from the human. That this would become the case, was also forecast by Boyle, for example, by showing how databases and copyright over software would become a *de facto* way of controlling information (Boyle 1996: 169–170). However, the legal constructs emerging for database control at that time are naturally not even close to the role that data has currently come to play. At the time of writing, it is furthermore still being debated whether data is a commodity in its own right or is covered by intellectual property rights. In a simplistic understanding of intellectual property rights, one could say no. The way in which data is currently controlled is not an object of intellectual property rights in the sense that there is no category in our current intellectual property rights legislation that states that *data* is an object (cf. Käll 2020). The linguistically closest we could get to this definition is the concept of database protection in copyright law. However, as we have learnt from the role of intellectual capital management in the previous chapter, what does it matter if IPR law does not recognize something as an object? What is more important here is the question of whether we can regard data, as information, being dematerialized from something else as a step towards individual commodification. This coding (cf. Pistor 2019), in its simplest understanding, makes it possible to trade with an object and convert it into capital value. The exact expressions of data commodification are not obvious, as the legal concepts of data commodification are still being created. As of now, data is already commodified. In the legal doctrine, it has long been understood as a remarkable development that the creation of information as objects of property tends to be established via contracts, in which companies in boilerplate contracts one-sidedly stipulate that individuals agree to data collection to access the service being offered (Radin 2013). However, as discussed in the previous chapter, the contract is just regarded as one of many legal tools that can be used to control intellectual assets.

For this reason, the commodification of data, like other information assets, has this tendency to be distanced from the processes that are required for its production. This implies a flattening out of the differences between the objects that may be considered as data, through law. If we consider intellectual property rights laws again, there is generally no difference made in copyright law between whether a literary work is of core interest to society and its cultural bonds, or if it is a work that no one will ever use. The same, with very few exceptions, also applies to patents. Copyright is therefore granted to works equally and the same applies overall to patentable inventions. In general, the same is true to trademark law, in which the only general boundary is that a mark to be protected by trademark law, should be possible to represent in a clear and precise manner and be distinctive in relation to the category for which it has been registered. This implies that one does not take into account either societal or business value when one grants intellectual property rights to certain phenomena. What is important is if something can be considered to be possible to capture as an object according to specific law. And if not, intellectual assets are controlled in other ways, and possibly later also reified as intellectual property objects in a narrower sense, as discussed in the previous chapter.

A way of thinking more affirmatively about this development is that it also makes visible a not so strict boundary between *body* and *mind*. As discussed, this divide has generally informed a way of perceiving "the" human, in which thinking has held a hierarchical position in opposition to the body. In this way, thinking has functioned as an informative practice for how to depict "human" activity from the behaviour of nonhuman others (e.g. Braidotti 2013: 172). When commodification of knowledge occurs, thinking is reshuffled from the domain of the individual human, making it less a unique basis from which humans can claim a position aginst all others. Instead it is those that control knowledge, via property, that rule.

Following this line of realizing how "the human" is already displaced via IPR, is furthermore a welcome break against the emerging discourses in law in relation to how to keep the human, or humanist values and rules, against the unfolding of AI. (c.f. Bratton 2021a: 105). Speaking with Boyle, anthropocentrism in AI can be detected in property discourse when

> (w)hy should the attempt to achieve *electromagnetic* artificial intelligence be the main locus of the philosophical and moral debate about the nature of consciousness? Many of the same issues are raised in transgenic species, biomechanical "wetware," or nonhuman animals, for that matter.
>
> (Boyle 1996: 152)

A variation on this kind of "fetishization" of the mind is arguably also how knowledge is perceived as something organic that needs sharing to grow. Such narratives are particularly visible in innovation theory (e.g. Open Innovation), as well as where such an understanding of knowledge is used to argue against the commodification of knowledge, as discussed in the previous chapter (also cf. Boyle 1996: 7). However, what all these narratives on the commodification of knowledge make very obvious is that knowledge is never disembodied. Instead, it continuously depends on different forms of bodies in order to be perceived as, for example, information, a work, an invention and so on. Furthermore, this process shifts when a new type of matter, such as digital bodies, may be utilized to embody knowledge. In this way, the force of intellectual property as a means of sustaining knowledge-based capitalism can, ironically, be understood as exactly that which also makes visible the materiality of "intangible" property objects. Through blockchain, for example we may also soon see an increasing number of layers of digitalization added to "physical assets" in order to make them both increasingly traceable and more tangible than they ever were without digital layers (Tapscott and Tapscott 2016, p. 159, also cf. Herian 2016a; 2016b). Through the development of such practices, one may argue that blockchain as a facilitator for the development of a smart thing appears to move further beyond property (see e.g. Esposito 2015: 1; Käll 2017). It also appears as if this movement of the concept of private property may be understood as an intensification of how control is pursued through property. This is because blockchain enables both further digitalization and control of physical elements (cars, parcels, entire cities). As this chapter suggests, this change in property control and information as a property object simultaneously challenges the matter of property as being about something abstract.

An important starting point for this chapter is consequently that the analysis of embodiment via "intellectual" property cannot stop with a mere understanding that such property is also always material. In fact, this realization is not necessarily so radical or even new. Rather, a practitioner of intellectual property law is well aware that the framing of the *intellectual* always connects to how successful one is in framing the *material*. Thus, questions of how to make successful claims of intellectual property involve the possibility of claiming that something is an invention and not a discovery, a work produced by a person. etc. (cf. Petrusson 2004: 114–115, 122–127). However, intellectual property still remains within a framework in which it is perceived to consider "knowledge" as its object of property. Furthermore, it is framed within theories that maintain that the capture of knowledge leads to the best growth of knowledge in a very general sense, as discussed in the previous chapter. This is the case, in spite of the narratives produced within the framework of the access to knowledge movement (e.g. Verzola 2010: 236–276). As briefly discussed, through this movement it has continuously been pointing out how the idea of intellectual property is a Western construct. Furthermore, it has been described as a construct which, as Vandana Shiva argues, produces a "monoculture of the mind" (1993). This, in turn, leads us towards the next theoretical setting of property, which is both a point of transcendence and a contestation in elaborating a concept of posthuman property – the domain of property and human personhood.

Progressive ideas of property and/as personhood

An effect of liberal individualism is that the concept of property is intrinsically bound up with the concept of personhood. As, for example, Radin argues, personhood includes the possibility to acquire objects that are "external" from oneself (1993: 195–196). However, this is an ambiguous relationship, as our dominant theories of property also prescribe that humans cannot be made external and owned. For this reason, one needs to find a limit between when something is external and nonhuman enough to be part of someone's acquisitions as a person (cf. Davies and Naffine 2001). As shown in the previous section, this, in turn, is part of a continuous process of rendering certain things external and others as internal to the human. This internal sphere also tends to be connected to an idea of privacy or inviolability. Examples of this internal, non-commodifiable sphere tend to focus on the boundaries of the body, which is why cases such as the one concerning John Moore's leukaemia string, embedded in his pancreas, stir up debates about the boundaries of property. Other property objects that have tended to live a life as being "more personal" in law are those things that are considered to be more closely related to the way in which humans live their lives in ways that are not directly transferable to market relations. Examples of such objects identified by Radin include wedding rings and homes (1996).

Another ambiguous construction that is resurfacing under advertising practises based on influencers, as will be further discussed in Chapter eight, is the dissolving boundaries between private and commercial personhood. As Davies and Naffine note, in Canada and parts of the United States, it has been resolved that a person has a proprietary interest in their "persona." According to them, an example of how the persona is connected to ownership is what has been called a "right of publicity," which consequently has primarily been about protecting famous persons (2001: 124). Such a right implies, for example, that a person may license or lease their image, in the sense of granting rights of commercial exploitation to another party (ibid.: 127). Davies and Naffine further point out the role played by the discourse of "self-ownership" in relation to this area (ibid.). Davies and Naffine show how the interests that persons may have in their commercial persona by tends to be legitimized by arguments concerning "the intrinsic separability" between "abstract elements of the self" and the actual person," it is possible to argue that this is not against the ideal of self-possession or non-commodification of the person (ibid.: 127). As has become clear during the more recent discussion of the establishment of increased data protection, such narratives on self-sovereignty and self-ownership over one's personal data are common ways to resort to when boundaries are legally erected against commodification. However, even when law operates with such conceptual narratives, it is still difficult to argue that a strict divide between property and personhood exists, not least from what we are witnessing in terms of the capture of personal data (Käll 2017: 2). Thus, early on, Radin argued that one can solve this dilemma by talking about categorising some categories of property rights as being bound up with personhood and that consequently should be subject to market forces to a lesser extent. And simultaneously, other categories of property rights are not to be perceived of as being bound up with persons and are left to the faith of the market. Consequently, one creates a divide between what Radin has called "fungible property" and "personal property" (1993: 197).

Against this backdrop we can, however, recollect again the story of John Moore.

What has intrigued scholars of critical intellectual property rights is that meanwhile a part of Moore's body, his pancreas, was not to be understood as his personal property – rights resulting from research on this same body part, was. Bhandar (2012) also places this case in further light of how the idea of what is personal and inviolable as being part of the human body and not property is something that consequently varies. As she states:

> [t]he body of the self-possessed legal subject in this instance becomes resolutely non-proprietary in relation to itself, while corporations engaged in the business of the life sciences potentially profit enormously from the bodily parts of the legal subject.
>
> (ibid.: 123–124)

Intellectual property rights in biotechnological inventions particularly highlights how the distinction between property and personhood fluctuates even within the property construct. This conundrum is specifically visible in relation to the human body, which Boyle also found to be ironic in the distinction made between animals and humans in relation to biotechnological research and the conception of transgenic species as discussed. As Boyle notes, one of the important theoretical limitations in patent law is the idea that patents cannot be granted to human beings (1996: 21–24).

So, the limits of personhood against property we now see eroding seems to be oriented around the pressing question of what should count as a human being? For example, many people did not see the oncomouse as human, despite the fact that it grew human genetic material (ibid.: 151; cf. Haraway 1997). But in Boyle's words, one could still consider them as a form of transgenic slaves (1996: 150–152).

A theoretical displacement of the human–nonhuman divide in property law via slavery in the strict sense is furthermore certainly not a new one to property. As discussed, e.g. by Bhandar, "[p]roperty law was a crucial mechanism for the colonial accumulation of capital, and by the late nineteenth century, had unfolded in conjunction with racial schemas that steadfastly held colonized subjects within their grip" (2018: 2). As Harris also notably points out in her famous article on "Whiteness as property" (1993), the function of slavery in the US implies that whiteness rather than, for example, a "human" body functioned as a boundary towards being understood as an object instead of a subject (Harris 1993: 1720). In a similar manner, Esposito shows how such gradation of humanity is manifested through the construction of slavery. He states this in the manner that the purpose of conceiving something as a thing is rather always one of "instrumental domination" based on the idea of the person. The purpose of the thing is to *serve* or at least *belong* to persons (2015: 17). This has also been developed into an idea, or even a *dispositif* of the person where "since a thing is what belongs to a person, then whoever possesses things enjoys the status of personhood and can exert his or her mastery over them" (ibid.). As he also points out, even if slavery is now considered as being abolished, it still appears in other forms of *de facto* slavery (ibid.: 6).

As discussed in Chapter 3, slavery is also again invoked to describe data colonialism and extraction for digital technologies. And, as one can assume, these questions are also increasingly relevant in relation to AI. However, even more so, the understanding of how what is human is organized under property in science, paves the way for engaging with the question of how to differentiate between the ownership of a certain embodiment of a transgenic species and the information over it, just like the case of John Moore's spleen. And ultimately, how does our understanding of what it is to be human also affect the boundaries even for seemingly progressive theories of property for personhood? Here we can then return to the particular note by Haraway where she suggests that the oncomouse as a phenomenon implies a form of inhabitation of life itself in which the temporalities are embedded in both communications enhancement and system redesign. In this move, in which different intellectual property rights and technological system collapse bodies, she advances the idea that life is becoming "enterprised up, where in the dyspeptic version of the technoscientific soap opera, the species becomes the brand name and the figure becomes the price" (1997: 11–12). Intellectual property can in a similar manner affirmatively also be understood to introduce a welcome conceptual rupture in the idea of self-ownership, particularly in the manner that intellectual property in biotechnologies introduces a disaggregated understanding of the human body, and consequently, the human (Bhandar 2012: 113). Such critical intervention furthermore facilitates an understanding of property as something that cannot be derived from the human body, yet is intrinsically connected to how a human body extends itself to the world (Keenan 2015: 67).

An important critique of ideas about how some things are intrinsically more important than others for personhood is that the importance of an object to one's personality may fluctuate (Radin 1993: 195). The opposite then is also true that the sacred wedding rings in Radin's example do not always represent a personal value that no one should be able to confiscate. On an individual level, a wedding ring can quickly become just a metal and stone piece, like any other, once a relationship has ended, or it can be confiscated by a fascist state displacing someone into becoming a migrant with no rights to hold things of financial value. Furthermore, ideas about what counts as a well-developed personality are naturally oversaturated by the society in which they materialize. Staying with more nonhuman aspects of this materialization, we can also contend that a wedding ring, of course, just like a mobile phone, also often depend on mining rare minerals to come into being as a personal property for someone else (cf. Wark 2019: 4). This bears interesting resemblances to the recent discussions of rare minerals for the digital society when it comes to the utilization of diamonds in engagement and wedding rings. A home is also built from both natural resources in construction, as well as in the planning of houses via workers and computer programmes, besides the values that inform the design of the same. What in this way may *feel* like a more personal property and is treated as such by law (for reasons of protecting certain humanist values) is not so personal if we consider the entire assemblage of bodies involved in bringing it into being, as well as affirming it as such.

For this reason, it is important to recall that the divide between persons and things executed through liberal ideology is also tightly bundled with the concept of free individuals (Davies and Naffine 2001: 1). While ideas of personhood work as a form of boundary creator in law, the "heart of liberal property theory" is still to affirm a "personal-continuity thesis" in which property is considered to be something necessary to ground people in a way in which they are in control of their environment. This grounding, in turn, is supposed to foster autonomy and personality (Radin 1993: 197). As Radin puts it: "[p]roperty is a property of persons; and this understanding is necessary for human freedom" (ibid.). Radin therefore suggests that a conceptual boundary for what could be commodified should be drawn with reference to what she refers to as "human flourishing" (ibid.: 198). She also develops this category to include "human beings" homes, work, food, education, health, as markers for where the boundaries of where the human body may be drawn (ibid.). This move can be understood as a call for a "progressive" theory of property, which is not only related to owning things in general but must take democratic ideals into account. Another example of such a theoretical intervention in property is the "Statement of Progressive Property" published in 2009 by the Cornell Law Review where it was argued that the dominating idea of property as "individual control over valued resources" is not suited to handling current property conflicts. Instead, the statement suggests that the concept of property needs to be replaced by a more progressive one, based on social responsibilities and obligations related to a democratic society (Alexander, Penalver, Singer, Underkuffler 2009; cf. Keenan 2015: 61). Further arguments made by these authors have included that besides from the already mentioned ideas on human flourishing and democracy, the concept of property should be attuned with certain notions of social obligation and virtue (Keenan 2015: 61). All these theories naturally imply a step forward in comparison to seeing property as being merely an economic concept and as subjects owning property as free and rational individuals without impacting each other or the environment surrounding them (ibid.). As Keenan points out, however, in making arguments such as those mentioned here, progressive property scholars largely uphold the status quo of property when they focus on merely increasing the responsibilities of property owners. As she puts it, such "[t]his scholarship ends up arguing for property to be more attentive to liberal ideas of equality and civic virtue, but not seeking to question, for example, the relationship between property and belonging, or between property and structural injustice" (ibid.).

In a similar manner, a dematerialized concept of the human, as well as a diminished boundary between persons and things, point towards a posthuman imaginary. In achieving such transgressed vision of boundaries between humans and nonhumans, there is however little to be celebrated if it means that both humans and nonhumans are dematerialized in order to sustain advanced capitalist desires. As posthumanist theory suggests – technologized body control is generally intensified in relation to technologies such as biotechnologies and information technology as a form of the "informatics of domination" (Haraway 1991: 161–162). The disaggregation of the human and the information in the hairy cell leukaemia case is an obvious example of how intellectual property rights fulfil the role of producing what counts as a human's private personal *sphere* or what counts as a human-based *thing*, as well as who is to control it, where the one who benefits from it is the actor who could be assigned a patent right and those the patent right holder is willing to license this patent to. As will be discussed next, the same ambiguous yet proprietary effects are found in the control of personal data in all its shapes and forms. From a posthumanist perspective, this is an important insight since it means that what is being practiced via such examples is not an innocent production of hybrids but a new form of capitalist control which also unfolds in racist, sexist and otherwise speciest ways.

Personal Data as Property: Private, Facial and Sensorial

The increased focus on data, both personal and non-personal, re-activates the conceptual discussions being pursued both in relation to property and personhood in general, and personhood and intellectual property in particular. Similar types of arguments that have been pursued in property theory are also explicitly prevalent in discourses on how data subjects should be allowed to control data about themselves. This tendency was already visible in EU legislation through the EU Data Protection Directive from 1995 (1995/46/EC) in which it was stipulated that while asserting the need for "the free movement of personal data," such flow should still be balanced against "a high level of protection for the privacy of individuals" (preamble p. 3). In brief, this construct is now also being expressed in the EU GDPR, implying the need to consider *data* (object) or more specifically "personal data" as sometimes being entangled with a *natural person* in accordance with Art. 4 of the GDPR. As Viljoen points out, this is problematic as the "attempt to reduce legal interests in information to individualist claims subject to individualist remedies are structurally incapable of representing this fundamental population-level purpose of data production (Viljoen 2021: 3). This advancement of data protection built around a conception of the human, and her right to privacy should, of course, also be read against the general development of the human-machine symbiosis of which many of us take part, when we use mobile phones as parts of our extended selves, unlocking them with finger or face prints. This also extends further into the development of AI. As Joler puts it:

> In our anthropocentric world, the territory of the human body and mind is one of the most explored and exploited extraction stratum. The process of quantification is reaching into the human affective, cognitive and physical worlds. Every form of biodata – including forensic, biometric, sociometric and psychometric – are being captured and logged into databases for AI training, psychological profiling, nano targeting and many other forms of data exploitation.
>
> (2020)

Even when laws set out to protect the interests of a data subject, it is therefore clear that this is with the backdrop of rendering a number of elements into information, that were not previously considered as being either internal or external to a person. Our biometric data is one such obvious example of a form of information that used to have a close connection with what was considered to belong to the human body. However, in general, *all* data collected about how we behave online was previously simply not technologically possible to collect, and not discussed as being part of either personhood or property. Consequently, we are here faced with a situation which is similar to the biotechnology setting where research has made it possible to treat something as information that neither formed part of the human body, nor was considered as property, if one is to lean on modern conceptions of persons and things. The legal resort in EU has however still been to embed equip "natural persons" with the tools to choose to consent to having their data be collected or not. As is uncontroversial to say, consent to data collection is of course not necessarily the strictest boundary a regulator can put in place to hamper processes of commodification of data, as hinted at above (c.f. Radin 2000; 2013). While the collection of data needs to be both proportionate and consensual in accordance with the GDPR, the reframing of the subject-object divide is however also so vast, both based on the practices in which they are carried out as well as in how new legal hybrid concepts such as "data subjects" is formulated.

Furthermore, the examples mentioned here just represent some of the everyday cases of data extraction and use. Something we have learnt from living through a global pandemic in digitally mediated societies is however how quickly even more pervasive forms of digital control could be rolled out. As mentioned in chapter two, early on, YouTube clips on drones patrolling rural China with messages to go home became part of our collective memory. Later, debates on COVID-19 tracking apps became a question for debate and policy decisions. On more seemingly innocent notes, we have encountered restaurants providing face-scanning screens for detecting the temperature of their guests. There were also a number of different initiatives being rolled out on vaccine passports to be downloaded on smartphones for everything from access to travel to public events. In this way, our human bodies and their potential connection to, or invasion by, nonhuman viral bodies are made further subject to a form of digital sensoring, which reaches beyond anything that could be captured by a traditional property-person debate. As a sidenote, the legal concept of privacy needs to be considerably adapted to be able to capture what is at stake in relation to digitalization in general (Lindroos-Hovinheimo 2021). This is something that also has become incredibly apparent under the COVID-19 response, where our health status and its incorporation into digital systems is more of a social good, or even requirement for access to the public sphere.

Another example of the vast implications of data, which reaches beyond the concept of the control a data subject can exercise, is the way that products such as the Amazon Echo device or other voice-enabled forms of AI is enabled. As Crawford and Joler put it, in relation to phenomena such as these:

> [i]t is difficult to place the human user of an AI system into a single category: rather, they deserve to be considered as a hybrid case. Just as the Greek chimera was a mythological animal that was part lion, goat, snake and monster, the Echo user is simultaneously a consumer, a resource, a worker, and a product.
>
> (2018)

Consequently, the anthropomorphic traits that objects such as the Echo, rides upon when they communicate via voices actualizes similar excess in the person–thing divide that the collection of information of the human body does. What seems like a simple property object from the position of consumer (and also laws that sorts it mainly under consumer protection for sale of goods) is in this way excessive to this form. Another way that this excess can be captured is also point at how Amazon Echo on its potential to be personal, and active, as opposed to how property objects were traditionally regarded. As such, the Echo's personal character is not only a commercial trick to make it feel desirable, since such appellation to the user is not anything new. Instead, what separates products that use data collection or other similar ways to personify their services, from previous forms of goods is that it *is* individual human users that are "collected, analysed and retained" (ibid.). Consequently, it is directly trained by the consumers, which also expands the database for human voices and the instructions used to train Echo to become even better (ibid.). This training furthermore occurs in a sphere, which in Western law has been considered both private and personal: the home (and even as private property, if it is inside a home which the private person owns). This in turn complicates both legal concepts such as the right to one's commercial persona and the right to one's personal data discussed here. Even if such concepts show that the fact that something can be personal, or part of personhood, while also being a commercial asset, mediated outside the traditional boundaries of the human body, the actual uses of information recasts further the conceptual divides between property and personhood.

Marilyn Strathern's article on the construction of reparations between two different clans in Papua New Guinea makes similar points in relation to the ambiguity of the person–thing divide. As contextually non-intuitive as this setting might seem in relation to questions of digitalization, Strathern's research shows how a strict emphasis of a person–thing divide may obfuscate societal questions to property. The binary thinking afforded by the person–thing divide in turn risks decentring questions regarding relationships and social belonging. The example she puts forward concerns the death of a clan member, which is understood as being a breach of performing care duties to the clan from which the dead clan member originated (the first clan). As a reparation to the first, an exchange from the second clan in which a woman of marriageable age is sent to the first clan was suggested. When reaching the court, this case was read in the language of how humans cannot be traded, as that counts as slavery (2004). As Strathern points out, this understanding of the person–thing divide is also interesting since it is not necessarily entirely fixed, as has been discussed later in the legal discipline. This is because the question of where a boundary of property is drawn is both fluctuating, rather than that human bodies as a whole cannot be transacted upon as property (ibid.). This is not least visible in the discussions about biotechnologies, as already discussed here.

The cases concerning data collection consequently again show how both the human body, as well as the appearance of domestic machines such as Amazon Echo, disrupts a pure idea of the human body, and its borders. In pursuing a posthumanist way of thinking, one could cherish such practices of a disaggregated understanding of the body. The reason for this is that it disrupts certain modern fantasies of what a normal human body is, as opposed to a nonhuman one. Consequently, disaggregated ways of considering embodiment, whether it be as a talking machine, or as in becoming partly informational, or digitally mediated, paves the way for considering the boundaries of "the human" as being less rigid or "pure." Thus, just like Bhandar, one may argue that these kinds of practices show just how instable the materiality of "the human" is (2012: 113). This in turn enables theorization not only about the composition of property beyond seemingly fixed subject-object boundaries, but about the role of commodification in both human and nonhuman lives. As such, this realization also paves the way for a deeper understanding of the fact that each human does not own every element of their body, not even in a limited sense such as their flesh, but certainly not in a broader high-tech cyborg sense including their data. In order to articulate a theory of property that brings these insights into further posthumanist light then involves asking if, and how, this disaggregated idea of property's subjects and objects, can be brought in line with the ethical endeavours of posthumanist theory.

Embodying Property beyond Humanist Materiality

Living under advanced capitalism implies that we live at a stage where the copy rather than the original has become the norm (Haraway 1991: 165, 150). As depicted by Haraway, every day our digital technologies are becoming more and more frighteningly alive. These realizations can be understood to rupture the conceptual ideas surrounding the property object. Such development becomes visible in the manner that advanced capitalism runs on resources described as "information" in which almost anything seems to be possible to turn into property as has been described here. This in turn changes not only the composition of the property object, but also the possibility to order, or govern, via property objects. The reason why this is so is because the mode that governance via information gives rise to, changes not only the object, but also what kind of control that can be exercised over a subject. This insight is important to formulating an idea of post-human property as something which motivates an understanding of property that goes beyond the assumption of both the individual as it has become disaggregated, or a dividual (Deleuze 1992), and beyond information as a thing. The reason for this is that posthuman property, as it is developed here, should be understood to incorporate both the commodification of disassembled bodies of persons and things, as well the emergence of a new form of control or logics of domination as described in Chapters 1 and 2.

From a posthumanist perspective, emphasis on the control enacted via property under information-centred logics of ordering, is welcome in the sense that it shifts the idea of property as something an individual can enjoy as a "being proper." This perspective, which advocates property as a means to order social and political spheres, fulfils ideals about patriarchal, feudal and capitalist control over other, non-proper subjects (Davies 2008: 12–13). The consequence of this is an opening up of property where both subjects and objects can be conceived of as "dividuals are always open to interaction, always ready to be detached from and attached to other dividuals" (Deseriis 2018). However, a first step to also moving towards such an idea in relation to proprietary control is to gather the conceptual lines that manage to outline property as a control form that goes both via and beyond its humanist ideals. Strathern, for example, also adds that the way out of the property discourse is not in advancing questions about the boundary of "the human" but rather the ideas of (a lack of) community that our late Western ideas of personhood are founded upon. As she shows in relation to the case discussed above, it can be easily judged via human rights discourse that humans cannot be objects for transactions and that the woman in the case should not be treated as an object for the clans to trade upon. However, this kind of reasoning also unsettles a deeper meaning of kinship and belonging which, in this case, is built around the generation of new blood in the separate clans over time. By refusing a transaction, a person like the person in this case, may win her subjectivity in a Western sense but lose her subjectivity and protection based on her membership of the indigenous community in question. And further, a different idea of community, not built upon a dominating idea of property, has been lost (Strathern 2004).

However, the concept of the body as a posthuman theoretical tool also has the capacity to move beyond the binaries identified here towards a less humanist understanding of property altogether. As prominently elaborated by Keenan, property can be thought to order bodies around part-whole belongings via affective characteristics as the force that *holds up bodies as space* (2015: 71–72). As we can recall from the introduction chapter, property in this sense can be conceived of as producing power by holding up certain bodies as space and, as such, reshuffles property theory to make property "less about the subject and more about the space in and through which the subject is constituted" (ibid.: 74). That property then becomes about creating part-whole connections (Cooper 2007; Keenan 2015) can be contrasted with the more general distinction of the individual versus the mass or as expressed in property law as persons versus property objects or private objects versus objects held in common. For example, in returning to the case of the status of the wedding ring in property theory, via a perception of property as productive of, and sustained by orders of, belonging we can also visualize how heterosexuality (and not only its traditional tokens such as wedding rings) can be understood as property as such as "relations of belonging are held up when wider social processes, structures and networks give them force" (Keenan 2015: 72). This includes "legal" institutions such as marriage but also social validation, which includes, as Keenan puts it: "accepting, supporting and celebrating couples who hold hands or kiss in public, through positive media representation, through the availability of appropriate sex education and safe sex materials, etc." (Keenan 2015: 73). Such insight can also be utilized to shift the discussion about whether data should be personal or proprietary to the benefit of seeing that commercial and societal interests in data are often not really about one individual, but about the aggregate of data produced and deduced from several individuals or their ties.

To exemplify the importance of which relations are being held up as property we can also recall what is now an ancient meme in which a person, David Thorne, suggests paying his overdue utility bills with a drawing of a spider sent to another person via e-mail. The very simple picture, which shows a seven-legged spider, was obviously rejected by the recipient, Jane Giles. Their polite mail exchanges, including the request by Thorne to have his spider drawing returned, if it was not going to be accepted as payment, became an immediate internet success and led to the crash of servers. The obvious pun in this story is how not everything can be made into something with a value to be appreciated on the market. Furthermore, it plays with the distinction and dissolution of the original and the copy in the sense that Thorne is asking to have the spider drawing to be returned. (Paying Bills with Spider Drawings 2008, as retold on the website: Know Your Meme 2009). As funny as this is, it also shows something serious in the question of the commodification of all things: the fact that it is never the commodity itself that implies something of value, but the way it is appreciated in the market or how it holds up relations in other ways. This can also provide an important lesson in how we now approach data-driven capitalism and "reclaiming" assets from the same. For example, we can contend that the right I have to receive the data collected about me, via the General Data Protection Regulation in EU, Article 15, is not in any sense a way for me to get my data "sent back" to me. The spider, so to speak, is at work somewhere else. This problematic is also considerably visible not least in how data is utilized in marketing, as will be discussed in Chapter 7 and Chapter 8, as it is the aggregate of information that is sold and utilized to feed advertisements back to the potential consumer that matters. Thus, a conceptualization of property boundaries cannot be expressed via restricting or reclaiming of knowledge, information, data, or possibly even in restricting data collection. Another way of expressing this is that it is the relationship between bodies that matters to the production of advanced capital, not the particular individuals. In order to understand how property control of information works here to produce part-whole belonging, as suggested by Crawford and Joler, we have to "move beyond a simple analysis of the relationship between an individual human, their data, and any single technology company in order to contend with the truly planetary scale of extraction" (2018). For this reason, the boundaries between property and "non- property" need to be rethought in a manner that has the capacity to highlight what is at stake in the articulation of property. It is also argued that by utilising the concept of the body, it is possible to show how the assumption of products of the mind as "disembodied" may be questioned. The next step to move further in such analysis is consequently to equip posthuman property with an idea of *entanglement*.

Part Three

Entanglement

The current stage of advanced capitalism runs on convergences, as made visible by recent innovations such as the Internet of Things, smart cities and robotics The plasticity of digital media, in particular, almost seems without limit as to what it can be attached to and transform. This is evident not least in the cultural expressions that tell stories about androids (Dick 1996 [1968]), avatars (Cameron 2009) and distributed intelligence (Jonze 2013). The so-called "4th revolution" (Floridi 2014) comes with a significant focus on various digital phenomena, such as artificial intelligence and smart objects, implying where the modes of governing discussed in Chapter 2, such as algorithmic decision-making, are being increasingly implemented into physical objects. The concept of entanglement in posthumanist theory is used here as a tool to highlight how the assumed divides between bodies may be questioned in relation to current developments in digital technology. What is special about these new entanglements is that they mix materialities that have been conceived of as separate, such as digital media with non-digital media, but also in how they transcend mind-body dualisms through the conception of other than humans as "smart" or having "intelligence." As Haraway contends, if there ever existed a boundary between different bodies, it was already transcended when information capitalism started to gain tract, in the late 20th century (1991: 150).

Philosophically, the mixing of matter previously considered to be separate also activates a need to further transcend dualist thinking, so customary in Western philosophy (e.g. Grosz 2017: 15–16) in order to capture the continuum of materialities that is now emerging. As Braidotti describes this philosophical understanding: "it conventionally fell into a discursive pattern of dualistic oppositions that defined the human mostly by what it is *not*. Thus, with Descartes: *not* an animal, *not* extended and inert matter, *not* a pre-programmed machine" (Braidotti 2019: 6–7). Entanglements of matter have therefore been actively used to produce alternative imaginaries of the posthuman condition. The technical, organic, political, economic, dream-like and textual aspects that begun to converge in late-twentieth century technoscience have been informative in the more than hybrid figures conceptualised, for example, by Haraway. As an example, she refers to the end-of-the-millennium seed, chip,

DOI: 10.4324/9781003139096-1c

gene, cyborg figures in the form of "the offspring of implosions of subjects and objects and of the natural and artificial" (Haraway 1991: 152).

The concept of entanglement in posthuman theory also functions as a means of connecting bodies with space, or how bodies in relation, constitute space. This convergence between posthuman bodies with each other and space significantly comes to us via some of the key themes of theorisation: the Anthropocene (e.g. Braidotti 2013) and its variations, Capitolocene (Moore 2017), Anthrobscene (Parikka 2014), Chthulucene (Haraway 2016), and many important variations of such descriptions of space (Yusoff 2019). To remind ourselves about the introduction chapter, one challenge in posthumanist philosophy, activated through such concepts, is to see how humans are not separate from each other or their environment. This non-separability is becoming visible not least now, when nature pushes back, moving the human race increasingly closer to extinction each day (Haraway 2016). The deeper relationality that is called for by posthumanist scholarship is of a theoretical kind; the Deleuzian-Spinozist way of thinking understands bodies as always positioning themselves via the extension or withdrawal from other bodies but are never only one (Deleuze Philippopoulos-Mihalopoulos 2014: 11 and passim). As such, the posthumanist perspective functions as a powerful tool to study how very particular bodies come to be entangled and form new materialities with spatial implications at surface, geological and atmospheric levels. When we study entanglements here, it is through a movement from subject to object to space via the digitalisation processes that actualise a convergence of all these phenomena.

Chapter 5

Posthuman Ecologies of Control
Platforms, Smart Cities and Smart Homes

The posthuman condition runs on convergences between materialities conceived of as separate (Braidotti 2019: 6–13). Our everyday lives have become so embedded in these convergences that we almost forget that there used to be a life without smartphones. However, as Greenfield reminds us, it was only about a decade ago that smartphones came to integrate and replace common items usually carried around in pockets and wallets, such as pictures of beloved ones or money (2017: 9–10). This movement towards smart lives, which became so prominent via smartphones and has now become well established via the Internet of Things (IoT), smart homes and smart cities, is of particular interest in understanding how property control unfolds, as they involve an entire eco-system of new actors compared to older media (cf. ibid.: 13). Whereas the elements surrounding our everyday lives were previously not exactly dumb, they were fixated in a more profound way as goods, buildings, streets and vehicles, and the actors providing them, at best, had an interest in their less static intangible values or continuous provisions of sustenance services. Now, our lively objects not only come in different layers as described in Chapter 3, but as integrated in eco-systems of control characteristic of platform capitalism (Srnicek 2017; Sadowski 2020).

This chapter also elaborates further how connections and boundaries between human and digital bodies increasingly converge under advanced capitalism. The focus here moves from information as an object towards its spatial characteristics through some of the most prominent emerging phenomena: platforms, smart cities and smart homes. As such, it is a precursor to the final chapters on AI. To achieve an understanding of what this stage of convergence, or entanglement, implies in terms of posthuman property control, the focus here is how the control of nonhuman bodies is produced via the interfaces or vectors (Wark 2004: note 315–316, Wark 2019: 2) between them, rather than the production of each of them as separate objects/commodities. As hinted at already in the description of advanced capitalism in the introduction, this type of interface control has to this stage of development, often been explored as a form of platform-based organization (Gawer 2011) and platform capitalism (Srnicek 2017).

DOI: 10.4324/9781003139096-5

Platform capitalism can be understood to include both an idea of the logics of capitalism in the current stage of development, as well as something that is narrower: as an innovation model, a format for knowledge and technology standardization or as platform-based business models. What is prominent for all these forms of arranging connections between different matter is that they operate under the idea of network logics, attaching more and more bodies together. As Bratton notes, "[p]latforms centralize and decentralize at once, drawing many actors into a common infrastructure" (2015: 46). As expressed by Sadowski, it is also common that entrepreneurs discuss their ventures in terms of creating entire "ecosystems," by which they mean: interconnected companies, platforms, apps, and devices. Hence, each device or platform inside this system is just understood as a minor, or insignificant, addition, to an environment. But: "as a whole, the swarm takes over, disrupts the equilibrium, and transforms the environment" (Sadowski 2020: 52). For this reason, this chapter does not aim to identify a single network of property control once and for all, but rather a type of ordering with certain characteristics that leverage on (the right) scale to produce capital.

In particular, this chapter also focuses on the concept of smartness to describe a particular stage of platform-based business organization, as a language for the utopian transformation of redesigning and optimising both objects and spaces for certain types of lives. Strictly related to the discussions of managing the openness of knowledge resources as discussed in the previous chapter, is the discourse on understanding how to treat knowledge as different elements, which can be constructed as larger *platforms*. For example, as Chesbrough has argued, the most developed form of co-creation between actors in an open innovation focused business model is the platform-based business model (2011). As will be unfolded here, this reshaping of digitalization operates around the logics of platforms and the materializations of digital objects and forms of control in manners similar to what has already been discussed but becomes even more sticky and prone to converge different practices, objects and spaces.

Platform-Based Logics as a Basis for Smartification

Platform-based business logics is at the core of the connection between different materialities such as information (data, communication, intellectual property rights), spaces, things and humans. What is characteristic of platforms compared to other types of markets or business models is that they follow a logic of modularity (Gawer 2011). In the simplest understanding of platforms, they can be understood as systems of Lego bricks. As is well known, Lego is different from many other toys in that it comprises bricks that (in their most basic form) can be combined in many different ways to build as expansive worlds as the otherwise spatial parameters afford. It is also characteristic for such bricks, just like platforms, that their value is expanded by adding more (or rather, the right) bricks to the system. Another simple form of platform-based logics can be found in technology platforms in which technologies are jointly pooled to sustain an industry standard. An example of this is the 3G standard for telecom, in which a number of patented technologies were shared and licensed under so- called FRAND (Fair, Reasonable and Non-Discriminatory) terms (e.g. Treacy and Lawrence 2008). Today, however, the platform as a concept and form of technology management has come to expand in virtually innumerable ways. If there was an old saying (from the late 2000s) that everything can be an app, that saying could today be translated into everything can be a platform.

In a by now famous conceptualization of platform capitalism, Srnicek argues that at the most general level platforms are digital infrastructures in which two or more groups interact. In this way, platforms are conceived as intermediaries, bringing together different users such as customers, advertisers, service provi-ders, producers, suppliers and physical objects (2017: 43). Srnicek also divides these platforms into advertising platforms, cloud platforms, industrial platforms and lean platforms (ibid.: 50–87). The identification of platforms as digital infrastructures has good purchase in relation to how to critically understand that data extraction is something that permeates digital platforms, which is also key to Srnicek's critical account. However, it also places an unnecessary binary between the digital and the non-digital elements involved in platformization, including understanding that nonhuman and human matter very much make up the infrastructure in these models, just like other business models. It also appears to have a comparatively narrower perception in relation to technology platforms in general, as it is not at all necessary to have a digital infrastructure to build a position as an intermediating actor over the design of scalable building blocks, as the Lego platform shows. The focus on data as an asset that creates and scales platforms is also slightly too narrow in considering how platform power is built on both intellectual property rights, contracts and many other forms of less tan-gible proprietary power (the design of the platform, its brand, etc.) as will be discussed further below.

Besides the scalability that comes from seeing a platform as an infrastructure that has the capacity of modularity, there is a deep connection between plat-form-based business models with a focus on "services" rather than the sale of goods (Chesbrough 2011: 107, Sadowski 2020: 62). As Sadowski puts it: "Uber offers 'transportation-as-a-service.' WeWork offers 'space-as-a-service.' Amazon Mechanical Turk offers 'humans-as-service'" (2020: 61). By not focusing solely on production or the sale of physical things, the potential for scaling is ridding businesses of matter. This is not least visible in the disposing of labour into an always-ready-to-pick-up-an-hour-of-work-here-and-there workforce. Even in cases with platforms such as Amazon, in which the original business model was to deliver something as physical as goods, work is increas-ingly made expendable via automation (cf. Srnicek 2017: 75–87). This is because the business model is to scale the network, and technologies developed for such a purpose (including technologies co-developed via Amazon Turk) make this type of business model technologically possible. Here, of course, digital technologies, play a vital function in how they can be used to connect bodies of different kinds, create databases, make possible design barriers between different platforms, etc.

To summarise the platform concept, it is generally utilized to argue that the platform functions specifically as a construction for designing environments largely from technological elements in order to connect and create increased network effects between different organizations, technological- and human bodies. This involves an understanding of information as different technological pieces and interfaces that can build on each other, thereby functioning as a *de facto* business practice connected to advanced capitalism. However, around 10–15 years from when platform-based business models started to become the topic of innovation theory in the manner described, they have evolved into the massive conglomerates that we see today. As Cohen writes, platforms can now be understood as creating territories defined by using protocols, data flows and algorithms to demarcate spaces and control their borders (2019: 235). Such expansion of the platform model as a vector of creating and controlling the connection between bodies and spaces has become particularly prevalent in the move towards smart cities and homes.

The City as a Platform and the Platformed Home: Smart Cities and Smart Homes

What is prominent about the latest forms of platforms is that they are moving away from specialising in infrastructure or communication, search or similar, towards being integrated in entire ecosystems of smart homes and – smart cities. The development that started with technological objects such as mobile phones has now spread to such an extent that there are advanced pilot projects that aim to make even entire cities smart. The idea of the smart city is said to have emerged from IBM and Cisco. As described by Sadowski and Bendor in 2008, an IBM top executive outlined the company's vision for a "Smarter Planet" in a speech to the Council on Foreign Relations (2019). The programme included several interrelated projects concerning water, energy and electronics. In 2009, Cisco similarly announced that it was working towards a "holistic blueprint for Intelligent Urbanisation," which later became known as "Smart+Connected Communities," connecting transportation, security and government administration (Sadowski and Bendor 2019). A smart city project that is increasingly gaining attention is the project being pursued by Alphabet (previously Google) through its Sidewalk Labs in which Alphabet as a market actor designed an entire city district in Toronto offering a corporate technology version of urban planning. This project envisioned an urban context where sustainability is foregrounded as what has been called out as a technochauvinist dream (Rogan 2019: 9). Thoroughly communicated in vision documents, a city plan was developed to cater to popular buzzwords such as community and sustainability, supported by data collection from its citizens and various autonomous enterprises (ibid.: e.g.

22). Furthermore, the visionary document of the Sidewalk Toronto plan directly likens both itself and other cities with technology platforms in the statement that: "The world's great cities are all hubs of growth and innovation because they leveraged platforms put in place by visionary leaders" (ibid.: 42 citing official Sidewalk document).

An often-cited example besides Alphabet/Google Sidewalk in Toronto is the case of Songdo in South Korea. As Gunel and Halpern write, even though Songdo has not achieved profitability, the embodiment of smartness still embodies "the idea of the narrative of the smart city as linking finance, high tech research, green infrastructure, and the perfectly customised consumer lifestyle" (2017: 11). Furthermore it "has already propagated through the financial news and the services of firms such as SAP, Siemens, Cisco, IBM, Morgan Stanley, and Arup and to many different locations from Rio's Operation's Centres to the Gherkin in London" (ibid.). As they further argue, since efficiency in terms of the environment is difficult to accurately assess, "[t]his is a future no longer described, but simply acted upon with zeal and speculative optimism" (ibid.). Greenfield makes a similar note in relation to the development of Songdo's remarkably limited vision in terms of design. As he puts it: "Even though it started from zero, and could have taken whatever shape its developers felt most appropriate Songdo's master plan replicates the formal order of a midsize American city of the mid-twentieth century" (2013: 663, also cited in Rogan 2019: 45).

As these ideas are becoming more pronounced and realized in practice, smart cities are emerging not only as a societal phenomenon but also as a core focus of research. Several international research projects have begun to explore the opportunities and challenges presented by smart cities, studying everything from waste management to the smart sharing of resources such as bicycles, office spaces and cars. In general, the focus on the "sustainable design" of a city is an often-recurring trope in these plans. In these visualizations, a prominent feature, as described by Mattern, is that the city as a space is understood in a fairly shallow way. This is despite the fact that when looking at urban communication networks, one can never focus on one specific media, but always media networks plugged into and dependent on other infrastructural networks as "our telecommunications networks need electricity; the Internet needs plenty of chilled water to cool the servers and roads to deploy its fiber-optic cable layers and service technicians, and all depend on some degree on bio-power" (Mattern 2015: xi–xii). As Mattern puts it: "[t]his 'urban enlightenment' includes open-data initiatives and urban informatics projects to aid in wayfinding, traffic flow, service and discovery, even the location of hazardous cracks in the sidewalk" (ibid.: x).

A precursor to this move is the understanding of the continuum between digital objects and spaces. Kitchin and Dodge (2011) suggest the concept of code/space for spaces that are intrinsically co-dependent of software to perform their role as spaces. As they argue, coded spaces may be perceived as spaces in which software makes a difference to space, for example, if the check-in area at an airport does not function, people cannot check in and the airport therefore prevents travel. If the code in the cashier function stops working at the checkout a supermarket, the supermarket also loses its sales function and may therefore be perceived as a warehouse and not a store (ibid.: 18). In their understanding, coded spaces can consequently be perceived of as such in particular when software creates a difference in the performance of the space, in case the code is there/not there. In code/space on the other hand, the relationship between the message and the code is so entangled that they cannot be separated. The relationship between them is so interdependent that if the code is not produced, space is not perceived as the desired perception of that space. The code is also understood as being part of a network of other materialities and consequently lacks power in itself. (Kitchin and Dodge 2011: 18). In a similar manner, Bratton describes the city layer of "The Stack" to be "filled with interfaces shifting between acceleration and enclosure, of both physical objects coursing through congested logistical routes and also data packets shuttled or throttled through glass wire and ambient electromagnetic fields" (2015: 150). As he further suggests, devices which includes apps at hand (or apps-as-hand) points our ways in food-finding, risk tabulation, and help us manage our personal finances, etc. (ibid.).

The engineering gaze on cities is something that increasingly also hits the "private" space of the home. This implies the introduction of digitized technologies into homes in which everything from home appliances to toys are interwoven with technologies that make them "smart" and pave the way for an external response. According to a recent report from ABI Research, almost 300 million smart homes will be installed globally by 2022. Thus, smart home devices and services will play an increasingly important role in smart city programmes (Wray 2018). In this way, network-connected and IoT devices are ideated to create a "nervous system" inside what has traditionally been considered one of the most private of spheres: the home (Duchich 2017–2018: 279). There are several examples of how smart homes are explicitly being connected to smart cities by technologies related to different types of utilities, such as homeowner energy consumption. Other now popular examples include smart home security cameras that can be embedded in both neighbourhoods and individual homes.

The phenomena that integrate the smart home with the city also include services that render the home into a market space. This may be exemplified by the increasing number of services for the delivery of goods directly to the home. Furthermore, in this way, objects generally found in homes, such as refrigerators and toys, are becoming marketing channels. Whereas citizens in non-digitized societies generally visit physical shops to supply the household with goods, in a smart city this is increasingly substituted by online ordering and different types of delivery services (including by drones) that render the home into a point of delivery, and a type of market, as the goods may be ordered online from a smart home device. The marketization of the home is also visible in the way that advertising, in turn, reaches citizens in their homes, through smart devices, and through algorithmically optimized messages. (Greenfield 2018) Companies such as Amazon are a great example of how this type of integration occurs as an integration both in the home (as for example via the Amazon Echo discussed in the previous chapter) and in relation to the delivery of goods to the home (e.g. Sadowski 2020: 25–29). This also brings us further into the layers with which the platform as a business model and infrastructure is now being mapped to cover the physical objects from which it used to distinguish itself.

The Logistics of Smartness

Much of the hype around smartness concerns elements of the city and home that consumers usually do not think much about. And as discussed in Chapter two, some of the technologies that make automation possible are not even visible to the human eye, such as lights unreadable to the human eye, perforating the city space (cf. Parikka 2021, Steyerl 2021). Besides questions of data management and communication between smart objects/environments, logistics is a fundamental aspect of the smartification of society. This can be most prominently exemplified by the increased awareness of how Amazon controls its supply chains/networks, but also other actors such as Walmart and sea ports. As Wark puts it in relation to Walmart, while it

> became famous for both selling very cheap consumer products and also for its ruthless exploitation of its workers and suppliers. On closer examination it is more of a logistics company, which succeeded also through using information to organise the flows of goods and labour through its distribution system. Walmart's infrastructure has a hub and spoke form, with box stores clustered around distribution centers. What is less well-known is that it has almost as many data centers as physical distribution centers.
>
> (2019: 8).

Another of these less visible technologies that has previously been mentioned as a core to facilitate platforms for smart objects, is blockchain. Tapscott and Tapscott, for example, suggest that blockchain can be understood as a ledger of things that could realize the long-envisioned world of technologists and science fiction writers alike in which "a seamless global network of Internet-connected sensors could capture every event, action, and change on earth" (2016: 152). Also, this folds into a general move of the commodification of information as assets – and property – through digitalization. As Tapscott and Tapscott argue, through blockchain technology, physical assets can become digital assets. "All documentation relating to a particular 'thing' can be digitised and continued in blockchain including patents, ownership, warranties, inspection certification, provenance, insurance, replacement dates, approvals, etc." (ibid.: 159).

An example of the digitalization of physical objects via blockchain is the type of service that is offered via Chronicled Open Source, which describes itself as a platform offering: "a toolkit that allows any brand, physical IP creator, product authenticator/customizer, or individual to assign a secure digital identity to a physical object by embedding an encrypted microchip and linking it to a blockchain record" (Chronicled website 2017). Chronicled Open Source further describes how this kind of use could be enabled by drones that are connected to parcels in order to deliver them seamlessly. They further present this product (service, platform) as a solution to the problem that parcel delivery is too inefficient as it is depends on human presence in order to run smoothly. Instead of relying on humans to be physically present to sign off the delivery etc., a drone could be utilized. Or, as Chronicled describes it: "encrypted microchips are used to give automated delivery drones a unique identity on the blockchain which IoT applications can use to allow or restrict drone access to locations such as a home or warehouse" (ibid.) It further describes that by having a technology verify a drone containing encrypted information fly to a connecting node, such as a door or a window with a chip, the chip in that node can verify the signature of the drone. It may then check its identity on the specific blockchain, confirm the access of the drone and consequently open the door/window (ibid.)

As discussed in Chapter two, the rationale behind encryption technologies is to enact openings and closures between different elements through a system of automated passwords. For this reason, it is not surprising that blockchain is now increasingly being theorized as a technology that could be utilized to produce locked connections between matter as diverse as persons and persons, persons and things, as well as things and things. This development folds into the transformation of physical things to *smart* or *intelligent* things. As the magazine *Forbes* writes, a combination of the development of the Internet of Things (IoT) and blockchain technology makes much sense in terms of improving the encryption needed in the IoT. This because a substantial part of the data that may be generated through IoT applications, such as smart home devices, is of a personal nature. Such data needs to be shared with other machines and services in order to be useful as a smart application. Blockchain creates a way to make possible such sharing more secure as it produces a barrier which a possible unauthorized actor would need to bypass (Marr 2018).

Blockchain also folds into sorting out logistics, or making logistics smart, especially in areas in which traditional logistics are more difficult to figure out. A recent example of this was made by Wang and her research into how Chinese rural economies are utilising blockchain to communicate trust to consumers in something so seemingly simple as the sale of chickens (Wang 2020). In this example, the chickens are tagged with an ankle strap that collects data about everything from how they move to what they eat, more or less like a FitBit, but for chickens. This data is then streamed into a system, which consumers can scan as they receive the (dead and consumption-ready) chicken, to verify its living conditions and its unbroken chain of delivery (ibid.: 35–65). As is discussed in the book, technologies of encryption and automation have been depicted as being important tools for creating food security in China, where the distances between food production and consumption are becoming increasingly vast and the population that needs feeding is similarly expanding. At the same time there is money to be made from supplying high-end products to a growing economically affluent group of citizens and expatriates, for example, in Shanghai and Beijing. Thus, there is a fear that the poorer food producers would try to sell produce more expensively by claiming they are of a higher quality than they actually are. The solution to this conundrum is to call for technology to build trust and minimize the risks of food production scams (ibid.: 35–65). What this also implies is that better logistics not only make possible smart cities and homes, but also smart villages, or what can be called a form of platform ruralism (Gil-Fournier and Parikka 2020).

Another way that a city platform emerges is via the so-called Digital Belt and Road Program as part of the Chinese Belt Road Initiative. The Chinese Belt Road initiative, in mirroring the historical concept of the Silk Road, was launched by the Chinese government in 2013, to promote further economic cooperation. It was also seen as a way of offering opportunities to develop sustainable development logistics. In order to achieve such a development, it was noted that accurate data needed to be collected, whereupon various kinds of technologies were developed to collect such data (e.g. Huadong et al. 2018). In this way, the project in itself can be understood as a form of an emerging platform for infrastructure.

From Smart Spaces to Posthuman Cartographies

The smart city, just like the knowledge-economy in general, is often heralded as being a solution to environmental crisis, or crisis in general (Rogan 2019). This means that, in abstract, it could also be a solution to several of the challenges that are outlined as the cause and effects of the Anthropocene. Critical accounts of smart cities and smart homes have however become increasingly prevalent in recent years. This is not least visible in the resistance against the Google Sidewalk project in Toronto, which was ultimately cancelled. What unifies many of the optimistic accounts of smart spaces, however, is that they tend to operate with a fixed idea of space, as something that can be predicted, engineered and optimized. As such, this understanding follows and expands the idea about an ideal human, and ideal human life, in harmonic entanglement with nature. The consequence of such ideals at worst are that they risk creating a totalitarian idea of society. Furthermore, the engineering of society can increasingly come to be handed over to the market in order to optimize for such a totalitarian understanding. Today, unfortunately, there are indications of the latter (see e.g. also Ducato 2020). Also, as described by Gunel and Halpern, smartness as a dominant method for engaging with possible urban collapse has become a catch phrase for an emerging techno-logical rationality "whose major goal is management of an uncertain future through a constant deferral of future results or evaluation through a continuous mode of self-referential data collection without endpoint" (2017: 11).

The appearance of a dissolving line between persons and the environment, in the way that the visionary documents such as in the Sidewalk project sets out, is furthermore reminiscent of how convergences between bodies are considered in the posthumanist field. Visser has argued that the establishment of "creative, smart, eco-cities" in itself is a posthuman and even a posthumanist vision (Visser 2018). In advancing such understanding, he builds on the idea from Hayles that a posthuman perspective privileges patterns of information over material instantiations, considers consciousness to be an epiphenomenon rather than a necessity for life, perceives of the human body as simply the first prosthesis we learn to manipulate, or replaces the body with other prostheses, and sees the human as seamlessly articulated with computer intelligences in which no essential difference is made between bodily existence and computer simulation (Visser 2018: 208). Based on this interpretation, he argues that top-down smart city initiatives in China, ignores "the human" as a disorganized creative force that cannot be captured under an information-centred modelling of the city (Visser 2018: 222–223).

When understanding posthumanism in this way, it is obvious that the entanglements between humans and space follow a form of logic in which we could again refer to an informatics of domination (Haraway 1991: 161–162) or to the process of dematerialization Hayles (1999). Smart cities, smart homes and the automation of logics all effectuate very particular entanglements between bodies and/as space, including top-down ideas of what it means to create an eco-city. As this chapter however points at, there are a number of risks in following such techno-optimist accounts of smartification of cities as well as other interrelated objects, from a posthumanist perspective.

For example, critical posthumanist theory has intervened in perspectives regarding space as fixed, in many ways prominently including the work of Braidotti (2002; 2011; 2013; 2019), as well as in recent work on law and space from a posthumanist perspective (Philippopoulos-Mihalopoulos 2014). What unifies all these perspectives is that they criticize a fixed concept of space as it theoretically can be understood as a form of ocularcentrism, a standpoint of early modernity in which an actor may provide a detached view of the world with a "God eye." As highlighted by Warf, such a perspective "presumes that each person is an undivided, autonomous, rational subject with clear boundaries between 'inside' and 'outside,' i.e. between self and other, body and mind. In geographic terms, ocularcentrism equates perspective with the abstract subject's mapping of space" (2008: 60). In a similar manner, spatial theory and spatio-legal theory have shown how fixed ideas of space obscure power. An example of insights from spatio-legal theory is the construction of spaces such as city parks and creates different impressions depending on who/what is experiencing the space. This, in turn, folds back to how subjectivity is shaped via certain normative and otherwise material orders.

In Haraway's words, an understanding of both space and vision, needs to be situated as it otherwise risks being nowhere while claiming to be everywhere at the same time, as a form of "god-trick" (1991: 191). In her view, the alternative to both these perspectives is in "partial, locatable, critical knowledges sustaining the possibility of webs of connections called solidarity in politics and shared conversations in epistemology" (ibid.: 198). As she points out: the world can neither speak for itself nor disappear in favour of a master decoder and "the codes of the world are not still, waiting only to be read" (ibid.) and "the world is not raw material for humanization" (ibid.: 192–193). Posthumanist perceptions of smart spaces necessarily need to enact a situated perception of the spaces in which digital technologies have now become embedded. To move in such a direction, it is worthwhile recalling the cartographic methods suggested by Braidotti: "[a] cartography is a theoretically based and politically informed reading of the present. Cartographies aim at epistemic and ethical accountability by unveiling the power locations which structure our subject-position" (2013: 164). For this reason, questions of sustainability promised by the smart city, need to be read against, for example, the property control embedded in them, as will be discussed in the following chapter.

A posthumanist cartographic approach could also entail creating a deeper map of the media city (Mattern 2015). In this type of mapping, we could ask ourselves which senses or sensations are being left out of the descriptions of digitized realities that we now encounter, or which life-worlds are going to vanish when replaced by something "smarter." Examples of maps for different or lost cities could show how cities (as well as other spaces) are always embedded in multiple media layers, not least sound, which tends to have been lost in time due to a lack of record(ing)s (ibid.: 21–26). This type of sensorial intelligence connected to smart cities will also be further discussed in Chapter 7.

Chapter 6

Digitized Space as Property

This chapter continues the focus on how property unfolds as spatial control in a way that is conceptually controversial compared to previous boundaries of property. The fact that property stands in direct relationality to space, as well as having the capacity to capture space as property, is both an uncontroversial and imperialist truth. After all, this is where much modern property theory starts, from an idea that persons can enclose lands, and even find *terra nullius* and turn it into property, in spite of other persons and species already living there. As pointed out by Davies: "[p]rivate property was (and is) constructed upon a series of assumptions, including that the socio-political human subject is existentially separate from the physical environment" (2020: 1105) This facilitates a view of space as something that can, and even *should*, be appropriated as private property. In relation to this, we shall recall that the fact that private property over land should at all be possible to claim as such, builds upon many layers of philosophical rationalizations. One of the more recently prominent threads is the idea of the Tragedy of the Commons as described by Garett Hardin. As discussed, this notion builds upon an understanding that if resources are held in common, they will be prone to overuse. As such, this fundamentally aligns with a basic Hobbesian understanding of individual humans as maximising their own resources and needs, whereby they will try to claim as much as they can from a common resource. For this reason, Hardin finds it feasible to recommend that persons, or rather the *homo economicus*, should own private property in lands so that they have an incentive to only exploit it to the degree it is sustainable (Hardin 1968).

This belief in individuals as best equipped to keep land as private property, instead of as a common resource is alive and kicking today. Following the identification of the Anthropocene this assumption immediately seems remarkable from a posthumanist perspective. First, because it is becoming clear that both humans and the environment are more conflated than modernist thought makes clear. And second, because property-controlled resource extraction currently fuels a stage where "nature pushes back" (c.f. Morton 2013; Haraway 2016). Consequently, there is reason to separate both the conceptual distinction between humans and their environments, and the material consequences of exploiting spaces via private

DOI: 10.4324/9781003139096-6

property. However, the concept of private property as a means of governing space still dominates in the Western world and wherever its order settles.

The spatial qualities of the proprietary control mediated via digital matter has a long history, not least in Lessig's understanding of code as law, as discussed in Chapter 2. Prominent in relation to digitalization is that the view of the possibility of owning a certain space is also translated into the concept of platforms, or web*sites*. A more recent discourse further paves the way for considering platform owners as digital landlords, consequently alluding to an idea that digital space is a space held as property that is never sold but just rented out (Sadowski 2020: 61–66). The spatial control that our digital landlords hold over us, just like in relation to physical property, is also not only an economic form of control, but also interests itself in governing our desires, as will be further discussed in Chapter 7 and Chapter 8. Cohen further argues that networked information technologies do not only call into being new virtual spaces but have called into place a new kind of networked space (2012: 33).

In this chapter, such ideas are taken seriously by considering the threads from Chapter 5 on platforms, smart cities and smart homes. Here we can also contend that it is not necessarily fruitful to consider public/or private space as a strict formal boundary to property, if it ever was, but rather *how* property becomes bundled up with/as space. This argument is made here through the conceptual apparatus in law that distinguishes between property, public space and private space. By also recollecting the cases from Chapter 5, this chapter points to how the control of smart cities, smart homes and platform-based business models is generally not only subject to the increased commodification of these spaces, but also reshapes how these spaces may come about as they become coded as property. A posthumanist understanding of property's spatiality is furthermore being developed by showing that it is not necessarily the networked space *per se* that is different in relation to the digital mediation of spaces the connections, or entanglements, they make possible. Instead, it is the manner in which property is formed as a layered form of control beyond the person–space distinction that here gives it a particularly posthuman character. Furthermore, it paves the way for the affective register of property taking place in all such layers, as will be discussed further in the concluding chapters.

Property versus Space

Critical property scholars such as Davies have pointed out that the division between private property over land and public, as well as private space, is a distinct feature of liberalist perceptions of law (Davies 2020: 1105). The public space that needs protection in liberal legal theory (whether seen as private property or not) tends to include the sanctity of the home, as well as spaces needed for cultural and political reproduction. These areas are part of what Radin has called a form of *contested* commodities, also aligned with her theory of personhood in property, as discussed in Chapter 4. The assumption that public space, just like private space, functions a boundary against commodification in property theory also has a long tradition in Western political thinking. The role of free public space has for example notably been elaborated by Arendt in her diagnosis of the human condition. In order to settle the rationality of human or Man as the political subject, space fulfils the vital place for politics in a democratic society (Arendt 1998[1958]: 22–78).

This tradition is reflected in property theory in which there are some limits as to the property interests that may take place in a space that is seen as common to all citizens. In spite of this, our public spaces are full of property interests and our commercialized spaces also hold the interests of the public that prevail over property rights (Radin 1993: 68). Examples of this is that there are usually regulations as to where marketing can take place in a city, and in what way. For example, we have recently seen an increase in regulations against sexist marketing in several major cities such as London and Stockholm (Jackson 2016; Derblom Jobe 2017). On the other hand, there is also the opposite effect in the regulation of cultural expressions such as graffiti (which as works of art could be subject to copyright protection) by claiming physical property rights, even to public goods such as state or regionally-owned trains and spaces (cf. Iljadica 2016). In Sweden, there is also strong protection of the natural commons, or rather the right to roam freely in nature. This right allows people to set up camping equipment in locations considered to be private property, as long as it is not seen as an intrusion of privacy (such as, being too close to someone's home). There are also restrictions on the privatization of beaches, meaning that no one can prevent anyone else from entering the water (sea or lakes) from the surrounding shoreline, whether or not it forms part of private property (see e.g. Bruncevic 2014).

Another Greek concept that already complexifies the conceptual boundary of space in property is the Greek concept of *oikos*. As Arendt writes, the idea of the household was distinct from the idea of the political sphere, or *polis*, since

> [t]he distinctive trait of the household sphere was that in it men lived together because they were driven by their wants and needs Natural community in the household therefore was born of necessity, and necessity ruled over all activities performed in it.
>
> (1998[1958]: 30)

The construction of the household in this way did not imply a zone of freedom for everyone included in it, as freedom was ultimately connected to the *polis*. Rather, it meant that economy was a cause for the household, and where politics was free from economics. The unfree state of the household is visible not least in the keeping of slaves in the household, as well as the very narrow definition of who was allowed to be part of the freedom of the *polis* (ibid.: 30–34). In modern times, in which the distinction has rather come to be between a public and private realm, the idea of economy as being separate from politics has been dissolved (Brown

2015), which s argued here is not least visible via the transformation of the concept of private property. In Arendt's conceptualization of the implications of spaces and the power derived from them under the Greek city-state, she shows that power over oneself and the community was never only located in a concept of property, which emerged thereafter. As she puts it, property was not first

> a fixed and firmly located part of the world acquired by its owner in one way or another but, on the contrary, had a source in man himself, in his possession of a body and his indisputable ownership of the strength of this body. Thus, modern property lost its worldly character and was located in the person himself.
>
> (1998[1958]: 70)

What this implies, among other things, is that the individualization of private property to the person, at least renders invisible other forms of status, which had previously granted persons a political standing. Interestingly, this older understanding of a person's connection and status as based on location also better connects with theories of property as a form of belonging (Cooper 2007; Keenan 2015), as well as the recuperation of other characteristics of status, such as whiteness (Harris 1993).

Cooper also argues that property can be fruitfully considered outside a rights and power understanding by perceiving property as being productive of belonging as both a person–thing and part–whole relations. This places property, not only outside the property-personhood discourse as discussed in Chapter 3, but also as a spatially sensitive concept. As an example, Cooper discusses the private school, Summerhill, where she identifies how property relations are formulated around five intersecting dimensions, including 1) belonging, 2) codification, 3) definition, 4) recognition and 5) power (Cooper 2007: 628). With this in mind, Cooper identifies shows how the perception of spaces in relation to private and public space and the possibility of seclusion varies between the bodies and space, even at this particular school and its sur-roundings can be considered as a form of property. To elucidate this claim, she points out how, while children may experience the possibility of escaping in groups into the forest as a way of acquiring solitude, a teacher, however, felt that this space was not private to him, considering the number of children who were present there (Cooper 2007: 641). The fixed ideas of private and public space are consequently unsettled in practices in which the liberalist divides of community are being displaced.

The understanding of property control as something that occurs in other ways than along the divisions between private and public divides is particularly interesting in relation to digitalization. The reason for this is not the least the way that there is a tendency to outline digital spaces as distinct from non–digital ones, as discussed in the previous chapter. However, there is also a tendency in law to mitigate property control both via legal tools embedded in sustaining the public sphere, as well as in relation to the private sphere. When space is considered more of as a continuum between matter, places and bodies, it becomes possible to highlight the extent to which property control resides in conflated spaces. The enactment of what could be coined as a form of property control over entangled spaces is visible in many ways. For example, certain digital technologies are allowed to form a spatial boundary around the nation-state (Keshavarz 2019); others are legitimate means of detecting and killing combatants on a battlefield (Arvidsson 2018); some are allowed to collect data in communication platforms, etc. This creates effects regarding which bodies are allowed to reside in which space, based on the properties of your body to which digital technologies can react. One of the latest examples is, of course, how special vaccine passports are being developed, to become yet another layer that a person needs to own in order to pass into certain areas. An irony of the Right to Be Forgotten (Case C-131/12, Google Spain vs. Agencia Espafiola de Proteccion de Datos (AEPD) (May 13, 2014)) was also that, in the end, Google could only be forced to remove the information from a search within the EU, based on the jurisdiction of the court. As such, this implies that limitations to someone's private property and a person's integrity are thoroughly spatially conditioned. In the establishment of digital privacy rights in the EU, it has also been noted that a general challenge is that digital spaces for communication, as opposed to physical spaces, are controlled through powerful technology companies (Edwards 2015).

Intellectual property rights are furthermore embedded in spatial references and fixations even on a surface level, which is their legislative framing. For example, the patent construction is still very dependent on nationalist registration systems in order to be conceived. The fact that the "locality" of intellectual property rights creates a problem for states and companies running on global transactions is also visible in the force with which the The WTO Agreement on Trade-Related Aspects of Intellectual Property Rights (TRIPS) agreement was conditioned for those who wanted to engage in trade under the World Trade Organisation. The spatial aspects of intellectual property rights are furthermore also obviously apparent in the idea of the public domain. As such, this domain is often understood as a space in which creativity can be freely exercised since copyrights have expired or are exempted under copyright law. Traditional examples of such exemptions in copyright doctrine are the parody exception, as well as private use. Research focusing on the concept of the commons has also suggested that, just as in the case of physical spaces, there should be an understanding that intellectual property rights need to be balanced against other interests. Some authors have even argued that common ownership of some resources may be more effective in relation to business interests than private ownership (Heller 1998; Heller and Eisenberg 1998).

However, as Cohen notes, the idea of the public domain ties in with a general conception of space as a sphere of free exchange and creation. This idea of the public domain therefore engages in an understanding that creativity can happen in all spaces (2012: 78). This, in turn, aligns with a flat understanding of both creativity and space, which undoubtedly assumes a view from above expressed as an abstract idea of knowledge creation. Similarly, property significantly divides space and very few areas are left from property's spatial fix or, as we can say if we want to be as blunt as possible: capital's need to nestle everywhere, settle everywhere and build connections everywhere (Marx and Engels 2015[1848]). This means that property goes to places and spaces where capital wants it to go, even if this is unthinkable in the general legal tradition of property. A telling example of the always excessive property control, as discussed from a different perspective in Chapter 2, is the construction of platform architecture as property control.

Spatial Property: Platform Architecture as Property

Platform architecture is omnipresent these days as we live in a society in which, as Cohen points out, dominant platforms use a plethora of legal constructs such as one-sided end-user license agreements and other boilerplate constructs and technical protocols to construct their operations as walled gardens. Within these walls, the interactions are strictly controlled in ways that reinforce their dominance over the conditions of data collection and knowledge production (Cohen 2019: 235). Consequently, platforms inhabit a very specific logic of spatial control with walls that open and close to make the garden flourish in the ways desired by the specific platform holder. And, if data is not the oil that these architectures run on, it at least appears to be both the seeds and flowers that make the garden blossom. The construction of platforms as an environment, or space, however, also occurs within a spatial layer that itself has specific characteristics and for this spatial form of control that we now take almost for granted.

As discussed in the introductory chapters, already from its emergence in 1969, the idea of the internet was understood as a network, or an entanglement, as a means of "subsuming heterogeneous networks while allowing those networks to function independently" (Zittrain 2006: 1975). Zittrain also points out that this structured openness of elements that become entangled as networks were constructed in such a way that they could be open to: "any sort of device: any computer or other information processor could be part of the new network so long as it was properly interfaced, an exercise requiring minimal technical effort" (ibid.: 1976). In this way, generativity – or the continuous sustainability of the internet space – was found to depend upon the connections it could make to other devices. Both Zittrain and Lessig also pointed out early on that there is a direct risk in controlling internet architecture in ways that makes it less "generative" as technological development could be harmed (Zittrain 2006; Lessig 1999: 223–225). This kind of reasoning in which openness is linked to the flow of information is something that we have now become well acquainted with via the innovation theories discussed in particular in Chapter 3. However, what surfaced in the form of the internet we see now was not an openness to all but exactly a control of interfaces through contracts, technological standards and other elements under the pretence that it is not openness as such that drives innovation but the design of openness and closure at exactly the right places in order to leverage intellectual assets, as discussed in Chapters 3 and 4.

An early example of this was when Android, iOS and Facebook constructed their business models through different levels of openness in many ways, for example, offering so-called *Software Development Kits*. These kits included different kinds of software packaged in a way that ascertains communication between different kinds of software and system files. A similar design tool that contributes to a harmonized architecture and that platform controllers may utilize and make available is the so-called Application Programming Interfaces, APIs. Such seemingly innocent requirements of design on technological elements facilitates how code may be utilized in a manner that produces a form of control, which one generally does not have over physical "spaces." As is also becoming increasingly recognized in the legal discipline, it is clear that it is problematic when it is large, multinational, information and communication technology companies that mainly control these architectures (Cohen 2012: 155–186; Käll 2014; Cohen 2019; Pasquale 2020). As such, this understanding not only paves the way for code as a new form of materiality of law, as discussed in Chapter 2, but also for the suggested concept of property as something that holds up bodies as space via technological architectures and more. In this way, it is not only the proprietary control of different assets, whether they can be called intellectual property rights, algorithms, data sets, contracts or gig workers, that determines how property can be detected over platforms, but also in the movements of which bodies (human and nonhuman) are made possible and how (cf. Keenan 2015: 163–165). This kind of holding up may be understood as unfolding as a specific form of design in which technological logics meet other norms such as racism, sexism, etc. to create a powerful system for privileging specific relationships between bodies over others.

Spatial Property: Holding up Certain Bodies as Platform Space

An example of how certain bodies, at least previously, were treated as normative on the Facebook platform, and consequently exceed our normal idea of property control, is the case of persons being excluded from Facebook because they did not use a "real name." To start with, the context of this case is that Facebook, as is well-known by now, employs certain community rules as a boilerplate for accepting members into its community. One of these rules state that a real name is needed to access, and participate in, the Facebook platform. This naturally separated Facebook from many other cyberspaces on which pseudonyms have been the norm, and still are, including other large platforms such as Twitter, Instagram and Snapchat. This "contractual" requirement was up for media debate as it became known how Facebook had required that people working as drag queens would use their "real names" instead of their drag names on Facebook. Facebook further threatened that if there was no such identification, the persons in question would have to close their accounts, and, in some cases, effectively shut down their Facebook accounts (Buhr 2014).

As an alternative to using their *real names* on Facebook, Facebook directed them to the alternative of using the construction *Facebook Pages* as a means of pursuing communication on the Facebook platform. The drag queens, however, refused such pursuits as they identified risks (of threats) if they had used their so-called real names on the Facebook platform but were not comfortable in using the Facebook Pages function as this is a function for *artists*, whereas they identified themselves as *persons* using their drag queen names (ibid.). As a response to the subsequent debate, Facebook continuously claimed that the reason for requiring legal names was to keep the community "safe." However, as was pointed out in a petition based on this case, persons defining themselves by assuming new names may be doing so simply to stay safe and protect themselves from actual harassment stemming from their choice of identity. As an example of such a group, apart from drag queens, one may specifically note groups of persons who identify themselves outside the gender binary having difficulty receiving recognition for the names they identify themselves with and therefore consider as real. To be specific persons identifying themselves as trans persons may be in a transitionary phase in which they no longer use their registered birth name, but where this name is still their legally registered name. Naming such persons by such names and even forcing such persons to use such names is widely understood as being an act of violence. Even if one could have understand the logics of directing drag queens drag queens to fan pages, there consequently are people who also are not using their legal names due to trans-identification. As of 2015, Facebook has changed their policy to take consideration like this into account. https://about.fb.com/news/2015/12/community-support-fyi-improving-the-names-process-on-facebook/

What this case also highlights is that the kind of power over subjectivity that platform companies hold, include who can be considered to be a legitimate subject and that, in this case, such power could also be linked to the power of gender/ing. Naming is also something that occurs along racialized and classist lines, as discussed by Benjamin (2019: 2–12) The racial aspects of naming and using one's real name, naturally also reaches a further intensity when one has to prove that the name one is using has a basis in legal documents. When platforms pose questions about what counts as normal personhood in using one's real name into their architecture, but also things like having a profile picture showing oneself and generally behaving in a certain way in accordance with the guidelines, they directly move engage in a form of property control that holds some bodies up while not holding up others.

Posthuman Property: Control and Belonging in Networks

Posthumanist theory suggests a critical account of power, based both in how matter comes to matter in general (Barad 2007), and advanced capitalism's role in these processes. As such this is a way of articulating both the capacities vested in matter to exist in certain ways, as well as in relation to other matter. Consequently, one can say that it is a way to view matter as both being performative in itself and in relation. Attending to the materiality of digital spaces in a posthuman sense, it becomes possible to highlight for example how the liquidity of data-driven spaces adds a layer of iterability and customization to things, coding part–whole belongings in increasingly different ways between individuals. This translates well to the perspectives in property theory that advances a way of considering property as a relational form of power, and a power over relations, stretching beyond the human–thing divide. From the perspective of attending to entangled aspects of digital technologies and humans, property perspectives that advance the question of belonging is therefore a fruitful way forward.

As has been discussed here, a property theory based in the role of matter and belonging creates a different view of property's function in digital spaces. With a traditional understanding of property, one can identify that privately owned spaces or buildings, roads or similar that form part of those spaces, are subject to property control. This translates also to digital architectures, where it early on was identified that proprietary control and closure of the internet, implies a form of market-based power over digital spaces. With a more posthuman take, based in property theories of belonging, we may however also see how digital spaces are made to produce and hold up certain bodies, and not others, *as* space. Such understanding then stands in sharp contrast to the liberal legal understanding of space and property's influence over it. This includes perceptions of space as something that cannot be appropriated by humans but rather as something that owns its inhabitants and is found in certain indigenous understandings of land (Davies 2020: 1105).

The relationality of property at play here therefore aligns also with the study on Summerhill conducted by Cooper, where she found that an adult perceived control and access to solitude in the forest differently from children, and that space therefore belonged differently to the adult, even if on the surface the adult had the same access to it as the children. In this way and other similar ways, the property control of digitally mediated spaces can be said to differ between how bodies belong to other bodies as space (also cf. Nakamura 2002; boyd 2012). The potential to consider property as a means of holding up bodies, also paves the way for an even more intersectional understanding of property power than is common in most property theoretical accounts (Keenan 2015: 71–72; cf. Crenshaw 2008).

Belonging as a concept of property, in turn, widens the understanding of property for personhood as advocated by Radin and discussed in Chapter 3. This is because it starts from social relations of belonging, such as between a child and its family and a collective identity and community (Cooper 2007: 629) In the case of platform-based business models and emerging smart objects and spaces, it is obvious that we can no longer distinguish between property and personhood. As Cohen puts it: "Networked space is not a unitary phenomenon or place; it can and does include a multiplicity of places and experiences, which in turn are connected to experienced, 'egocentric' space in many different ways" (Cohen 2012: 41). To then consider property in this way enables a productive understanding of how entanglements between human and digital bodies are shaped via property in complex ways.

In this chapter, the idea is advanced that property functions as a force that "holds up bodies." This in turn makes it possible to consider property as a form of effective power that hinders or makes bodies move. Exactly how such a holding up of bodies occurs depends on both the materialities of the bodies employed and the affective forces they activate or are activated by. Property is consequently suggested to involve the production of entanglements rather than as a separation between bodies, and control over objects, only. The relational character that property is suggested to have along the lines of posthumanist theory, should not in itself be understood as something univocally good. As pointed out particularly well by many feminist theories, relational perspectives as such do not evaluate the particular relation (see e.g. Svensson 1997; Nedelsky 2011). So, to say that property performs a more deeply relational function, is not to say that this relationality produces a desired type of belonging. This point may seem a bit banal, but it is still a vital aspect from a critical perspective of digitalization, since concepts of "community" or "sustainability" are deeply relational concepts, that are being put in use to advance everything from smartphones, social medial platforms, and smart cities. As discussed, a relational concept of property has explanatory value for what types of control that are being developed in such contexts as such. However, in order to move a concept of property towards posthumanist ideas of belonging (including posthumanist notions of sustainability and community), the questions of interest remain in confronting *how* bodies are held up to sustain advanced capitalism. Furthermore, it begs the ethical question of how such forms of property control can be iterated.

To move towards such question of how bodies are held up, or rather "what a body can do," is therefore the focus of the final part that engages further with posthumanist ethics.

Part Four

Ethics

Our digitally mediated lives are increasingly being connected to a call for a new, or at least a strengthened, form of ethics. This call is both visible in relation to digital technologies in general, as well as for emerging artificial intelligences in particular. In fact, it has become so obvious that an increased focus on ethics is needed that large platform companies have their own ethics departments. The understanding that there is a lack of boundaries against advanced capitalism has also been identified as being especially pressing in relation to the recent developments of artificial intelligence, algorithmic governance and the emergence of robots (Pasquale 2020; Dyer-Witheford et al. 2019; Kalopkas 2019) As is becoming increasingly recognised also in the general literature, the call for ethics can imply anything from making technologies more opaque, to a redistribution of resources that shifts colonialist tendencies of data extraction (Couldry and Mejias 2019; Amoore 2020).

In calling for a posthumanist ethics via an expanded understanding of property, we therefore continue to follow the threads elaborated in the previous chapters of this book. This implies keeping the focus on how the differences between bodies are being displaced and re-entangled via advanced capitalism. However, it also includes the more affective and affirmative dimension of posthumanist ethics, which, as Braidotti puts it, aims to reinvent a lost people in forming new alliances via and beyond humanist registers (Braidotti 2019: 164). This ethical impulse is not least also highlighted in how to create knowledge and draw together bodies in ways that escape, or at least have the potential to escape, the logics of surveillance, platform entanglements or simply the informatics of domination. Barad is instructive in advocating such openness as "a matter of differential responsiveness (as performatively articulated and accountable) to what matters"(2007: 380). In more concrete terms this implies we must continuously attend to "what matters and is excluded from mattering" (ibid.: 380). Another way in which knowledge creation is understood differently in posthumanist theory, and as a form of ethics, is the way that new convergences between matter can also be understood as an opportunity if they pave the way for a more deeply relational or kinnovative (Haraway 2016: 209) ontology in which "[w]e must find ways to celebrate low birth rates and personal,

DOI: 10.4324/9781003139096-1d

intimate decisions to make flourishing and generous lives (including innovating enduring kin – kinnovating) without making more babies." In this way, the practices of knowing, reach beyond saving the human from the threats of control by machinic species, and towards cross-species becomings, responding to the challenges posed by advanced capitalism in the Anthropocene.

Chapter 7

Artificial Intelligence for Advanced Capitalism

Artificial intelligence is emerging in multiple and more diffuse ways than most sci-fi and capitalist dreams alike can imagine. The hopes include visions of increased capabilities for humans to gain *superintelligence* from what could be framed as digital-neurological technology, or in the words of Elon Musk, "neural lace." In more detail, such neural lace is described as implying "tiny brain electrodes" that could be used to upload and download our thoughts (Winkler 2017). The establishment of such pathways often builds further upon the disembodied understanding of information depicted by Hayles in 1999, in which an "entity that may flow between carbon-based organic components and silicon-based electronic components to make protein and silicon operate as a single system" (1999: 2). Already at that point, there were vivid imaginaries of the possibility that it could soon become possible to extract human memories from the human brain and import them directly to computer disks (ibid.: 13).

A trend in law and business literature, probably worthy of a study in its own right, is also to describe the coming smartification of society through made-up scenarios of a future in which objects communicate seamlessly while humans go on with their increasingly (capitalist) efficient lives (e.g. Hildebrandt 2015; Tegmark 2017; Rogan 2019; Bastani 2019: 1–12). The risk that one day the human species would have to cede its place as the exclusive species of thinking to technological bodies has been articulated in both science and science fiction. As also described by Beth Singler:

> [w]ith artificial intelligence, we have long told stories about the end of the world at the hand of our "robot overlords". In the Terminator series (pictures from which still dominate the press's discussions about AI) the prophecy of Skynet's awakening – aka "Judgement Day" – relies on familiar religious language and tropes.
>
> (Singler 2021: 162)

Related to these actual or coming inventions are questions as to what could happen if human brains instead had to become faster to even keep up with machines (Hayles 1999: 290). The Turing test, famously developed by Alan

DOI: 10.4324/9781003139096-7

Turing in the 1950s, was designed to be able to separate a human from a machine via an assessment of verbal performance. To put it simply, if the human carrying out the test could not make this separation, it was proved that the machine could think (ibid.: xi). Bratton argues that this can be understood as a form of AI-anthropocentrism which is an effect of AI anthropomorphism

> definable as the notion that AI is intelligent to the extent that it is human-like. This goes back at least to the Turing test, in which a speculative AI was asked to "pass" as a human, and to pretend to think *how humans think that humans think* in order to qualify as intelligent. What Turing meant as a sufficient condition of intelligence has become instead, especially in popular culture, a necessary condition: a threshold, an ideal, a norm against which real AI is measured.
>
> (Bratton 2021 1: 94)

At the same time, there are still vivid discussions regarding what should be considered as AI. Dyer-Witheford et al. show that one can see tendencies in these discourses in dividing AI into a narrower definition of AI. As they further point out, such forms of AI are already here. The other, more far-reaching AI would then be of the kind that would ultimately be capable of "full human emulation" is yet to come (2019: 1). Both "narrower" and more full-scale automation technologies are however important in pinpointing what *de facto* existing and emerging AI capitalism will look like. This includes considering "narrow AI" in the sense of technologies that are already present in our own lives, for example: robot delivery vehicles in warehouses, killer drones, as well as background technologies in smartphones, computers, search engines, social media feeds, etc. (ibid.: 2). All these technologies play a role in what Dyer-Witheford et al. call "actually existing AI-capitalism" (ibid.). This term aims to capture the ambiguities by which AI enthusiasm enfolds in a phase of the experimental and uneven adoption of related automation technologies. What is clear, however, is that data is currently being captured and utilized to produce technologies that are in sync with the dominating forces of capturing surplus value, as described throughout this book.

In critical accounts of AI, there are at least two large streams of how to approach the potential in AI for a leftist project leading away from strictly capitalist aims of creating surplus value. One of these streams is the so-called accelerationist stream of theory, which sees the development of automation as an inevitable force to end both work and capitalist accumulation (ibid.: 7). Affirmative takes on technology like these also resonate to some degree with the view of technological development advanced by posthumanist theorists. A recent example of such posthumanist affirmative stance to technology involves the writings on xenofeminism. As the collective of authors suggesting a xeno-feminist view show, there might be benefits from a feminist perspective to consider how natural biology and social reproduction can be administered through new technologies (Laboria Cuboniks 2018; Hester 2018; ibid.: 6). A second form of intervention to AI capitalism includes a more critical understanding of how the automation of capital does not necessarily imply the end of capitalism. As Dyer-Witheford et al. point out, capital is already an automatic subject and, via the form afforded by artificial general intelligence, it would not only dispense of human labour but also humanity as such (2019: 158). This is also the stage at which AI capitalist endeavours fruitfully can be read against the idea of transhumanism as it is imagined by Nick Bostrom: as a transcendence of the human. Whereas Bostrom depicts this as an integrated force in the human (Bostrom 2005), the automation of capital in transcending the human is rather here understood as an embedded force of capitalism. In producing a critical account of such capitalism, Dyer-Witheford et al. suggest that leftist perspectives also need to take account of the racist assumptions and output in relation to accelerationist perspectives, which in themselves prevent a blank belief in automation as a means of (fully automated, luxury) communism (2019: 160–162). In one way, the transcendence, or at least: transformation, of the human via technology is, as discussed throughout, something that has been viewed in positive light by posthumanist theories as it integrates an understanding of the human as something susceptible to enhancement when it is considered as embedded in "the flexible, adaptive structures that coordinate our environments and the metaphors we ourselves are" (Hayles 1999: 290). The question, however, is rather if, and how, this may be done while both breaking with and pushing further the critical project and ethics of posthumanist theory.

As of now, there is an increased amount critical research carried out to pinpoint the risks in advancing capitalism via AI, including against how AI is being used as a means of automating work, whether reproductive or productive. As such, this tightly follows the Marxist and feminist Marxist tradition of capital and capitalism both, and are valid starting points also for highlighting ethico-political dimensions of AI via posthumanist theory, to support the critique of advanced capitalism. While it is vital to keep automation in mind in order to critically understand the power and forms of control embedded in the smartification of society, the way that bodies are made possible and make possible certain flows are furthermore vital for a posthumanist conception of both AI and ethics. This implies that besides commodification and exploitation of labour in the more traditional sense, a posthumanist ethico-political stance is also interested in how the human and non-human are produced via affective registers. Throughout this book, we have encountered many ways in which we can speak of the affective aspects that digital objects are engaged with, and where practices related to AI emphasize this further. For examples, as discussed in Chapter 2, the coding of images for data sets that enable machine-learning, can continue certain types of sexist and racist biases. This kind of affective ordering however also gets a more explicitly affective character in human/robotic interactions, ranging from robopsychology to affective computing (Ferrando 2019: 114).

A posthumanist understanding of the affects involved in AI however also moves beyond the human-centred ways in which these technologies unfold. This involves finding ways to move towards an ecology of affects, which involves such things as energy and minerals are fundamental to "knowledge"-based capitalism, as discussed throughout. Such focus does not need to fall under the (often simplified and misunderstood) vitalism, as suggested by Bennett (Bennett 2010). Rather, it is the actual orderings of AI, as well as their potential to order via the existing, and other forms of affect that is of interest here. The question as to whether AI has agency is hence not the question here. Instead, the aim is to ask which new forms of affects might be unfolding under increased automation, and which risks and opportunities do they give rise to from a posthumanist perspectives. This chapter then will suggest some such examples with the aim of showing how it is not only the possibility of machinic superintelligence in a "mind-oriented" way that is at play in AI, but also very much sensorial intelligence and capture.

Sensorial Intelligence

As I write this chapter, during what is hopefully the beginning of the end of a global pandemic, a possibly low-resolution observation is that many human senses have come to be displaced, if not made illegal or illegitimate. It has been a year where touch has given way to distance and with this many other sensations connected with connection in-between bodies.

At the same time, digital systems scan the surroundings for humans to detect possibly harmful sensing such as through COVID-19 tracking apps or measuring body temperature at airports or restaurants. Indeed, the touch to unlock our smartphones, so revolutionary just a few years ago is now replaced with face identification, as discussed in Chapter 2. Consequently, even the machines are soon able to sense without humans touching them. Instead, the individual human touch, and soon even the individual face, is being substituted by data aggression and analysis to identify general patterns. The shift towards a non-human touch, and nonhuman gaze, are hence both involved in constructing a nonhuman sensorial intelligence. As discussed in Chapter 5 in relation to smart cities, what particularly renders a city smart is that it is embedded with sensors that are utilized to transfer data about everything from the atmosphere, waste, electricity and traffic flows into networked computer systems in which algorithms make sense of how to best organize the city from the input received. This same of sensing is also prevalent in social media feeds running to optimize user's experiences based on how their mood appears (based on both individual and general user behaviours).

The concept of ambient intelligence has also functioned as a descriptive term for the development where intelligence is brought to everyday environments in a way that makes them sensitive to other bodies. In particular, this field is connected to advancements in sensors and sensor networks and how they relate to artificial intelligence (Cook, Augusto, and Jakkula 2009). As Cook et al. put it in 2009:

> [T]he basic idea behind Ambient Intelligence (AmI) is that by enriching an environment with technology (e.g., sensors and devices interconnected through a network), a system can be built such that it acts as an "electronic butler," which senses features of the users and their environment, then reasons about the accumulated data, and finally selects actions to take that will benefit the users in the environment.
>
> (ibid.: 278)

As they further point out, since ambient intelligence is related to "real-world, physical environments," an effective use of sensors is vital in the way that algorithms otherwise have nothing to attach to (ibid. 280).

To recollect these aspects, we can again return to the example in Chapter two on how scanning technologies such as LiDAR is used to make the city readable for autonomous vehicles. This can then furthermore be understood not only to materialize the environment in which the autonomous vehicle moves but to enable smart vehicles to sense and be sensed by their environment as pulses of light and sound, as well as other technologies used to map the city as "one, intensive, complex landscape of dynamics and navigation" (Parikka 2021: 186). LiDAR technology participates in this sensing of the environment by sampling its surrounding at a rate in the range of 5–20Hz, which is comparatively much lower than other sensors such as cameras (20–60Hz) or WiFi adapters (100Hz) (ibid). Also, as suggested by Parikka, WiFi can generally be understood as an effective sensor for detecting the outline of bodies (ibid.). Manaugh notably also describes how the use of 3D scanning mechanisms such as LiDAR sensors in autonomous cars enable a very specific navigational way of mapping the city as an ecology of flickering machines that capture "extremely detailed, millimetre-scale measurements of the surrounding environment" (2015). Parallel to the development of autonomous vehicles utilising the LiDAR system, Elon Musk's system for Tesla has, however, been developed as a means of navigating the environment solely through machine learning (see e. g. Eady 2020), which places the sensorial form of intelligence at an earlier stage (in extracting data sets and classifying reactions based on such). In either case, however, the reading of the environment by an autonomous vehicle is created by the transmission and reception of information or images of the space surrounding the vehicle (Parikka 2021: 25).

This process of making the environment measurable also connects to a shift in logics related to computation and control, as discussed in Chapter 2. In the case of LiDAR, while changes to space may not be visible for objects other than autonomous vehicles, they alter both the composition and readability of this space with the object of materialising the movements of autonomous vehicles. The readability also aligns with the conceptualization of algorithmic governance, as discussed in the same chapter as "this form of governance is intent on collecting as much data as possible in order to establish robust correlations; in other words, instead of decoding underlying essences, this mode of governance works by way of establishing connections, patterns, and, no less crucially, predictions," as discussed by Kalopkas (2019: 2). In a similar manner, Chandler and Fuchs have pointed out how "[a]lgorithmic governance seeks to find patterns and relationships, enabling new ways of seeing, sensing, responding and adapting to life in its complex emergence" (Chandler 2018: 2). Judging from how smart cities are unfolding today, we can safely say that much of the sensoring capacities of making environments smart is all about arranging flows for the purpose of very specific types of optimization, as discussed in Chapter 4. Quite often, these kinds of optimization ratio-nales fold into a form of terraforming in the way described by Sadowski, in which smart technologies are deployed in ways of creating the conditions for a specific model of human life that changes how people live and interact with their environments (Sadowski 2020: 52). Or to put it in more direct terms: "Smart tech is a way of terraforming society for digital capitalism to thrive" (ibid.).

This is also the stage at which the sensorial forms required to achieve data collection and machinic response move further into an affective form, as it actively shapes the desires of bodies, as a form of affective intelligence.

Affective Intelligence and Movement of Bodies

It has been widely discussed that a characteristic of advanced capitalism is its logic of working on an affective register, which is why Karppi suggests that this variation of capitalism is termed *affective capitalism* (Karppi et al. 2016). This is visible in terms of both the management logic that stresses that workers need to be committed to their status as employees to a larger extent than before (e.g. Brown 2015; Karppi et al. 2016). Seminal works such as Naomi Klein's *No Logo* (2000; Hardt and Negri's theories in *Empire* (2000); and Massumi's *Politics of Affect* (2002) are all examples of how the sale of goods has been dis-placed by the sale of branded experiences or a space of consumption rather than a consumption of goods. The affective turn to commodity production is, in essence, a part of an economy driven by creating scarcity when com-modities are in abundance in relation to the total amount of humans and their actual needs for survival. Western capitalism has therefore shifted from marketing products and services based on price and focuses instead on experiences in the form of brands protected by trademark rights. This turn to the emotions of the consumer in relation to the sale of products, in itself, collapses a number of ideas of society, in which one dissolving boundary is, again, the distinction between political and commercial space (Klein 2000). As is clear to most of us now, our algorithmically optimized social media feeds accelerate this development even further.

The decoding of affect in a narrower sense, as feelings, or excess of feelings, also play a vital role in developing AI. As outlined in Chapter 2, facial recognition is one of many techniques by which governance under AI unfolds. Facial recognition in turn also has a history as affect recognition via the face. As discussed by Crawford, the American psychologist Paul Ekman was early on trying to establish a connection between how one person could decode the feelings of another person by reading that person's facial expression. In the beginning of the research, Ekman was trying to establish a universal framework for interpreting emotions from faces. His initial research study from 1967 in Papua New Guinea, however, showed (as is obvious today) that facial expressions are not easy to interpret, especially outside their cultural context. The reason why Ekman chose to base his initial study in Papua New Guinea, as told by Crawford, was that the Fore people of Okapa, living there, had been living in isolation from most of the rest of the world. This for him made them ideal test subjects for certain ideas of what constituted "natural" human behaviour. Ekman's theory was that since the Fore people had lived with little contact to Westerners or mass media, they would be able to prove that their recognition and display of core expressions would show the universality of such expressions. This hypothesis was however refuted when it turned out that Ekman's flashcard experiments with the Fore people, failed (2021: 151–152). After more research and the use of photographs and in mapping and modelling expressions, his research however came to more defined conclusions of the way that affects can be mapped onto the face. Together with others, this has come to pave the way for the type of affective intelligence that is part of AI today: not the least via facial recognition technologies (ibid.: 151–179). As Crawford points out, the possibility of detecting feelings via faces is however still inherently tricky. She therefore argues that the automation of affect recognition is currently not delivering the promises it sets out (ibid.: 176–179). In relation to this, it should however be noted that the affective aspects of AI reaches further than the possibility to recognize feelings via automation. As discussed, many partial technologies that make up automated digital technologies today: personal data collection, datasets, algorithms and their outputs such as behavioural advertising, dating apps etc. have clear affective effects. A way to recognize how such affective aspects of AI has effect already today is just via applying a wider concept of affect as being something that orient bodies, draw them together, or apart, rather than as a form of "feeling recognition" (e.g. Philippopoulos-Mihalopoulos 2013; Philippopoulos-Mihalopoulos 2015: 11; Braidotti 2013: 192–194).

Affect also disperses into the neoliberal culture in which one is constantly reminded about how to be a better and more joyful person through training apps, health trackers and by building communities that thrive on interactions such as hearts and likes, as well as the interpretation of the same (cf. Jungselius 2019). Our intelligent products are furthermore full of emotional and otherwise affective messaging such as described by Tapscott and Tapscott when they point out the possibilities of the increasingly intelligent traits of objects by the question (and answer): "Feeling lonely? You can always talk to your house" (2016: 161). Furthermore, the utterance of "I love you so much" by the six-year-old girl to Alexa, the Amazon assistant, who helped her order a dolls house, in itself deserves a recognition of the emotional aspects involved in AI capitalism (Karppi and Granta 2019: 869).

The apps surrounding us to foster our well-being also constantly push us to move our bodies in particular ways, including becoming fitter, for example, through FitBits tracking our movements throughout the day and aspiring to certain goals. From the start, the FitBit device, and now many other devices following its lead, may also track our sleep, either in a normal setting or placed in sensitive mode, which enables "extremely detailed sleep reporting" (ibid.). This now also involves the possibility of tracking one's own breathing. Recently, iPhones have also started being equipped with these kinds of health reminders, including logging one's screen time and which apps one is using most, as well as automatically lowering the music one is listening to if one is not meeting an ear health goal that Apple has set for the user (without previous notice). Furthermore, health apps are, of course, also connected to the sharing of affective messages via our digital communities, both on their own and to our regular apps, by the possibility of sharing our results and hashtag them with tags such as #fitspo and #strongisthenewskinny, further emotionally enhanced via reactions such as likes, hearts or a range of emojis.

A popular reference regarding this is the female robot/robot-like characters who become love objects to male film characters. Just recall the widely cited film *Her* by Spike Jonze, in which the character Theodore is pictured as a lonely man about to go through the final stages of his divorce. At this point he decides to buy himself a new operating system, OS, being sold as the first one in the world to have artificial intelligence. This operating system comes with a female face, or more specifically, a voice, the voice of Samantha. As the story unfolds, Theodore becomes romantically attached to Samantha and starts spending more and more time with her. The more-than-human intelligences vested in Samantha as a powerful operating system are furthermore put into use to help Theodore in ways that others have not been able to. Samantha, however, finally fails to be the perfect girlfriend when it is revealed that she has not been faithful to Theodore, but has also provided her services to many others, as operating systems are intended to do, after all (meanwhile the same does not apply in human relationships, as the sub-text reveals).

More monogamous companions can be found in digital assistants like Apple's Siri who, in spite of the allegedly gender-neutral name, is both described in, and performs, a very gendered type of communication (Hester 2016). In support of this, one can notice the manner in which Apple advertized Siri in stating that: "Siri understands what you say, knows what you mean and even talks back" (Apple's website Siri, 2015). As Frank Pasquale points out in relation to *Her*, what could also be highlighted is the "extraordinary evocation of an increasingly likely future in which billions of conversations captured by data-hoarding firms and governments are used to design an operating system (OS) that simulates a witty, supportive lover or a devoted friend" (Pasquale 2020: 204). These desires are, in turn, obviously coded into the system, reflecting very particular desires, and optimising in relation to them (ibid.: 20). Building on a feminist understanding of care and emotional labour, we can clearly identify the extreme heterosexual and patriarchal assumptions in films such as *Her*, but also, of course, in the apps surrounding us, feeding content that affirms already dominant desire lines. These heterosexual and patriarchal assumptions apply to both humans and nonhumans alike as the definitions of what a machine does, as opposed to a human (woman), sheds light on.

The data derived from private person's use of social media has an even more obvious emotional, and even sexual, character when one considers how it is/ has been used in dating or sex apps such as Tinder and Grindr. For example: Tinder (while it is kept secret exactly how it works) has an algorithm that decides which profiles to suggest as options for a user. The user then performs the renowned swipe (left or right). The swiping has as such been called out as an unfair dating logic by some (as it is apparent that one only has a few seconds to make an impression, which tends to make certain shallow characteristics more desirable than others). However, what is then possibly more problematic is the way that data has been analysed by a user's behaviour and profile attention, to suggest matches based on those. And even if one does not find it to be a problem, it is still an example of how automation takes on affective characteristics. Other less obvious, but today well-known, examples from social media platforms range from Facebook to TikTok, in which the loading pages have become increasingly personalized. For example, the "For You" page of TikTok can suggest many different types of videos to stream based on how you have engaged with content on the platform before, without getting repetitive. Actually, it is probably one of the easiest to explain cases of how personal data and algorithms work together to keep a user affectively engaged online, or as my nine-year-old child so accurately put it: is that why I only get shown funny videos?

Obviously, the affective aspects of AI capitalism also come through via the regimes of behavioural advertising. Here we can again remind ourself about Zuboff's take on the aspect of advanced capitalism and its relation to surveillance capitalism and its trade in "behavioural surplus." As discussed, data that is captured from persons' behaviours online, are here fed into producing "prediction products" (2018: 8). or an assessment of behaviour as "behavioural future markets" (ibid.: 8). This is particularly evident in relation to behavioural marketing practices where the business model of social media platforms, like

Facebook, early on was to sell user data to data brokers/advertising agencies. Such entities later resold more fine-grained data to companies that wanted to advertise on the Facebook platform, where Facebook could offer target groups based on the which customer base the company wished to reach (Turow 2011; Dempster and Lee 2015). As the Cambridge Analytica case further shows, it was not only information in terms of sales of goods that could be provided via Facebook. Also, information about political behaviours, and how certain users reacted to messages, how they interact with news, what kind of pages they follow etc. could be made the basis for a finer analysis of which their political orientation is. The sale of such information to political analysis companies like Cambridge Analytica proves how powerful it can be to use this information to enforce beliefs amongst voters. Furthermore, this can also be understood as a use of behavioural surplus that runs on affective registers in the manner that the sharing and engaging with content on Facebook very much is an expression of emotional politics (c.f. Mouffe 2005).

Furthermore, many of the "innovative" projects in the gig economy are based on the semi-autonomous aspects of consumers rating a service that someone has performed for them. Today one cannot even visit a state-run enterprise in Sweden, such as the package-delivering service offered by the Nordic post (PostNord), without being asked to rate the experience afterwards. In fact, even when the package delivery system has been transformed into a "fully automatic" experience where one goes to a locker full of mysteriously sized individual boxes to use one's phone Face-ID to open one's Bank ID to open the post app to open the box with the package (via a code), one is still asked to give feedback on the experience afterwards. In its most extreme examples, negative customer ratings can lead to delisting and in this way a form of the effective firing of a person as has been described by Ducato in the case of Uber transport services (Ducato 2020). Consequently, the move towards augmented intelligence very often comes with explicit emotional undertones as well as actualized bodily governance that move bodies in one way and not another. These are both examples of affect in the posthumanist sense. To this, they should consequently be considered when formulating a concept of ethics for resisting AI capitalism. As also Ferrando notes, these technological fields of research and vision are interesting to the affective turn connected to Spinozan and posthumanist theory, engaging in affects in social, political, cultural and cybernetic spaces (2019: 114). As the next section will show, an attention to the role of affect in AI capitalism is not necessarily the focus of what we can call "actually existing AI ethics," represented in both scholarship and in the recent efforts to govern such aspects in the European Union.

Actually Existing AI Ethics

The general ethical impulse of AI stands in direct relation to technologies that are included under the concept. As discussed, there is a tendency to primarily focus on those kinds of technologies that ultimately create a form of super-intelligent machine. However, as of today, artificial intelligence outperforms human intelligence in many domains, consequently decentering the individual human in a number of activities (Bostrom 2014: 14–16). Recent projects such as the High-Level Expert Group in Artificial Intelligence, constructed by the European Commission, addresses AI in this more differentiated sense, where it is not one ultimate form of AI that needs to become ethical, but many related technologies (European Commission High Level Expert Group on Artificial Intelligence 2019). The group's work is in this sense highly relevant to reflecting on the opportunities and risks of AI. During spring 2020, the group published a document called Ethics Guidelines for Trustworthy AI that sets out to mitigate some of these potential risks, while capturing the benefits of AI (ibid.). The guidelines outline that in order to build a trustworthy AI system, three main criteria must be fulfilled: 1) it should be lawful; 2) it should be ethical; and 3) it should be robust (from both a technical and social perspective) (ibid.: 2–5). However, it is also interesting to note that the guidelines already stated in the first section that they will not deal with questions of what constitutes "lawful" AI. In their definition of what constitutes ethical principles of AI, however, they state that it is to be based on fundamental rights (ibid.: 2). Furthermore, they stipulate that AI ethics should be co considered a sub-field of applied ethics with an increased focused on issues related to "development deployment and use of AI." In doing this, it is suggested that AI ethics should be focused on identifying how AI can create a good life of individuals in relation to e.g. "quality of life, or human autonomy and freedom necessary for a democratic society" (ibid.: 9).

Starting off in "fundamental rights" as they are enshrined in the EU treaties, the EU charter and international human rights law, the working group identifies five relevant fundamental rights for ethical principles towards trustworthy AI: 1) Respect for human dignity; 2) Freedom of the individual; 3) Respect for democracy, justice and the rule of law; 4) Equality, non-discrimination and solidarity; 5) Citizens' rights (ibid.: 10–11). The guidelines further connect these types of ethics to what they refer to as a long tradition in Europe of safeguarding such values through, for example, human rights (ibid.). As ethical principles for AI, it is also pointed out in particular that AI needs to comply with 1) Respect for human autonomy; 2) Prevention of harm; 3) Fairness; and 4) Explicability (ibid: 11).

Such an understanding of the direct link between ethics, human rights and democracy is not unexpected, considering that the legal discipline has suggested similar orientations (Hildebrandt 2015, Pasquale 2020). As Pasquale also points out, there seems to be a trend in AI ethics in which one is solving the idea of a machine producing certain unwanted normative effects by building rules into the machine. As an example, he discusses the famous idea that one might design a machine to produce paper clips and its logics of automation is designed in a way that it does not stop until it has turned all available material on Earth into such clips. So, in relation to this case, one could then design into the machine a kind of anti-maximization rule (Pasquale 2020: 213). This belief in integrating law into AI itself as a form of ethical response can also be connected to the idea, as Chandler and Fuchs put it, that "ethical accountability is increasingly perceived as residing in machines, which results in automated decision-making. Knowing and sensing seems to become a unified algorithmic procedure that resides across the human/machinic divide" (Chandler and Fuchs 2018: 6). This had also been suggested as a way of creating better data protection, so-called legal protection by design (Hildebrandt 2015: 214–217).

The problem with such a movement of rules into machines, as Pasquale points out, is that even ordinary rules (in a text and court-oriented understanding of law) are always in conflict with other rules, existing or potential (ibid.). Pasquale therefore suggests that a key question for AI ethics, law and policy is to figure out how to keep humans in the loop of AI. To do this, he suggests four new laws of robotics to increase the possibility of human monitoring, intervention and responsibility (ibid.) The four laws to sustain such ethics suggested state that:

1   Robotic systems and AI should complement professionals, not replace them (Pasquale 2020: 6).
2   Robotic systems and AI should not counterfeit humanity (Pasquale 2020: 7).
3   Robotic systems and AI should not intensify zero-sum arms races (Pasquale 2020: 9).
4   Robotic systems and AI must always indicate the identity of their creator(s), controller(s), and owner(s) (Pasquale 2020: 11).

This view is a more critical form of ethics compared to the type of ethics suggested in the EU AI Ethics guidelines. The reason for this is that it cuts to some core issues about what could happen to labour under increased automation (particularly point 1). However, even though Pasquale points out that there can be no uniform idea of what a universally good rule is (a point which very much corresponds with a posthumanist situated perspective of law and knowledge), he is still in keeping with the idea that robots and AI should support humans and humanity. While this is naturally better (for humanity, in general) than putting paper clip making robots in charge, it still builds upon the assumption that there will be a consensus about what humanity is and should entail. Such assumptions of humanity's character are also visible in his third and fourth suggestion which seem to accept both private ownership and wars, as long as they are carried out in an ethical way. These might be just pragmatic suggestions based on the current world-order, but it is nevertheless a standard with much Western and liberal humanist baggage.

A variation of this kind of humanist ethics is also the turn to the (human) self, as a minimum boundary for ethics. An example of this is the use of the concept of the bounded self as something that is needed in order to be in a relational setting, as a prerequisite for privacy. Couldry and Mejias, for example, suggest that a new form of ethics to counter data colonialism must start from an understanding of the self to counter the questions of surveillance to which some of these technologies give rise (2019: 151–155). To do this, they further ask for a renewed understanding of the boundaries of the self and, by extension, also the social world, and set out a definition of autonomy of the self as important, which in its essence implies: "the self's minimal integrity, or boundedness, without which the self would not be a distinct site of experience at all" (ibid.: 155). In alliance with a Hegelian understanding of freedom rather than the dominating liberalist perception of freedom, they argue that this concept of autonomy may lead to a "more socially grounded notion of freedom, based in the mutuality of social life" (ibid.: 157).

However, in these kinds of views, the bigger ecological as well as capitalist picture is still not being entirely accounted for. As discussed in a recent research paper, researchers at the University of Massachusetts, Amherst, carried out a life cycle assessment for training several large AI models. This study resulted in the findings that a process such as this can emit more than 626,000 pounds of carbon dioxide. This equals almost five times what an average American car emits over nearly five lifetimes (including the production of the vehicle) (Hao 2019). It has also been pointed out that advances in hardware and methodology for training neural networks depend on the availability of exceptionally large computational resources that necessitate similarly substantial energy consumption. For this reason, these models have a high environmental cost in terms of hardware, electricity, as well as cloud computing time (Strubell et al. 2019). Instead of focusing on what AI will do to the human, and the superiority of human intelligence, a more deeply relational ethics should also consider its effects on the possibility of the endurance of bodies beyond the human (but the human too, considering things are not looking great in the face of the Anthropocene).

Ethics beyond Artificial Human Intelligence

In light of the emergence of the thoroughly extractivist and surveillant practices we now see emerging around AI, it can certainly be tempting to dust off the old bounded self and erect some new, if at least, minimal, boundaries for what is needed for a human to flourish (cf. also Radin 1993 and Cohen 2012: 223–266). However, at this point it seems evidently clear that the practices of advanced capitalism emerge as biopolitics and necropolitics simultaneously and in many complex ways (cf. Braidotti 2013: 9; Mbembe 2003). These developments flatten out the differences between humans, and other matter, such as machines and render us all posthuman, but not in the same way. The lasting differences between "us the humans" is visible for example in the way that algorithms are racist (Noble 2018) and technology in general too, including digital communities (Nakamura 2002, boyd 2012, Benjamin 2019). Even more so, this racism is embedded via the minerals extracted, via the real oil needed to keep the new oil afloat. The heavily racialized borders of the EU, if not controlled via waters and the ships patrolling them, are also controlled through facial recognition technologies, biometric passports, emerging viral passports and similar digital inventions (Keshavarz 2019, Lee-Morrison 2019). This means that we cannot talk about human rights, ethics, the self (privacy, private spaces) etc. without recalling that "even" the EU, which prides itself as being a guardian of human rights, is not so humanist depending on your own assigned status (even if you are a human on the paper). For example, it was clear, already before increased digital fencing, that people are dying at European borders despite the supposed human rights that we have signed up for and pride ourselves of sustaining. For this reason, there simply cannot be an ethics that is not also an ethico-politics against the lethal use of AI in an extended necropolitical sense. And furthermore, the return to the human cannot happen via the hope that programmers with new knowledge will be able to pursue a fully-fledged, intersectionally sensitive understanding of societies into machines (even if that would certainly be welcome, too).

In spite of this, we now see that the idea of human and the human control of intelligence technologies returns in both governance documents like the ethical guidelines in general, and in the idea of ethical judgment as a human-centred practice in particular. To put it bluntly, it is as if the struggle over ethics in relation to being able to critically assess AI is about designing a more and more elaborate Turing test, just to safeguard "human" control, even though it is human control that has allowed the Anthropocene, Capitolocene etc. to unfold. Couldry and Mejias caution against post-anthropocentric understandings of the current forms of power, including advanced capitalism. In particular they point out the danger of using insect metaphors since no one thus far has shown that human beings *are* collective animals "in a zoological sense". They even go as far as stating that pretending that humans are collective animals may "divert attention from the human costs of capitalism's new social order" (2019: 157). What such ideas fundamentally misinterpret, and miss out on, is that the distinction between human and non-human bodies serves current forms of capitalism perfectly in relation to, for example, the concept of property as something legitimately held by "humans," yet does not mean anything when it comes to stopping human extinction. This is because it was never about the human as such, but always about extracting surplus via capitalism and other orders of domination. In relation to this, it should, however, be noted that Couldry and Mejias also point to the indifferences between data subjects dominated by data colonialism (ibid.; cf. Käll 2017). In staying within an understanding of the human and the bounded human self, the entire field of conventional property theory and humanist assumptions risks being repeated.

Central to moving towards a posthumanist idea of ethics is to emphasize how AI, just like other advanced technologies, is embedded in many layers of matter, but also in affective registers. From a posthumanist perspective, such attention to affects is then core, as ethics is all about how bodies can compose, move and relate to each other. Affect here, it deserves to be repeated, does not imply a move towards vitalism but an empirically oriented way of understand why certain assemblages are composed in a particular way, and how to move towards a posthumanist idea of privileging certain compositions over others. This also means that while a "relational" or collectivist perspective is advocated as opposed to a (property-owning), it is important to stress that collectivism in itself is just the ontological starting point. Everything is always collective, the question is how to produce and sustain a posthumanist collectivity.

A posthumanist collectivist focus is particularly pertinent in the consideration of AI ethics as AI discourses and practices are full of both artificial emotions and technologies for movement. Market-based practices in which big data, personal data and data are utilized to analyse relations while using them for the exploi-tation and production of very particular specific desires is an example of such affect-orientated aspects of the technologies that are entangled with AI. For example, Ferrando suggests that we can also highlight other needs, including a reconsideration of technology as eco-technology. In this endeavour she argues that eco-technology implies rethinking technology "not in separation from the environment, but as part of the environment" (2019: 118). She also grounds this in the cycle of material existence in which "technological objects come from the Earth – for instance, in their embodiments made of minerals and metals, among other materials – and, once disposed of, will go back to it" (ibid.). Such ethics become more about a form of terraforming in which the term *terraforming*, usually referring to transforming the ecosystems of other pla-nets to enable Earth-like life, instead becomes and articulation for the fact that in the face of the Anthropocene "we will need to terraform Earth if is to remain a viable host for its own life" (Bratton 2019: 8).

At this time, the need for such sociolegal engineering is vital but will still not emerge from a natural scientific impulse alone. Whether we live in a post-truth society or not, the question of whether other ways to envision AI for the sake of terraforming the Earth or not, is a question about which forces can be unleashed. To move in this direction is to move both affectively and materially at the same time since bodies never act alone. What drives bodies to act is both their material dispositions and what makes them create and catch speed from other bodies. Ethics in a posthumanist sense pushes us further in another imagination of what AI can be for and who should be in control over it than traditional ethics, in that it collapses the distinction between humans and nonhumans, internal and exter-nal bodies, as well as in relation to law and justice. This implies we need to move through but beyond the "human-in-the-loop" figure that has recently surfaced as an ethical response by displacing the necessity and role of the superiority of "the human" entirely.

In speaking with contemporary philosophy, this fall of the superior, even "the political" human, can be understood to lead to the loss of both human and politics entirely. To speak with Agamben we could say that the human falls from its role as a living a political entity to become bare life, or *homo sacer*

(Agamben 1998). This form of life, or *zoe,* is a life shared between all who are not human, for example animals. Hence, it could possibly also be ascribed to AI, in all or some of its emerging forms (also cf. Darling 2021 on the possibility of likening robots and AI to animals). This implies that there can be reason to start more from a theorization of finding connections, rather than establishing new conceptual phenomena to settle on what an ethical account of AI could be. In particular, the question might not be who is human or not, but rather how to combine human, nonhuman, and inhuman forces to create a planet or more that remains habitable for other than capital. As Braidotti suggests, it is actually by the loss of this position, the turning of us all into *zoe,* that we can create a relational ethics in which the endurance of multiple species is the focus. This also then implies taking a relational approach as both the starting and ending point, not as something the bounded self may choose to be a part of but is inevitably a part of (2019: 166). Both the human and thinking capacities of the human in this sense become about understanding how bodies are composed and kept together. This, in turn, is a move towards Posthuman Property as affective property.

Chapter 8

Posthuman Affective Property

Affect in its narrow sense, as a human expression of emotions, is often understood to be excluded in both jurisprudence and law under liberalist societies. Judges, for example, in accordance with the dominating idea of adjudication, should settle cases based on the objective facts and not on their gut feeling. However, in spite of this, legislation deals with affective expressions in many ways, and consequently, so do traditional forms of law. This is evident when it comes to the fields of marketing, freedom of speech legislation, as it is exactly the affective aspects that marketing particularly appeals to. Freedom of speech, in turn, veils itself under the idea that speech occurs on a political level and not on an emotional level (Massumi 2002; 2015; Hardt and Negri 2000), but not least when we live in an age in which political speech often appeals to the emotions. Also, the right to carry out certain forms of speech, and not others, is an example of an explicit protection of certain possibilities to affect and not to affect. Political forms of speech as well as marketing can in this way be understood as two types of expressions that appeal to affective registers. The turn to more emotional forms of affecting can in this wider sense of affect, be seen as a particular mode of such expressions today.

In property legislation, an obvious expression on affective control can also be found in trademark legislation. The reason for this is that trademarks as intellectual property rights protect parts of what can be communicated as a brand. What can be included under such rights has come to expand in recent times, just like for other intellectual property rights. In recent history, the trademark right used to cover word marks such as slogans and the names of products, as well as figurative marks. As a result of for example recent developments in the European Union (Directive (EU) 2015/2436), a trademark can now cover anything that can be sufficiently represented in an application. Theoretically, this includes sounds, colours, scents, etc., creating the possibility of having more aspects of a larger brand protected, rather than individually separable marks. Trademarks in this way develop into sustaining entire brandscapes, full of capitalist desires. Legislation on the collection of data can furthermore also be understood to, at least implicitly, deal with the output of data as an affective form of power. Even in a narrower sense, we can consequently argue that several elements with affective force are currently being protected under different kinds of legislation, including forms of control of data (Käll 2017).

DOI: 10.4324/9781003139096-8

However, the affective aspects of property in a posthuman sense are much wider than what can be included in legislation on property rights (and even data regulation rights). In following the understanding that property is something that brings (the right) bodies together, as discussed in Chapter 6, the form of capitalism that thrives on creating such connections produces a continuous form of excessive affective control. Furthermore, this form of control is not limited to creating bonds between humans but reaches both the atmosphere and deep layers of the Earth, in how it draws together bodies, exhausting most of them, and continues the automation of capital. Thus, this final chapter sums up the connection between posthuman property and the affective aspects of capitalism as an excessive form of governing that runs on the connections between bodies. In building on this understanding of control, the chapter suggests that a fruitful way forward is to understand how property works on new registers that connect bodies, whether through code, machines, different types of intelligence or other types of digitally mediating technologies.

Controlling How Posthuman Bodies are Held Up

There are many ways in which our legal concepts of property fail to limit advanced capitalism. Of course, it is both naïve and born out of some kind of faith in liberalist ideas of property that one was ever planning to limit capitalism when private property is made possible and legal. However, positivist perceptions of law still consider both property and other concepts of law such as marketing, freedom of speech and data regulation, as being explicit tools to prevent capitalist control from unfolding in unchecked ways. Even for the sake of continuing a liberalist tradition of law, one therefore needs to understand how a new form of control is emerging. This force takes place via the de/materialization of bodies (cf. Hayles 1999) and by bringing them together or apart (Cooper 2008), for example, in holding them up as space (Keenan 2015). What is then the reason for *not* considering property as having this kind of affective capacity, which seems to mirror the form of capitalism emerging today? An answer might lie in how the human, and human personhood, functions as a conceptual boundary against property today. An idea of property as a more fluid form of control that does not in itself hold anything (human) sacred, consequently runs against liberal humanist values of both human subjectivity and law. To imagine property as something that does not automatically stop, for example, at the human body, nor at the data transpiring from my movements on the internet, can sit uneasily with agendas focused on hindering commodification, via currently more established legal tools. Therefore, it needs to be stressed that to consider property as an excessive form of control is not the same as saying that it is a desirable order, but rather saying: property was always like this. Or rather: there was never a time when property was not about making certain bodies come together and others not.

In order to configure property in this sense, we must necessarily shift towards an understanding that there is no beginning or end to this process but just a continuous flow of power between bodies. This is not the same as saying that there is no end to capitalism, to racism, to sexism, etc. The forces between bodies vary, and they vary just because they are in relation to each other and shift the strength of the forces between them (Deleuze 1988). As a comparison of how all matter stands in relation to each other, we can take the example where Marx discussed the relationality of bodies by stating that a sugar cone is, as a body, heavy, and for this reason has a weight. However, one cannot see or feel how much the sugar cone weighs without putting it in relation to something. To make this assessment, we take, for example, iron, whose weight we also have made into a relative tool for which to measure the weight of the sugar cone. This relationship between bodies does not show the value of certain goods, such as a linen coat, as this value is produced as something external to that body. The existence of economic value therefore appears as something external to the body (Marx 2013[1969]: 13]: 50). However, it is just the fact that something external is integrated into a commodity that gives it value and weight against other bodies (ibid.: 51).

To exemplify using a conundrum that is now emerging in relation to social media, which has not been covered much in research, we can consider the concept of influencers. Influencers are persons (and to that, automated influencers exist too) who share pictures, messages and other content via social media platforms. Very often this includes marketing messages such as clothes they "like" and similar. As per recent developments in marketing law, influencers are increasingly forced to mark certain things as advertisements so that consumers can distinguish between an influencer's commercial messages and non-commercial messages (e.g. Commercial Practices Directive 2005/29/EC Appendix: 22). However, the entire idea that an influencer runs their popularity around is the fact that they can assemble many others to engage in their digital persona. It is this engagement that, in turn, generates the possibility of selling advertisements as part of the general content. Consequently, the feed, officially owned as intellectual property (in all its layered elements) is a form of property of the influencer, (which however further tends to be contractually controlled by the platform), and the way that it works is via drawing the right bodies to each other. Furthermore, the affective aspects of influencers are also that they, as private persons, can act in ways that are otherwise regulated in marketing laws or similar regulations. This implies, for example, that an influencer can act in sexist or racist ways as long as such actions are not contractually regulated by a platform owner, or it does not cross the limits of free speech. The ways that certain poses or behaviours in this way can ride on dominant forms of desire imply a form of leveraging on affect that reaches beyond what property, marketing and data regulations can capture.

In this way, the conceptual boundaries for private property are again transgressed by capitalism itself. Consequently, property rights as coded and controlled by law become even less visible, or sensible. The transformation of property in itself is not necessarily something that is necessarily *felt* by those of us experiencing it. Rather the way that information is dematerialized, and our lives are enmeshed in digital technologies, occur in a manner that makes us feel comfortable, if anything at all. The changing boundaries of property control taking place here is alluring in this sense, as it works on an affective register that makes it hard to either see or resist. In returning to the property versus personhood divide, one can easily imagine how it would be more noticeable and felt, being forced to sell one's body parts turned into commodities to be sold at a market. Or, as in the intellectual property case of *Moore v. Regents*, how the tangibility of the body part, that later is used to have information extracted, invokes a feeling of a clearer conflict between one's private persona and property. To surgically remove a body part for the purpose of turning it into property is hence likely to *feel* worse, than being dazzled by the charming atmosphere of influencers, their perfect homes – relationships, attire, make-up and so on. Looking at it from an abstract perspective, or a view from nowhere, there is of course nothing wrong with creating environments that "feel" good for the bodies that occupy it. In fact, as Philippopoulos-Mihalopoulos points out, this is the dream of all orders of governance: to become so integrated with the bodies it incorporates that it disappears of their sight (Philippopoulos-Mihalopoulos 2013). However, the engineered atmosphere that both these types of phenomena are entangled with here are affective in the sense that they exploit emotional aspects to draw bodies together. In this constructed intimacy between bodies, the connections and feelings (no matter how sincere they might be) are still converted into capital.

For this reason, property in the digitally mediated society also needs to be understood as a control form that reaches beyond legal conceptual divides between property, marketing and other expressions, in order to convert emotions into capital. In such a transition of property, we still remember that property is, of course, always affective in the sense that it keeps bodies together or apart. A clear example is the story that returns over and over here in how, by legally defining property rights as something that a human can hold over a thing, one defines a certain affective bond excluding others. What is new in the posthuman condition is that the affective registers of property can be played out with a bigger force, as well as in more subtle ways. This "humanist-posthuman" excess of affective control is particularly visible in the emotional capitalism taking place in social media platforms. Emotional exploitation and control is however not the only way in which we can speak about an affective turn of property in relation to digitalization and beyond. The next step is to also be able to place the wider role of affect in relation to property control beyond the emotional control over humans.

Posthuman Property as Affective Property Beyond the Human

As has been recounted throughout this book, posthuman property is a form of control that exceeds the common idea of private property, as it transcends our understanding of the human and the human body. This shaping and drawing together of bodies is an affective process, which has always overwritten conceptual boundaries of property law, as discussed in the previous chapters. The digital economy, however, intensifies this affective characteristic of property in the way that affect becomes both a commodity and a radiating materiality of commodities, bringing bodies together, for the creation of monetary value. This is the discourse of property as always being about exploitation and distribution of part-whole connections, but in ways that involve many more bodies than those of humans and their senses of belonging.

Posthuman property creates particular ways of belonging in how it displaces both anthropocentric understanding of matter and relations while producing new ones. Property here is no longer about an object that can be defined by human-made law, over which persons can have control. Consequently, the affective shape of posthuman property also exceeds the human emotional spectrum. What makes this form of property particularly posthuman is furthermore the continuous process of extraction from both human and nonhuman bodies. Such a process is, as discussed, particularly visible in the way that information is dematerialized and turned into a commodity. It also gains intensified speed when data is utilized for different forms of AI. Posthuman property is furthermore productive in the sense that it uses its extracted resources – whether it is datasets, people seeking company in dating apps, or minerals – to draw bodies together into a posthuman condition.

In considering property to have this affective capacity, it also becomes possible to consider property, and property control, without the human. This is by no means a new thing in terms of property control, as the company after all can take the shape of persona *ficta* that has the legal capacity to own things. The theoretical conundrums surfacing in intellectual property law from time to time like: "can a monkey have copyright in a selfie it took?" or "will AI be able to get patents or copyrights to objects it innovates/creates?" are just two recent and standard examples of how the "nonhuman" owner already exists both theoretically and practically today. These questions obviously riff on the assumption that there exists a person–thing divide and hence whether a "thing" can come to take on the human role and own other things. This is however not an interesting question from a posthumanist perspective. The reason for this is that it is one thing to base a concept of ownership on a legal concept that ultimately falls back on human responsibility, and another to consider the ways in which property exceeds also the human that is supposed to be in the loop (somewhere). Whether or not we believe that automation will end both work and capital accumulation, someone will still be in control of these processes. It is the way that such control will be carried out, the distribution of who will have a place and who will not, that is the focus for creating an alternative vision of property. The point that posthuman property makes shows that property has very little to do with how a thinking human (a person) can own something (a thing) and is much more about how the advanced capitalism we live under (or if it is something worse) controls which forms of life are at all possible.

In understanding the distribution of bodies as property at work as a form of affective control, one furthermore paves the way for highlighting (and changing) orders of domination. As discussed, the modern concept of property traditionally includes an idea of objects that are considered as commodities in an industrial capitalist sense. Property scholars such as Harris, have shed light on why it is pertinent to consider also whiteness as a form of property. Doing so furthermore aligns with an affective line of thinking about property. Connecting such ideas of property with posthumanist theory in general, and the digitalized society in particular, implies that racism, sexism and speciesism, as well as other orders deeply related to capitalism, can be considered as internal to property. As also discussed, such affective orders are currently being explored in several disciplines related to both the digitalization of society, as well as artificial intelligence, although not under the concept of property.

Crossing over the human and nonhuman binary, including related divisions such as human versus nature and subject versus object, informs posthumanist thinking and advanced capitalism alike. If what separated humans from nonhumans was a distinction between the degree to which one could control (and not be controlled as) property, the increased commodification and control of *all* bodies may be understood as a flattening out of differences built upon the human and nonhuman divide. The transversal of such binaries, however, tends to be made invisible in information-centred discourses. Information is then understood as something that can be captured and controlled via intellectual property rights, trade secret rights, or protected via data protection regulations, product reliability protection, consumer sale of goods laws, anti-discrimination regulations and similar. Even when relational or critical interventions are called for in these areas, they tend to stay within assumptions that divide human and nonhumans along humanist lines. This is visible in how "natural resources" and "physical" property in general are excluded from evaluations of the vastness of property control in digitally mediated societies, or more narrowly about digital media. Meanwhile, as discussed throughout, the ecological aspects of both digitalization in general and emerging AI in particular are becoming increasingly known. These processes are also bundled up with the exploitation of both humans and resources, sometimes very similar to more explicitly colonialist times. The question then becomes: how can we move towards an understanding of property as an entanglement, or rather, an ecology that breaks up with continuous colonial and postcolonial processes?

Here, one needs to be ready to face that the question might possibly not be one of property or no property but rather which form it can and should take. As Bratton puts it: "In order to govern geopolitical flows, emergent geopolitics requires good and sufficient information about what it governs so as to identify and enforce the broad outlines of any plan" (Bratton 2019: 58–59). For this reason, the property forms and objects discussed here could naturally also be put in use to *plan* a more sustainable ecology. To this it may be noted that Davies suggests that "[m]ovement of property away from its colonial emphases can (also) be promoted by inflecting it with different ethical language, one that emphasizes mutuality rather than rights and control" (Davies 2020: 1112–1113). This points exactly at the deeply relational role that property *always* plays, but also in shifting it towards a direction where bodies can assemble in a more durable manner.

As pointed out, the mere insight into understanding all forms of matter as co-relational and co-dependent beyond the humanist perspective in itself also changes which relationships can be seen and emerge. Understanding that both human and nonhuman bodies are connected and create ecologies is the first move towards posthumanist ethics. As Braidotti puts it: "The bodily self's interaction with his or her environment can either increase or decrease that body's *potentia*" (Braidotti 2019: 178). Making cartographies that can account for alternative connections beyond the current forms of power are ethical moves as such. Finding and understanding how bodies can gain or regain power come from many directions that usually are not understood to form part of digitalization, AI etc. (Vickers and Allado-McDowell 2021: 9–36; Crawford 2021: 9–14).

The posthumanist relational ethics also comes with the capacity of an affirmative non-exhaustive characteristics. The ethical move is to get going, and put the motion back into e-motion, as Braidotti puts it (2019: 181). Even if property draws bodies to each other, in a manner that will exhaust them all, there is also endless potential for new relationships to take place. Some bodies, as well as entire species, may die and others have been killed already, but this is not a reason for passivity, but for turning towards other and new becomings. This, of course, does not mean surrendering to an accelerationist logic. Affirmative ethics as the power to move on, and to move differently, is not the same as affirmation in our daily use of the term, but as a way of recuperating and collectivising in order to unleash something livelier than capital. Helping us in this task is, of course, capital itself, when it transforms us all into commodities, including our very communism, as Hardt (2010) put it. However, it is also in this phase that we realize there is nothing left to own, nothing left to control, but other worlds, already waiting.

Property or Something Worse: Moving towards Posthumanism via Posthuman Property

There is a popular saying by Fred Jameson that it is easier to imagine the end of the world than to imagine the end of capitalism. In the same manner, it now seems easier to reimagine old legal rules on fairness, accountability, transparency and ethics in new technological settings that have long surpassed such ideas of governance, than it is to imagine the end of property. The question has become even more complicated under advanced capitalism in which property control unfolds in multiple ways, through the claiming of more and more elements as business assets, as well as through *de facto* control of both human and nonhuman bodies. "Capital as property frees land from its spatial fixity. Information as property frees capital from its fixity in a particular object" (Wark 2019: 124). However, the affective capacity of property also makes it into something worse. This is so because when materialities such as land and information were transformed into capital, there was still an idea in law that those objects could be defined and limited. Consequently, a response from a legal theorist on problems caused by private property could be to limit the concept of property further in scope and time. Now this is no longer possible. The reason for this, as has been discussed throughout, is based on several factors and complex layers of how property control is constructed. It seems today as an impossible question to answer how one would even imagine a construction for limitation, and redistribution, of property when property is no longer about sharing a predefined thing or a certain type of an immaterial object, but functions as a dispersed order of control that reaches deep into the control over our intimate desires. This lack of oversight is a problem in the sense that what we are facing now is both property in the traditional sense, as well as something worse.

However, it is still around the question of the redistribution of property that a posthumanist perspective needs to remain, in order to fulfil the ethical goals of moving towards a radically sustainable future (cf. Braidotti 2013: 191–194). This need is determined in the way that posthuman bodies cannot avoid it: they must keep redistributing their matter, keep belonging partially to some bodies, while not to other bodies. This is what it means to remain in being, whether one remains on the spot or moves nomadically in space. Some parts of one's body are still bound to move, as long as there are other bodies present. This need is, however, also indetermined in the manner that bodies constantly fight over *how* distribution occurs and between what and whom. It is for this reason that it becomes even more vital to consider questions of distribution in a posthuman sense, in order for posthumanist belonging to take place.

What makes a "simple" call for the redistribution of the wealth derived from our posthuman bodies more complicated than usual is that the overview assumed in law, and legal theory, from where to draw lines and limits, is limited (by power or other matter). Hence, we cannot provide a single or objective answer for what to do, even if such an answer was desirable. What we can do however, is to provide maps for the ways that property effectuates itself in this posthuman era, and attempt to capture and redistribute the resources differently.

A first step in this direction is, then, to acknowledge that the question for property theory is no longer to circulate around conceptual boundaries of what is human and what is nonhuman, persons or things, personhood or property, but which connections are activated, which forces are unleashed. What can therefore be rediscovered here, is a thoroughly materialist conception of both property and law. This is a future in which the excessive potentiality vested in each posthuman body, in the encounter with other bodies, implies that something always escapes: we do not know what a body can do (Deleuze 1988: 18). That is the message of both fear and hope, as well as the movement towards a redistribution of bodies along the lines of posthumanist ethics.

References

Arvidsson, Matilda (2018). Targeting, gender and international posthumanitarian law and practice: Framing the question of the human in international humanitarian law. *Australian Feminist Law Journal 44(1)*: 9–28.

Books, Book Chapters and Articles

Adkins, Lisa, Cooper, Melinda, and Konings, Martin (2020). *The Asset Economy*. Cambridge/Medford: Polity Press.

Agamben, Giorgio (1998). *Homo Sacer: Sovereign Power and Bare Life*. Stanford, California: Stanford University Press.

Ahmed, Sara (2008). Open forum imaginary prohibitions: some preliminary remarks on the founding gestures of the 'new materialism'. *European Journal of Women's Studies 15* (1): 23–39. https://doi.org/10.1177/1350506807084854.

Alexander, Gregory S., Peñalver, Eduardo M., Singer, Joseph W., and Underkuffler, Laura S. (2009). A statement of progressive property, *Cornell Law Faculty Publications*, 11. http://scholarship.law.cornell.edu/facpub/11.

Amaro, Ramon (2021). Machine learning, surveillance and the politics of visibility, in Vickers, Ben, and Allado-McDowell, K., Eds., *Atlas of Anomalous AI*. Ignota Books.

Amoore, Louise (2020). *Cloud Ethics: Algorithms and the Attributes of Ourselves and Others*. Durham/London: Duke University Press

Arendt, Hannah (1998[1958]). *The Human Condition*. Chicago/London: The University of Chicago Press.

Arvidsson, Matilda (2021). Maskininlärning och rättsligt beslutsfattande: Migrationsrättsliga frågor och AI, in Noll, Gregor, Ed., *AI och rätten*. Lund: Studentlitteratur.

Barad, Karen (2007). *Meeting the Universe Halfway: Quantum Physics and the Entanglement of Matter and Meaning*. Durham/London: Duke University Press.

Barlow, Perry (1996). A declaration of the independence of cyberspace, online at: www.eff.org/cyberspace-independence.

Bastani, Aaron (2019). *Fully Automated Luxury Communism – A Manifesto*. London: Verso Books.

Benjamin, Ruha (2019). *Race After Technology*. Medford: Polity Press.

Bennett, Jane (2010). *Vibrant Matter, a Political Ecology of Things*. Durham/London: Duke University Press.

Bentham, Jeremy (1846). Principles of the civil code, Classical Utilitarian Website (CUWS), available at www.laits.utexas.edu/poltheory/bentham/pcc/index.html.

Bhandar, Brenna (2012). Disassembling legal form: Ownership and the racial body, in Stone, M., Wallrua, Illan, and Douzinas, Costas, Eds., *New Critical Legal Thinking*. Oxon/New York: Routledge.

Bhandar, Brenna (2018). *Colonial Lives of Property: Law, Land, and Racial Regimes of Property*. Durham/London: Duke University Press.

Bhandar, Brenna, and Goldberg-Hiller, Jonathan (2015). *Plastic Materialities: Politics, Legality, and Metamorphosis in the Work of Catherine Malabou*. Durham/London: Duke University Press.

Bietti, Elettra (2020). From ethics washing to ethics bashing: A view on tech ethics from within moral philosophy, DRAFT – Final Paper Published in the Proceedings to ACM FAT★ Conference (FAT★ 2020), available at https://papers.ssrn.com/sol3/papers.cfm?abstract_id=3513182.

Birch, Kean, and Muniesa, Fabian (2020). *Assetization: Turning Things into Assets in Technoscientific Capitalism*. Cambridge, MA: MIT Press.

Bostrom, Nick (2005). A history of transhumanist thought, available at www.nickbostrom.com/papers/history.pdf.

boyd, danah (2012). White flight in networked publics? How race and class shaped American teen engagement with MySpace and Facebook. In Chow-White, Petet A., and Nakamura, Lisa, Eds., *Race After the Internet*. Oxon/New York: Routledge.

Boyle, James (1996). *Shamans, Software, & Spleens, Law and the Construction of the Information Society*. Cambridge, MA: Harvard University Press.

Boyle, James (2003). The second enclosure movement and the construction of the public domain, available at http://scholarship.law.duke.edu/cgi/viewcontent.cgi?article=1273&context=lcp.

Braidotti, Rosi (2002). *Metamorphoses, Towards a Materialist Theory of Becoming*. Cambridge/Malden: Polity Press in association with Blackwell Publishers Ltd.

Braidotti, Rosi (2011). *Nomadic Subjects, Embodiment and Sexual Difference in Contemporary Feminist Theory*, 2nd ed. New York: Columbia University Press.

Braidotti, Rosi (2012). *"Becoming-world" in After Cosmopolitanism*. Hoboken: Taylor and Francis.

Braidotti, Rosi (2013). *The Posthuman*. Cambridge/Malden: Polity Press.

Braidotti, Rosi (2019). *Posthuman Knowledge*. Cambridge: Polity Press.

Bratton, Benjamin (2015). *The Stack, On Software and Sovereignty*. Cambridge, MA: MIT Press.

Bratton, Benjamin (2019). *Terraforming*. Moscow: Strelka Press.

Bratton, Benjamin (2021a). Synthethic gardens: Another model for AI and design, in Vickers, Ben, and Allado-McDowell, K., Eds., *Atlas of Anomalous AI*. Ignota Books

Bratton, Benjamin (2021b). *The Revenge of the Real*. London/New York: Verso Books.

Brians, Ella (2011). The 'virtual' body and the strange persistence of the flesh: Deleuze, cyberspace and the posthuman, in Guillaume, L., and Hughes, J., Eds., *Deleuze and the Body*, Edinburgh: Edinburgh University Press.

Brown, Wendy (2015). *Undoing the Demos*. Brooklyn, NY: Zone Books.

Bruncevic, Merima (2014). *Fixing the Shadows, Access to Art and the Cultural Commons*. Gothenburg: Gothenburg University.

Bruncevic, Merima (2017). *Law, Art and the Commons*. Oxon/New York: Routledge.

Bruncevic, Merima, and Käll, Jannice (2016). *Modern Immaterialrätt*. Stockholm: Liber.

Burk, Dan L. (2014). Copyright and the architecture of digital delivery. *First Monday* 19 (10) available at http://firstmonday.org/ojs/index.php/fm/article/view/5544/4123.

Butler, Judith (2011). *Bodies that Matter*. Oxon/New York: Routledge.

Chandler, David (2018). Digital governance in the anthropocene: The rise of the correlational machine, in Chandler, David and Fuchs, Christian, Eds., *Digital Objects, Digital Subjects: Interdisciplinary Perspectives on Capitalism, Labour and Politics in the Age of Big Data*. London: University of Westminster Press.

Chandler, David, and Fuchs, Christian (2018). Introduction, in Chandler, David, and Fuchs, Christian, Eds., *Digital Objects, Digital Subjects: Interdisciplinary Perspectives on Capitalism, Labour and Politics in the Age of Big Data*. London: University of Westminster Press.

Chesbrough, Henry (2003). *Open Innovation: The New Imperative for Creating and Profiting from Technology*. Boston: Harvard Business School Press.

Chesbrough, Henry (2011). *Open Services Innovation*. San Francisco: Jossey-Bass.

Chon, Margaret (1993). Postmodern progress: Reconsidering the copyright and patent power. *DePaul L. Rev.* 43: 97, available at http://via.library.depaul.edu/law-review/vol43/iss1/3.

Chun, Wendy Hui Kyong (2011). *Programmed Visions, Software and Memory*. Cambridge, MA: MIT Press.

Cohen, Julie E. (2012). *Configuring the Networked Self, Law, Code, and the Play of Everyday Practice*. New Haven: Yale University Press.

Cohen, Julie E. (2019). *Beyond Truth and Power: The Legal Constructions of Informational Capitalism*. Oxford: Oxford University Press.

Cook, Diane J., Augusto, Juan C., and Jakkula, Vikramaditya R. (2009). Ambient intelligence: Technologies, applications, and opportunities. *Pervasive and Mobile Computing* 5(4): 277–298.

Coole, Diana, and Frost, Samantha (2010). Introducing the new materialisms, in Coole, Diana, and Frost, Samantha, Eds., *New Materialisms, Ontology, Agency, and Politics*. Durham/London: Duke University Press.

Cooper, Davina (2007). Opening up ownership: Community belonging, belongings, and the productive life of property. *Law and Social Inquiry* 32(3): 625.

Cooper, Melinda (2008). *Life as Surplus, Biotechnology and Capitalism in the Neoliberal, Era*. Seattle: University of Washington Press.

Couldry, Nick, and Mejias, A. Ulises (2019). *The Costs of Connection: How Data Is Colonising Human Life and Appropriating It for Capitalism*. Stanford: Stanford University Press.

Crawford, Kate (2021). *Atlas of AI: Power, Politics, and the Planetary Costs of Artificial Intelligence*. New Haven: Yale University Press.

Crawford, Kate, and Joler, Vladan (2018). Anatomy of an AI System The Amazon Echo as an anatomical map of human labor, data and planetary resources, available at https://anatomyof.ai.

Crawford, Kate, and Paglen, Trevor (2019, September 19). Excavating AI: The politics of training sets for machine learning, available at https://excavating.ai.

Crenshaw, Kimberlé (2008). *Mapping the Margins: Intersectionality, Identity Politics and Violence against Women of Color*, in Bailey, Alison, and Cuomo, Chris, Eds., *The Feminist Philosophy Reader* (pp. 279–309). New York: McGraw-Hill..

Cubitt, Sean (2016). *Finite Media: Environmental Implications of Digital Media*. Durham/London: Duke University Press.

Darling, Kate (2021). *The New Breed: How to Think about Robots*. Dublin: Penguin House

Davies, Margaret (2002). *Asking, the Law Question*, 2nd ed. Sydney/Melbourne/Brisbane: Law Book Co. of Australasia.

Davies, Margaret (2008a). *Property: Meanings, Histories, Theories*. Oxon/New York: Routledge-Cavendish.

Davies, Margaret (2008b). Feminism and flat law theory. *Feminist Legal Studies* 16: 281–304.

Davies, Margaret (2017). *Law Unlimited, Materialism, Pluralism and Legal Theory*. Abingdon/New York: Routledge.

Davies, Margaret (2020). Can property be justified in an entangled world? *Globalizations* 17(7): 1104–1117.

Davies, Margaret, and Naffine, Ngaire (2001). *Property as Persons. Legal Debates about Property and Personality*. Aldershot/Burlington: Dartmouth Publishing Company and Ashgate Publishing Limited and Ashgate Publishing Company.

Deleuze, Gilles (1988[1970]). *Spinoza, Practical Philosophy*. San Francisco: City Lights Books.

Deleuze, Gilles (1992[1968]). *Expressionism in Philosophy: Spinoza*. New York: Zone Books.

Deleuze, Gilles (1992). Postscript on the societies of control, available at www.jstor.org/stable/778828.

Deleuze, Gilles (2002[1995, 1965, and 1972]). *Pure Immanence: Essays on A Life*. Brooklyn: Zone Books.

Deleuze, Gilles (2016). Vi och Spinoza, in Montan, F. and Spindler, F., Eds., *Att läsa Spinoza*. Hägersten, Sweden: Tankekraft Förlag.

Deleuze, Gilles, and Guattari, Félix (2013[1998]). *A Thousand Plateaus, Capitalism and Schizophrenia*, Trans. Massumi, Brian. London/New York: Bloomsbury Publishing Plc.

Dempster, Craig, and Lee, John (2015). *The Rise of the Platform Marketer: Performance Marketing with Google, Facebook, and Twitter, Plus the Latest High-Growth Digital Advertising Platforms*. Hoboken: Wiley Press

Deseriis, Marco (2018). The politics of condividuality. *Technoecologies*, available at https://transversal.at/transversal/0318/deseriis/en.

Dolphijn, Rick, and van der Tuin, Iris (2011). Pushing dualism to an extreme: On the philosophical impetus of a new materialism. *Continental Philosophy Review* 44: 383–400.

Dolphijn, Rick, and van der Tuin, Iris (2012). *New Materialism: Interviews & Cartographies*. Open Humanities Press, e-book, available at http://quod.lib.umich.edu/cgi/p/pod/dod-idx/new-materialism-interviews-cartographies.pdf?c=ohp;idno=11515701.0001.001.

Douzinas, Costas, and Gearey, Adam (2005). *Critical Jurisprudence, the Political Philosophy of Justice*. Oxford and Portland, OR: Hart Publishing.

Ducato, Rossana (2020). Private ordering of online platforms in smart urban mobility: The case of Uber's rating system, in Finck, Michèle et al., Eds., *Smart Urban Mobility*. Berlin/Heidelberg: Springer.

Duchich, Stefan (2017–2018). These walls can talk! Securing digital privacy in the smart home under the fourth amendment. *Duke L. & Tech. Rev.* 16: I.

Dyer-Witheford, Nick, Mikkola Kjosen, Atle, and Steinhoff, James (2019). *Inhuman Power: Artificial Intelligence and the Future of Capitalism*. London: Pluto Press.

Elkin-Koren, Niva (2005). What contracts can't do: The limits of private ordering in facilitating a creative commons. *Fordham Law Review* 74.

Esposito, Roberto (2015). *Persons and Things*. Cambridge/Malden: Polity Press.

Ferrando, Francesca (2019). *Philosophical Posthumanism*. UK/New York: Bloomsbury Academic.

de Filippi, Primavera, and Hassan, Samer (2016). Blockchain technology as a regulatory technology: From code is law to law is code. *First Monday* 21(12).

de Filippi, Primavera, and Wright, Aaron (2019). *Blockchain and the Law, The Rule of Code*. Cambridge, MA: Harvard University Press.

Drahos, Peter, and Braithwaite, J. (2002). *Information Feudalism: Who Owns the Knowledge Economy?*New York: The New Press.

Dvorak, Tomás, and Parikka, Jussi (2021). *Photography Off the Scale*. Edinburgh: Edinburgh University Press.

Edwards, Lilian (2015, December). Privacy, security and data protection in smart cities: A critical EU law perspective. *CREATe Working Paper*, 11.

Floridi, Luciano (2014). *The 4th Revolution: How the Infosphere is Reshaping Reality*. Oxford: Oxford University Press.

Foray, Dominique (2006). *The Economics of Knowledge*. Cambridge/London: The MIT Press.

Foucault, Michel (1984). *The Foucault Reader, An Introduction to Foucault's Thought*, Rainbow, P., Ed. New York: Vintage Books.

Foucault, Michel (2002[1966]). *The Order of Things, An Archaeology of Human Sciences*. London: Routledge.

Fuchs, Christian (2019). Karl Marx in the age of big data capitalism, in Chandler, David, and Fuchs, Christian, Eds., *Digital Objects, Digital Subjects: Interdisciplinary Perspectives on Capitalism, Labour and Politics in the Age of Big Data* (pp. 151–164). London: University of Westminster Press.

Gawer, Anna (2011). Platform dynamics and strategies: From products to services, in Gawer, A., Ed., *Platforms, Markets and Innovation*. Cheltenham, UK: Edward Elgar.

Gianopoulou, Eleni, Yström, Anna, Ollila, Susanna, Fredberg, Tobias, and Elmqvist, Maria (2010). implications of openness: A study into (all) the growing literature on open innovation. *Journal of Technology Management & Innovation* 5(3): 162–180.

Glavå, Mats, and Petrusson, Ulf (2002). Illusionen om rätten- juristprofessionen och ansvaret för rättskonstruktionerna, in Askeland, Bjarte, and Bernt , Jan Fridthjof, Eds., *Erkjennelse og engasjement: minnesseminar for David Roland Doublet, 1954–2000*. Bergen: Fagbokfrolag.

Glavå, Mats, and Petrusson, Ulf (2008). Law in a global knowledge economy: Following the path of Scandinavian sociolegal theory. *Law and Society, Scandinavian Studies in Law* 53: 94–133, available at www.scandinavianlaw.se/pdf/53-5.pdf.

Goodrich, Peter (1999). The critic's love of the law: Intimate observations on an insular jurisdiction. *Law and Critique* 10: 343–360.

Goodwin, Peter (2019). Wage-workers, not slaves: Reflections on Jack Qiu's chapter, in Chandler, David, and Fuchs, Christian, Eds., *Digital Objects, Digital Subjects: Interdisciplinary Perspectives on Capitalism, Labour and Politics in the Age of Big Data*. London: University of Westminster Press.

Graham, Mark, and Haarstad, Håvard (2011). Transparency and development: Ethical consumption through Web 2.0 and the internet of things. *Information Technologies & International Development* 7(1).

Granstrand, Ove (1999). Intellectual capitalism – An overview. *Nordic Journal of Political Economy* 25.

Granstrand, Ove (2000). The shift towards intellectual capitalism – The role of infocom technologies. *Research Policy* 29: 1061–1080.

Granstrand, Ove, and Holgersson, Marcus (2014). The challenge of closing open innovation: The intellectual property disassembly problem. *Research-Technology Management* 57(5): 19–25.

Greenfield, Adam (2006). *Everywhere: The Dawning Age of Ubiquitous Computing*. Berkeley: New Riders Publishing.

Greenfield, Adam (2013). *Against the Smart City*, 1.3 ed. New York City: Do projects.

Greenfield, Adam (2018). *Radical Technologies and Everyday Life*. London/NY: Verso Books.

Grosz, Elizabeth (2017). *The Incorporeal, Ontology, Ethics, and the Limits of Materialism*. New York: Columbia University Press.

Günel, Gökçe, and Halpern, Orit (2017). FCJ-215 demoing unto death: Smart cities, environment, and preemptive hope. *Fiberculture Journal*, available at https://twentynine.fibreculturejournal.org/wp-content/pdfs/FCJ-215HalpernGunel.pdf.

Gustafsson, Håkan (1998). Immanence of law, in Hirvonen, Ari, Ed., *Polycentricity, The Multiple Scenes of Law*. London/New York: Pluto.

Guattari, Félix (1995[1992]). *Chaosmosis, an Ethico-Aesthetic Paradigm*. Bloomington/Indianapolis: Indiana University Press.

Guattari, Félix (2008[1989]). *The Three Ecologies*. London/New York: Continuum.

Gunneflo, Markus (2016). *Targeted Killing: A Legal and Political History*. Cambridge: Cambridge University Press.

Gustafsson, Håkan (2002). *Rättens polyvalens. En rättsvetenskaplig studie av sociala rättigheter och rättssäkerhet*. Gothenburg: Gothenburg University.

Gustafsson, Håkan (2011). *Dissens, om det rättsliga vetandet*. Göteborg: Jure Förlag AB.

Halberstam, Jack, and Livingston, Ira (1995). Introduction: Posthuman Bodies, in Halberstam, Jack, and Livingston, Ira, Eds., *Posthuman Bodies*. Bloomington and Indianapolis:Indiana University Press.

Haraway, Donna (1991). *Simians, Cyborgs, and Women. The Reinvention of Nature*. London: Free Association Books.

Haraway, Donna (1997). Modest_Witness@Second_Millennium. FemaleMan©_Meets_Oncomouse™. London/New York: Routledge.

Haraway, Donna (2008). *When Species Meet*. Minneapolis: University of Minnesota Press.

Haraway, Donna (2016). *Staying with the Trouble, Making Kin in the Chthulucene*. Durham/London: Duke University Press.

Hardin, Garett (1968). The tragedy of the commons. *Science* 162(3859): 1243–1248.

Harding, Sandra (2015). *Objectivity and Diversity, Another Logic of Scientific Research*. London/Chicago: The University of Chicago Press.

Hardt, Antonio (2010). The common in communism, available at http://seminaire.sam izdat.net/IMG/pdf/Microsoft_Word_-_Michael_Hardt.pdf.

Hardt, Michael, and Negri, Antonio (2019). *Empire*. Cambridge: Harvard University Press.

Harris, I. Cheryl (1993, June). Whiteness as property. *Harvard Law Review*: 1707–1791.

Hayles, N. Kathrine (1999). *How We Became Posthuman, Virtual Bodies in Cybernetics, Literature, and Informatics*. Chicago: The University of Chicago Press.

Heller, Michael A. (1998). The tragedy of the anticommons: Property in the transition from marx to markets. *Harvard Law Review* 111: 3621–3688.

Heller, Michael A., and Eisenberg, Rebecca (1998). Can patents deter innovation? The anticommons. *Biomedical Research. Science* 280(5364): 698–701.

Herian, Rob (2018). *Regulating Blockchain: Critical Perspectives in Law and Technology*. Oxon/New York: Routledge.

Hester, Helen (2018). *Xenofeminism*. Cambridge/Medford: Polity Press.

Hildebrandt, Mireille (2015). *Smart Technologies and the End(s) of Law*. Cheltenham UK/Northampton, MA, USA: Edward Elgar.

Hildebrandt, Mireille (2020). *Law for Computer Scientists and Other Folk*. Oxford: Oxford University Press.

Hohfeld, Wesley (1913). Some fundamental legal conceptions as applied in legal reasoning. *Yale Law Journal* 23: 16.

Hohfeld, Wesley Newcomb (1946). *Fundamental Legal Conceptions as Applied in Judicial Reasoning*. Yale University Press.

Huadong Guo, Jie Liu, Qiu, Yubao, Menenti, Massimo, Chen, Fang, Uhlir, Paul F., Zhang, Li, van Genderen, John, Liang, Dong, Natarajan, Ishwaran, Zhu, Lanwei, and Liu, Jiuliang (2018). The Digital Belt and Road program in support of regional sustainability . *International Journal of Digital Earth* 11(7): 657–669.

Huizingh, Eelko K. R. E. (2011). Open innovation: State of the art and future perspectives. *Technovation* 31(1): 2–9.

Hydén, Håkan (2020). The sociology of digital law and artificial intelligence, in Priban, Jirid, Ed., *Research Handbook on the Sociology of Law*. Cheltenham: Edward Elgar Publishing.

Iljadica, Martha (2016). *Copyright Beyond Law: Regulating Creativity in the Graffiti Subculture*. Oxford: Hart Publishing.

Joler, Vladan (2020). New extractivism: An assemblage of concepts and allegories, available at https://extractivism.online/.

Jungselius, Beata (2019, 9 September). "She liked the picture so I think she liked it." Unpacking the social practice of liking. *Netcom* 33–31/2, available at http://journals.openedition.org/netcom/3849.

Kaldor, Mary (2000). *Nya och gamla krig*. Göteborg: Bokförlaget Daidalos.

Käll, Jannice (2014). *Virtuell tjänsteinnovation? Plattformar för information i gränssnittet mellan ICT och automotive*. Gothenburg: Gothenburg University.

Käll, Jannice (2017). A posthuman data subject? The right to be forgotten and beyond. *German Law Journal* 18(5).

Käll, Jannice (2018). Blockchain control. *Law Critique* 29: 133–140. https://doi.org/10.1007/s10978-018-9227-x.

Käll, Jannice (2020). Governing space through autonomous vehicles, in Finck, Michèle et al. Eds., *Smart Urban Mobility*. Berlin/Heidelberg: Springer.

Käll, Jannice (2021). The potential for new materialist justice through Nordic feminist perspectives of law. *Nordic Journal of Law and Society*, forthcoming.

Kalopkas, Ignas (2019). *Algorithmic Governance, Politics and Law in the Posthuman Era*. Cham: Palgrave Macmillan.

Kapczynski, Amy (2010). Access to knowledge: A conceptual genealogy, in Kirkorian, G., and Kapczynski, A., *Access to Knowledge in the Age of Intellectual Property*. New York: Zone Books.

Karppi, Tero, and Granta, Yvette (2019). Non-artificial non-intelligence: Amazon's Alexa and the frictions of AI. *AI & SOCIETY* 34: 867–876,

Karppi, Tero, Kähkönen, Lotta, Mannevuo, Mona, Pajala, Mari, and Sihvonen, Tanja (2016). Affective capitalism: Investments and investigations. *Ephemera Journal*, 16(4): 1–13.

Keenan, Sara (2015). *Subversive Property, Law and the Production of Spaces of Belonging*. Oxon/New York: Routledge.

Keshavarz, Mahmoud (2019). *The Design Politics of the Passport: Materiality, Immobility, and Dissent*. London: Bloomsbury Visual Arts.

Kirkorian, Gaëlle, and Kapczynski, Amy (2010). *Access to Knowledge in the Age of Intellectual Property*. New York: Zone Books,

Kitchin, Rob (2014, April–June). Big Data, new epistemologies and paradigm shifts. *Big Data & Society*.

Kitchin, Rob, and Dodge, Martin (2011). *Code/Space: Software and Everyday Life*. Cambridge, MA: MIT Press.

Klein, Naomi (2000[1999]). *No Logo, Taking Aim at the Brand Bullies*. Toronto: Knopf Canada.

Laboria, Cuboniks (2018). *The Xenofeminist Manifesto: A Politics for Alienation*. London: Verso Books.

Lee-Morrison, Lila (2019). *Portraits of Automated Facial Recognition: On Machinic Ways of Seeing the Face*, Bielefeld: Division of Art History and Visual Studies.

Lefebvre, Hénri (1991[1974]). *The Production of Space*, Donald Nicholson-Smith trans. Oxford: Basil Blackwell.

Lessig, Lawrence (1999). *Code and Other Laws of Cyberspace*. New York: Basic Books.

Lindholm-Schulz, Helena (2002). *Krig i vår tid*. Lund: Studentlitteratur.

Lindroos-Hovinheimo, Susanna (2021). *Private Selves: Legal Personhood in European Privacy Protection*. Cambridge: Cambridge University Press.

MacCormack, Patricia (2012). *Posthuman Ethics, Embodiment and Cultural Theory*. Burlington/Farnham: Ashgate.

Madero, Marta (2010). *Tabula Picta*. Philadelphia: University of Pennsylvania Press.

Madison, James M. (2009). Notes on a geography of knowledge. Legal Studies Research Paper Series. Working Paper No. 2009–2009. University of Pittsburgh School of Law.

Markou, Christopher, and Deakin, Simon F. (2019). Ex machina lex: Exploring the limits of legal computability, in Deakin, Simon, and Markou, Christopher, Eds., *Is Law Computable? Critical Perspectives on Law + Artificial Intelligence*. Hart Publishing.

Marx, Karl (2013[1969]). *Kapitalet, kritik av den politiska ekonomin*, vol. 1. Lund: Arkiv Förlag.

Marx, Karl, and Engels, Friedrich (2015[1848]). *The Communist Manifesto*, trans. Moore, S. Milton Keynes, UK: Penguin Random House.

Massumi, Brian (2002). *Parables for the Virtual*. Durham: Duke University Press.

Massumi, Brian (2015). *The Politics of Affect*. Cambridge: Polity Press.

Mattern, Shannon (2015). *Deep Mapping the Media City*. Minneapolis: University of Minnesota Press.

Moore, Jason W. (2017). The Capitalocene, Part I: on the nature and origins of our ecological crisis. *The Journal of Peasant Studies 44(3)*: 594–630.

Mbembe, Achille (2003). Necropolitics. *Public Culture* 15(1): 11–40.

Moll, Joanna (2019). *The Hidden Life of an Amazon User*, available at https://ars.electro nica.art/outofthebox/en/amazon/.

Moore, Phoebe V. (2019). E(a)ffective Precarity, control and resistance in the digitalised workplace, in Chandler, D. and Fuchs, C. Eds., *Digital Objects, Digital Subjects: Interdisciplinary Perspectives on Capitalism, Labour and Politics in the Age of Big Data* (pp. 151–164). London: University of Westminster Press.

Morton, Timothy (2013). *Hyperobjects: Philosophy and Ecology after the End of the World*. Minneapolis: The University of Minnesota Press.

Mouffe, Chantal (2005). *On the Political*. Oxon/New York: Routledge.

Moulier-Boutang, Yann (2011[2007]). *Cognitive Capitalism*. Cambridge: Polity Press.

Nakamura, Lisa (2002). *Cybertypes. Race, Ethnicity, and Identity on the Internet*. New York: Routledge.

Nedelsky, Jennifer (2011). *Law's Relations: A Relational Theory of Self, Autonomy, and Law*. New York: Oxford University Press.

Negri, Antonio (2019). The appropriation of fixed capital: A metaphor? in Chandler, Dave, and Fuchs, Christian, Eds., *Digital Objects, Digital Subjects: Interdisciplinary Perspectives on Capitalism, Labour and Politics in the Age of Big Data*. London: University of Westminster Press. https://doi.org/10.25969/mediarep/11944.

Nietzsche, Friedrich (2005[1883–1885]). *Thus Spoke Zarathustra*. New York: Barnes & Noble Books.

Noble, Safiya Umoja (2018). *Algorithms of Oppression: How Search Engines Reinforce Racism*. New York: New York University Press.

Parikka, Jussi (2014). *The Anthrobscene*. Minneapolis: University of Minnesota Press.

Parikka, Jussi (2015). *A Geology of Media*. Cambridge, MA: MIT Press.

Parikka, Jussi (2021). On seeing where there's nothing to see: Practices of light beyond photography, in Dvorak, Tomás, and Parikka, Jussi, Eds., *Photography Off the Scale*, Edinburgh: Edinburgh University Press.

Pasquale, Frank (2015). *The Black Box Society, The Secret Algorithms That Control Money and Information*. Cambridge, MA: Harvard University Press.

Pasquale, Frank (2020). *New Laws of Robotics, Defending Human Expertise in the Age of AI*. Cambridge: Harvard University Press.

Pasquinelli, Matteo (2018). Metadata society, in Braidotti, Rosi, and Hlavajova, Maria, Eds., *Posthuman Glossary*. London: Bloomsbury.

Petrusson, Ulf (2004). *Intellectual Property and Entrepreneurship, Creating Value in an Intellectual Value Chain*. Gothenburg: Center for Intellectual Property Studies.

Petrusson, Ulf, Rosén, Henrik, and Thornblad, Tobias (2010). Global technology markets, the role of open technology platforms. *Review of Market Integration* 2: 333–393.

Philippopoulos-Mihalopoulos, Andreas (2013). Atmospheres of law: Senses, affects, lawscapes. *Emotion, Space and Society* 7: 35–44.

Philippopoulos-Mihalopoulos, Andreas (2015). *Spatial Justice: Body, Lawscape, Atmosphere*. Oxon/New York: Routledge.

Pistor, Katarina (2019). *The Code of Capital: How the Law Creates Wealth and Inequality*. Princeton, NJ: Princeton University Press.

Poster, Mark (2001). *What's the Matter with the Internet?* Minneapolis: Minnesota University Press.

Pottage, Alain, and Sherman, Ben (2013). *On the Prehistory of Intellectual Property in Concepts of Property*, in Howe, Helena, and Griffiths, Jonathan, Eds., *Intellectual Property Law*. New York: Cambridge University Press.

Qiu, Jack Linchuan (2019). Goodbye iSlave: Making alternative subjects through digital objects, in Chandler, D. and Fuchs, C., Eds., *Digital Objects, Digital Subjects: Interdisciplinary Perspectives on Capitalism, Labour and Politics in the Age of Big Data* (pp. 151–164). London: University of Westminster Press.

Radin, Margaret Jane (1993). *Reinterpreting Property*. Chicago: The University of Chicago Press.

Radin, Margaret Jane (1996). *Contested Commodities*. Cambridge: Harvard University Press.

Radin, Margaret Jane (2000). Humans, computers and binding commitment. *Indiana Law Journal*, 75: 1125–1162.

Radin, Margaret Jane (2003). *Information Tangibility i Economics, Law and Intellectual Property, Seeking Strategies for Research and Teaching in a Developing Field*. Boston: Springer Science and Business Media.

Radin, Margaret Jane (2013). *Boilerplate, The Fine Print, Vanishing Rights, and the Rule of Law*. Princeton: Princeton University Press.

Rogan, Kevin (2019). Anti-intelligence: A Marxist critique of the smart city, available at www.academia.edu/39125907/Anti_intelligence_A_Marxist_critique_of_the_smart_city.

Rose, Carol M. (1990). Property as storytelling: Perspectives from game theory, narrative theory, feminist theory. *Yale Journal of Law & Humanities* 2: 36–57. Available at http://digitalcommons.law.yale.edu/cgi/viewcontent.cgi?article=2821&context=fss_papers.

Rustad, Michael L., and Kulevska, Sanna (2015). Reconceptualizing the right to be forgotten to enable transatlantic data flow. *Harvard Journal of Law and Technology* 28: 349.

Sadowski, J., and Bendor, R. (2019). Selling smartness: Corporate narratives and the smart city as a sociotechnical imaginary. *Science, Technology, & Human Values* 44(3): 540–563. doi:10.1177/0162243918806061.

Sadowski, Jathan (2020). *Too Smart, How Digital Capitalism is Extracting Data, Controlling Our Lives, and Taking Over the World*. Cambridge, MA: MIT Press.

Schollin, Kristoffer (2008). *Digital Rights Management, the New Copyright*. Stockholm: Jure.

Selkälä, Toni, and Rajavuori, Mikko (2017). Traditions, myths, and utopias of personhood: An introduction. *German Law Journal* 18(5): 1017–1068.

Shiva, Vandana (1993). *Monocultures of the Mind*. London/New York/Penang: Zed Books Ltd and Third World Network.

Singler, Beth (2021). When AI prophecy fails, in Vickers, Ben, and Allado-McDowell, K., Eds., *Atlas of Anomalous AI*. Ignota Books.

Spindler, Fredrika (2013). *Deleuze: Tänkande och Blivande*. Munkedal: Glänta Produktion.

Srnicek, Nick (2017). *Platform Capitalism*. Cambridge/Malden: Polity Press.

Steyerl, Hito (2021). A sea of data: apophenia and pattern (mis-)recognition, in Vickers, Ben, and Allado-McDowell, K., Eds., *Atlas of Anomalous AI*. Ignota Books.

Strathern, Marilyn (2004). Losing (out on) intellectual resources, in Pottage, A. and Mundy, M., Eds., *Law, Anthropology, and the Constitution of the Social: Making Persons and Things* (Cambridge Studies in Law and Society, pp. 201–233). Cambridge: Cambridge University Press.

Strubell, Emma, Ganesh, Ananya, and McCallum, Andrew (2019). Energy and policy considerations for deep learning in NLP, available at https://arxiv.org/abs/1906.02243.

Svensson, Eva-Maria (1997). *Genus och Rätt: En Problematisering om Föreställningen av Rätten*. Uppsala: Iustus.

Svensson, Eva-Maria (2013). Boundary-work in legal scholarship, in Gunnarsson, Åsa, Svensson, Eva-Maria, and Davis, Margaret, Eds., *Exploiting the Limits of Law: Swedish Feminism and the Challenge to Pessimism*. Farnham: Ashgate.

Swan, Melanie (2015). *Blockchain: Blueprint for a New Economy*. Sebastopol: O'Reilly Media, Inc.

Tapscott, Alex, and Tapscott, Don (2016). *Blockchain Revolution. How Technology Behind Bitcoin is Changing Money, Business, and the World*. New York: Penguin Random House.

Teece, David J. (2000). *Managing Intellectual Capital*. Oxford: Oxford University Press.

Tegmark, Max (2017). *Life 3.0, Being Human in the Age of Artificial Intelligence*. New York City: Vintage Books.

Terranova, Tiziana (2011). *Network Cultures*. London: Pluto Press.

Thiele, Kathrin (2014). Ethos of diffraction: New paradigms for a (post)humanist ethics. *Parallax* 20(3): 202–216.

Treacy, Pat, and Lawrence, Sophie (2008). FRANDly fire: Are industry standards doing more harm than good? *Journal of Intellectual Property Law & Practice* 3(1).

Tsing Lowenhaupt, Anna (2017). *The Mushroom at the End of the World: On the Possibility of Living in Capitalist Ruins*. Princeton: Princeton University Press.

Turow, Joseph (2011). *The Daily You: How the Advertising Industry is Defining Your Identity and Your Worth*. New Haven: Yale University Press.

Vatanparast, Roxana (2020). The infrastructures of the global data economy: Undersea cables and international law. *Harvard International Law Journal Frontiers* 61.

Valverde, Mariana (2014). The rescaling of feminist analyses of law and state power: From (domestic) subjectivity to (transnational) governance networks. U.C. Irvine L. Rev. 4: 325. https://scholarship.law.uci.edu/ucilr/vol4/iss1/15.

Verzola, Roberto (2010). Undermining abundance counterproductive uses of technology and law in nature, agriculture, and the information sector, in Kirkorian, G., and Kapczynski, A., Eds., *Access to Knowledge in the Age of Intellectual Property*. New York: Zone Books.

Viljoen, Salome (2021). Democratic data: A relational theory for data governance. *Yale Law Journal* 131(2): 577–654.

Visser, Robin (2019). Posthuman policies for creative, smart, eco-cities? Case studies from China. *Economy and Space* 5(1): 206–225.

Wang, Xiaowei (2020). *Blockchain Chicken Farm, And Other Stories of Tech in China's Countryside*. New York: Farrar, Straus and Giroux.

Warf, Barney (2009). From surfaces to networks, in Warf, Barney, and Arias, Santa, Eds., *The Spatial Turn: Interdisciplinary Perspectives*. Oxon/New York: Routledge.

Wark, MacKenzie (2004). *A Hacker Manifesto*. Cambridge/London: Harvard University Press.

Wark, MacKenzie (2019). *Capital is Dead: Is This Something Worse?*London/New York: Verso.

Weizman, Eyal (2019). *Forensic Architecture: Violence at the Thresholds of Detectability*. New York: Zone Books.

Wilhelmsson, Thomas (1994). En social avtalsrätt? Några kommentarer. *Juridisk Tidsskrift* 3.

Wilhelmsson, Thomas (2001). *Senmodern Ansvarsrätt, Privaträtt som Redskap för Mikropolitik*. Uppsala: Iustus.

Wolfe, Cary (2010). *What is Posthumanism?*Minneapolis: University of Minnesota Press.

Wolfe, Cary (2016). "Life" and "the Living," Law and Norm, in Braverman, I., Ed., *Animals, Biopolitics, Law: Lively Legalities*. Oxon/New York: Routledge.

Yusoff, Kathryn (2019). *A Billion Black Anthropocenes or None*. Minnesota: University of Minnesota Press.

Zittrain, Jonathan (2006). The generative internet. *Harvard Law Review* 119: 1974.

Zuboff, Shosana (2019). *The Age of Surveillance Capitalism: The Fight for a Human Future at the New Frontier of Power*. London: Profile Books Ltd.

Non-Academic Articles

Buhr, Sarah (2014, 18 September). Facebook Won't budge on letting drag queens keep their names. *Techcrunch*, available at http://techcrunch.com/2014/09/18/facebook-wont-budge-on-letting-drag-queens-keep-their-names/.

Burgess, Matt (2020, 10 December). Co-op is using facial recognition tech to scan and track shoppers. Available at www.wired.co.uk/article/coop-facial-recognition.

Derblom Jobe, Michelle (2017). Nu förbjuds sexistisk och rasistisk reklam i Stockholms stad. Available at www.svt.se/nyheter/lokalt/stockholm/nu-forbjuds-sexistisk-och-ra sistisk-reklam-i-stockholms-stad.

Eady, Trent (2020). Tesla's deep learning at scale: Using billions of miles to train neural networks. Available at https://towardsdatascience.com/teslas-deep-learning-at-sca le-7eed85b235d3.

The Economist (2017, 6 May). Fuel of the future: Data is giving rise to a new economy. Available at www.economist.com/briefing/2017/05/06/data-is-giving-rise-to-a-new-economy.

Hao, Karen (2019). Training a single AI model can emit as much carbon as five cars in their lifetimes: Deep learning has a terrible carbon footprint. *MIT Technology Review*, available at www.technologyreview.com/2019/06/06/239031/training-a-single-ai-model-can-emit-as-much-carbon-as-five-cars-in-their-lifetimes/.

Jackson, Jasper (2016). Sadiq Khan moves to ban body-shaming ads from London transport. London mayor wants to stop running ads that promote unrealistic body expectations and demean women. *The Guardian*, available at www.theguardian.com/media/2016/jun/13/sadiq-khan-moves-to-ban-body-shaming-ads-from-london-transport.

Käll, J. (2017, 27 March). Google and Facebook can't just make fake news disappear, fake news is too big and messy to solve with algorithms or editors because the problem is … us. *Backchannel*, available at https://backchannel.com/google-and-facebook-cant-just-make-fake-news-disappear-48f4b4e5fbe8.

Levy, Stephen (2014, 21 November). Hackers at 30: "Hackers" and "Information Wants to Be Free." *Wired*, available at www.wired.com/story/hackers-at-30-hackers-and-information-wants-to-be-free/.

Manaugh, Geoff (2015, 11 November). The dream life of driverless cars. *New York Times*, available at www.nytimes.com/2015/11/15/magazine/the-dream-life-of-driverless-cars.html.

Madrigal, Alexis C. (2014, 27 March). In defense of Google flu trends. *The Atlantic*, available at www.theatlantic.com/technology/archive/2014/03/in-defense-of-google-flu-trends/359688/.

Marr, Bernard (2018,28 January). Blockchain and the internet of things: 4 important benefits of combining these two mega trends. *Forbes*, available at www.forbes.com/sites/bernardmarr/2018/01/28/blockchain   -and-the-internet-of-things-4-important-benefits-of-combining-these-two-mega-trends/2/#6cbb70c512dd.

Privacy International (2020). Facewatch reality behind marketing discourse. Available at https://privacyinternational.org/long-read/4216/facewatch-reality-behind-marketing-discourse.

Thomke, Stefan (2001). *Millennium Pharmaceuticals Inc.* Harvard: Harvard Business School.

Winkler, Rolfe (2017, 27 March). Elon Musk launches neuralink to connect brains with computers. *The Wall Street Journal*, available at www.wsj.com/articles/elon-musk-launches-neuralink-to-connect-brains-with-computers-1490642652.

Wall Street Journal (2017,27 March). Startup from CEO of Tesla and SpaceX aims to implant tiny electrodes in human brains. Available at www.wsj.com/articles/elon-musk-launches-neuralink-to-connect-brains-with-computers-1490642652.

Wray, Sarah (2018, 15 June). Why the smart city starts increasingly at home. *Smartcitiesworld*, available at www.smartcitiesworld.net/special-reports/special-reports/why-the-smart-city-could-increasingly-start-at-home.

EU Directives, Regulations and Other Communication

Directive 95/46/EC of the European Parliament and of the Council of 24 October1995 *on the protection of individuals with regard to the processing of personal data and on the free movement of such data.* "EU Data Protection Directive."

Directive *2001/29/EC of The European Parliament and Of The Council of 22 May 2001 on the harmonisation of certain aspects of copyright and related rights in the information society. "The Infosoc Directive."*

Regulation 2016/679 of Apr. 27, 2016, on the Protection of Natural Persons with Regard to the Processing of Personal Data and on the Free Movement of Such Data, and Repealing Directive 95/46/EC (General Data Protection Regulation), 2016 O.J. (L 119) 1 (EU) [GDPR].

Ethics Guidelines for Trustworthy Artificial Intelligence, European Commission, Independent High-Level Expert Group on AI, 8 April 2019, available at https://digital-strategy.ec.europa.eu/en/library/ethics-guidelines-trustworthy-ai.

EU Proposal 2021/0106 (COD) for a Regulation laying down harmonised rules on artificial intelligence (Artificial Intelligence Act): Regulation of The European Parliament and of the Council Laying Down Harmonised Rules On Artificial Intelligence (Artificial Intelligence Act) And Amending Certain Union Legislative Acts, Brussels, 21.4.2021.

Court Cases

US

Moore v. Regents of the University of California, U.S. Supreme Court of California, 51 Cal. 3d 120:271Cal. Rptr. 146; 793 P.2d 479, (1990).

Sony Corp v. Universal Studio Inc, U.S. Supreme Court, Case 416 U.S. 417 (1984).

Kelley v. Chicago Park District, Nos. 8–3701 and 8–3712 (7th Cir. Feb. 15, 2011).

EU

Case C-131/12 Google Spain and Google EU:C:2014:317 *"The Right to Be Forgotten."*

Other Official Governance Documents and Reports

IP/10/1462. *European Commission sets out strategy to strengthen EU data protection rules*, available at http://europa.eu/rapid/press-release_IP-10-1462_en.htm?locale=en.

MEMO/10/542. *Data protection reform – frequently asked questions*, available at http://europa.eu/rapid/press-release_MEMO-10-542_en.htm?locale=fr.

European Commission. *Factsheet on the Right to Be Forgotten ruling* (C-131/12), available at http://ec.europa.eu/justice/data-protection/files/factsheets/factsheet_data_protection_en.pdf.

European Parliament Draft Report with recommendations to the Commission on Civil Law Rules on Robotics (2015/2103 (INL)).

European Commission (2019). Independent High-Level Expert Group on Artificial Intelligence. *Ethics Guidelines for Trustworthy AI.*

Blogs, Instagram Posts and Podcasts

Apple: Siri, a function of Apple iOs, available at www.apple.com/ios/siri/ (accessed 4 February 2015).

Google: Google self-driving car project, available at www.google.com/selfdrivingcar/ (accessed 12 October 2016).

Chronicled: An open registry for the internet of everything, available at http://chroni
cled.org/index.html (accessed 31 March 2017).

Chronicled: Drone case study, available at http://chronicled.org/drone-case-study.html
(accessed 26 October 2016).

Facewatch website: available at www.facewatch.co.uk (accessed 11 February 2021).

Fitbit website: available at www.fitbit.com/se/zip (accessed 5 November 2016).

Fitbit: Fitbit help – how do I track my sleep? available at https://help.fitbit.com/arti
cles/en_US/Help_article/1314 (accessed 5 November 2016).

Herian, R.Anything but disruptive: Blockchain, capital and a case of fourth industrial
age enclosure – Part I, available at http://criticallegalthinking.com/2016/10/18/a
nything-disruptive-blockchain-capital-case-fourth-industrial-age-enclosure-part/.

Herian, R.Anything but disruptive: Blockchain, capital and a case of fourth industrial
age enclosure – Part II, available at http://criticallegalthinking.com/2016/10/19/a
nything-disruptive-blockchain-capital-case-fourth-industrial-age-enclosure-part-ii/.

Know Your Meme: Paying bills with spider drawings: Seven legged spider, available at
https://knowyourmeme.com/memes/events/paying-bills-with-spider-drawings-se
ven-legged-spider (accessed 28 March 2021).

Talks

Hester, H.Inhuman symposium – Helen Hester, available at www.youtube.com/watch?
v=ZSBefHq7C_o (accessed 15 January 2016).

Interview with Elon Musk: We are already cyborgs (2016, 3 June). Code Conference,
available at www.youtube.com/watch?v=ZrGPuUQsDjo (accessed 2 April 2017).

Art Works, Poems and Films

Gil-Fournier, Abelardo, and Parikka, Jussi (2020, August). *Seed, Image, Ground*. Video
essay commissioned by Fotomuseum Winterhur, available at www.fotomuseum.ch/
en/situations-post/seed-image-ground/.

Jonze, Spike. *Her* (2013). Available at www.imdb.com/title/tt1798709/ (accessed 12
November 2016).

Index

Printed in the United States
by Baker & Taylor Publisher Services